THE REAL MEANING
OF OUR WORK?

THE REAL MEANING OF OUR WORK?

Anne Holdorph

Jewish Youth Clubs in the UK, 1880–1939

PETER LANG

Oxford • Bern • Berlin • Bruxelles • Frankfurt am Main • New York • Wien

Bibliographic information published by Die Deutsche Nationalbibliothek.
Die Deutsche Nationalbibliothek lists this publication in the Deutsche
National-bibliografie; detailed bibliographic data is available on the Internet
at http://dnb.d-nb.de.

A catalogue record for this book is available from the British Library.

Library of Congress Cataloging-in-Publication Data

Names: Holdorph, Anne, 1983- author.
Title: The real meaning of our work? : Jewish youth clubs in the UK,
    1880-1939 / Anne Holdorph.
Description: Oxford ; New York : Peter Lang, [2017] | Includes
    bibliographical references and index.
Identifiers: LCCN 2017027959 | ISBN 9783034322133 (alk. paper)
Subjects: LCSH: Jewish youth--Great Britain--Societies and
    clubs--History--19th century. | Jewish youth--Great Britain--Societies and
    clubs--History--20th century. | Jews--Great Britain--Social life and
    customs. | Jewish Lads' & Girls' Brigade (Great Britain)--History--19th
    century. | Jewish Lads' & Girls' Brigade (Great Britain)--History--20th
    century.
Classification: LCC DS135.E5 H65 2017 | DDC 369.4089/924041--dc23 LC
record available at https://lccn.loc.gov/2017027959

Cover image: London Jews in Wartime – the work of Youth Clubs in Stepney,
London, 1942. Source: Wikimedia Commons (part of Ministry of Information
Second World War Official Collection).

Cover design by Peter Lang Ltd.

ISBN 978-3-0343-2213-3 (print) • ISBN 978-1-78707-426-2 (ePDF)
ISBN 978-1-78707-427-9 (ePub) • ISBN 978-1-78707-428-6 (mobi)

© Peter Lang AG, International Academic Publishers, Bern 2017
Wabernstrasse 40, CH-3007 Bern, Switzerland
info@peterlang.com, www.peterlang.com, www.peterlang.net

This publication has been peer reviewed.

Printed in Germany

Contents

Acknowledgements

The production of this book is indebted to Tony Kushner, who has provided constant support and guidance and without whom this book would not have been completed. I would also like to thank Joan Tumblety who has provided additional help and support. Thank you to the lovely people at Peter Lang and the anonymous reviewers who helped to turn this from a thesis into a book.

Thank you to the individuals and organisations who have supported this work financially: the University of Southampton, the Spalding Trust, the Catherine MacKichan Trust and the Stapley Trust. I would also like to thank Eleanor Quince for helping me to secure funding to complete this work.

Finally, I would like to thank my friends and family who have suffered through my PhD with me, in particular Lucy Hounsham, Becky Holdorph, Holly Dunbar, Kay Hughes, Emma Merriott, Emma Morris, Luke Hall, Ed Jellard and Charlotte Medland, who have provided much needed advice, guidance, proofreading and attention.

Judaism, Masculinity and Femininity, 1880–1939

The end of the nineteenth and beginning of the twentieth century marked a key period in the creation of youth clubs across the UK, the most high profile of these being the Boys' Brigade and the Scout and Guide Associations. From the 1880s clubs for girls and boys emerged in towns and cities. The clubs were primarily for those aged 14 and older, although some also catered for younger people. Philanthropists and social workers saw this age group as particularly vulnerable and in need of guidance. There were groups that catered for political interests, such as Zionism, groups that considered themselves to be educational and those that were social in nature. This book will focus on social clubs, which played a particularly important role, enabling philanthropists to exercise control, although not always successfully, over young people who were seen as particularly vulnerable to negative influences. Fears of deterioration of the British population, highlighted by perceived military failure in the Boer War and the poverty surveys of Booth and Rowntree, resulted in clubs for boys emphasizing military drill and physical fitness. Girls' clubs emphasized moral and social purity. Many clubs included a religious element and were often explicitly supported by the churches. The Boys' Brigade for example, placed an emphasis on 'the advancement of Christ's Kingdom' and the Girls' Friendly Society claimed a strong connection with the Anglican Church, boasting the Archbishop of Canterbury as one of its patrons.[1] As a result of such Christian underpinning, Jewish youth were often excluded from these clubs. Wealthy Jewish

---

[1]   Donald M. MacFarlane, *First For Boys: The Story of the Boys' Brigade, 1883–1993* (London: The Boys' Brigade, 1993), p. 6 <http://www.boys-brigade.org.uk/ffb.pdf> [accessed 2 April 2013]; and Vivienne Richmond, '"It is not a Society for Human Beings but for Virgins": The Girls' Friendly Society Membership Eligibility Dispute 1875–1936', *Journal of Historical Sociology*, 20 (2007), pp. 304–27 (p. 304).

philanthropists created their own clubs for Jewish youth, which mirrored those within the Christian community. Much like in Christian clubs, Jewish groups used religion in order to promote acceptable identities amongst young people.

Within the Jewish community, the process of creating acceptable identities had a particular focus on immigrant Jews, rather than solely on the working classes. As a result of the focus on immigrants, the process was termed at the time and in subsequent scholarship 'Anglicization'. This was not a simplistic process. David Feldman has argued that there were a variety of ways in which competing bodies, including philanthropists, Zionists, and revolutionaries sought to exercise control over the immigrant population.[2] The Yiddish newspaper *Di Poylishe Yidel*, for example, encouraged its readers to learn English in order to read certain literature to contribute to their revolutionary cause and the anarchist newspaper *Der Arbayter Fraynd* implored readers to unite with the English working classes and adopt their customs and language, while the *Machzike Hadath*, an organization to which some of the most religiously Orthodox belonged, believed that Anglicization was the duty of Jews who had been welcomed into England. This demonstrates that despite many similarities, including the importance of learning English, numerous institutions contributed to the process of Anglicization amongst the immigrant community.[3] Tananbaum added to this by stating that the ways in which these groups targeted certain sections of immigrant society was nuanced by gender.[4] It is the Anglicizing efforts of philanthropists that I will primarily refer to, in particular those philanthropists who came from the middle and upper-classes of Anglo-Jewry. Their efforts aimed not only to make immigrants into 'Englishmen' but were designed to 'shape and cultivate [immigrants]

---

2   David Feldman, *Englishmen and Jews: Social Relations and Political Culture 1840–1914* (London: Yale University Press, 1994), p. 347.

3   Feldman, *Englishmen and Jews*, pp. 329–52.

4   Susan Tananbaum, 'Making Good Little English Children: Immigrant Welfare and Anglicization Among Jewish Immigrants in London, 1880–1939', *Immigrants and Minorities*, 12 (1993), 176–99 (p. 177).

in a mode and image that both Jews and Britons would applaud'.[5] Indeed, communal institutions run by Anglo-Jewish elite, including youth clubs, adopted this ethos. Immigrants experienced this Anglicization from a number of institutions, from education to poor relief and Livshin noted that the combined efforts of Anglo-Jewry meant that the pressures were 'too strong not to have their effect'.[6] Her view, however, does not take into account the control that the immigrants were able to exert over the process and the meanings that they took from this. Those who had settled in the UK were not a homogenous group, but rather included a variety of ages, nationalities, religious observances and cultural traditions who left their homes for a number of reasons, primarily a combination of poverty and persecution. Most came from the Russian Empire and the majority of their children were either very young on arrival to the UK or born shortly after their arrival. Some were more traditional than others, and their politics were far from unified. Such variations meant that some were more eager to become Anglicized than others. Additionally, individuals were able to 'resist the influences of institutions and messages they disliked' through aligning themselves with one of the number of Anglicizing influences.[7] As a result, immigrant Jews were not submissive participants in the process of Anglicization. For children and young people, this process is further complicated. Many young people, especially second generation immigrants and those who arrived as infants were keen to become more Anglicized, and as a result more modern, and exerted pressure over their parents to do the same. As a second generation immigrant living in Manchester recalled 'we wanted to emancipate ourselves and to make ourselves more modern ... and to get rid of all these old things'.[8] In contrast, young people who arrived

---

5   Eugene C. Black, *The Social Politics of Anglo-Jewry 1880–1920* (Oxford: Basil Blackwell, 1988), p. 104.

6   Rosalyn Livshin, 'The Acculturation of the Children of Immigrant Jews in Manchester, 1890–1930', in *The Making of Modern Anglo-Jewry*, ed. by David Cesarani (Oxford: Basil Blackwell, 1990), pp. 76–96 (p. 93).

7   Feldman, *Englishmen and Jews*, pp. 348–9.

8   Manchester Jewish Museum (hereafter MJM), J268, and Livshin, 'Acculturation', p. 88.

in the UK as older children or who were the eldest sibling often resisted Anglicizing influences, for example, by maintaining spoken Yiddish.[9] The varied responses to Anglicization, both from adults and young people, has an impact on the study of Jewish youth clubs, in particular when looking at membership of the clubs – the voluntary membership of clubs likely did not include young people who were resisting Anglicizing elements. As a result, it is important to note that club membership was not necessarily an exact replica of the overall Jewish demographic.

The religious activities at Jewish boys' and girls' clubs reveal much about the nature of Jewish childhood in the UK before the Second World War, as well as pressures felt by the Jewish community as a whole. The period from the mid-1880s to 1939 witnessed the introduction, and later the growth of the various youth clubs, and as such provides a good period for the study of such groups. Religion will be defined, following Peter Connolly, as 'any beliefs which involve the acceptance of a sacred, trans-empirical realm and any behaviours designed to affect a person's relationship with that realm'.[10] Whilst by no means the only definition of religion, it allows both belief and observances to be considered as a religious act, and thus includes the range of activities that the club leaders themselves viewed as 'Jewish' rather than purely secular. This study will look at religion in Jewish youth groups, including uniformed clubs such as the Jewish Lads' Brigade and the Scouts and Guides, and examine the way in which religion was used to promote British (and within it, gendered) identities. The broad educative experiences of Jewish youth outside of formal schooling have been underrepresented in academic studies. This book will begin to address this gap and start to create a fuller picture of Jewish childhood. Not only did religious programming include activities designed to promote physical fitness and patriotism amongst all young people, it also sought to promote acceptable gender identities. I will use the term 'religious programming' to include any element of the clubs' activities that contained a religious dimension using the Connolly's definition mentioned. This study will contribute not only

9   Livshin, 'Acculturation', p. 86.
10   Peter Connolly, *Approaches to the Study of Religion* (London: Continuum, 1999), pp. 6–7.

to the study of Jewish history, but also to childhood and youth studies, history and wider social history.

To successfully examine the influence of the clubs' activities in promoting identities, it is important to look at the Anglo-Jewish community as a whole. The remainder of this section will explore British Jewry in the late nineteenth century. Influenced by the wave of mass immigration from Eastern Europe, the Jewish community in the UK was facing a time of intense change. By the early twentieth century, the existing community was working on behalf of immigrant Jews to provide social and economic assistance, combining Jewish and Victorian approaches to charity. I will examine the effect the immigrant community had on the Jewish population as a whole, exploring, in addition, gender identities within the UK and the Jewish sphere.

Immigration and the Anglo-Jewish Community

By the middle of the nineteenth century Jews in Great Britain had made progress towards social and political inclusion and acceptance. In 1829, Roman Catholics were admitted to parliament, which left the Jews as the only major religious minority who were still subject to political discrimination. From there, the struggle for full Jewish emancipation took approximately thirty years. Political discrimination officially ended in 1858 when Lionel de Rothschild was elected as the first Jewish Member of Parliament.[11] The period following Rothschild's election until the 1880s has been seen as 'a golden age, when Jews were in harmony with their surroundings'.[12] The Jewish community had gained not only the right to stand as MPs, but also

---

11   See Michael Clark 'Jewish Identity in British Politics: The Case of the First Jewish MPs, 1858–87', *Jewish Social Studies*, 13 (2007), pp. 93–126 (pp. 93–4); and U. R. Q Henriques, 'The Jewish Emancipation Controversy in Nineteenth Century Britain', *Past and Present*, 40 (1968), pp. 126–46 (p. 126).

12   Clark, 'Jewish Identity', p. 95.

to own land and enter into professions which had previously been barred to them as a consequence of the religious oaths required for entry.[13] For the established Jews of the late nineteenth century, this progress was at the forefront of their minds. Faced with an influx of Eastern European Jewish immigration, which occurred between the 1880s and the First World War, middle and upper class Anglo-Jewry was naturally anxious to ensure they did not lose their freedom and status.

Between 1881 and 1914 the number of Jewish immigrants to the UK reached its peak with an estimated 120,000 to 150,000 Jews settling permanently in Britain.[14] Primarily from Eastern Europe, the large number of impoverished 'aliens' who arrived created a Jewish community that was more visible than ever before. Established Anglo-Jewry considered the immigrant group a threat to the progress that had been made during the course of the century as the immigrants 'reminded British Jews of their lowly and foreign born origins, worse still they reminded the Gentiles'.[15] Those who had worked hard for political gains feared that the highly visible, poor and distinctly foreign looking immigrants would challenge the carefully cultivated Anglo-Jewish image, and thereby threaten the material and political benefits that came with it. The threat of the newly arrived immigrants was perceived as immense. For established Anglo-Jewry the religious and social identities of the immigrants was a matter that required immediate attention in order to protect their status in society. Tananbaum noted that 'most Anglicizers directed their efforts at children or through their mothers' as this achieved 'rapid results'.[16] They thus targeted differences between 'native' and 'immigrant' education and worship, especially with social policies that were highly gendered.

13   See Clark, 'Jewish Identity', and Henriques, 'Jewish Emancipation'.
14   Todd M. Endelman, *The Jews of Britain, 1656–2000* (London: University of California Press, 2002), p. 127.
15   Geoffrey Alderman, *Modern British Jewry* (Oxford: Oxford University Press, 1992), p. 126.
16   Susan L. Tananbaum, *Jewish Immigrants in London 1880–1939* (London: Pickering and Chatto, 2014), p. 9.

The style of religious worship of the immigrant Jews and Anglo-Jewry was very different. An 'English' synagogue service would have been an alien experience for the immigrant Jew:

> The solemn atmosphere, English language sermons, begowned clerics, choral music and stately architecture of English synagogues were unfamiliar, intimidating and smacked of Christian influence – in addition to which the membership fees were beyond the reach of all but the most successful newcomers.[17]

The role of the Chief Rabbi was controversial amongst immigrants. In Eastern Europe Jewish communities typically had their own local rabbinical authority. The Chief Rabbi, however, viewed the whole of the British Empire as one large community. The position of the Chief Rabbi on many issues caused the immigrant community to develop feelings of distrust towards powerful figures within the Anglo-Jewish religious sphere. Specifically his conservative position on trade unions and his refusal to let rabbinical groups determine what constituted *Kosher* food resulted in the increased alienation of immigrant Jews from the religious praxis of the native-born Jews.[18] For immigrant Jews, the very notion of the Chief Rabbi was different from their experiences of Judaism at 'home' and helped to increase the sense of distance between them and Anglo-Jewry.

The response of the immigrant Jewish community to the differences in worship was to introduce their own 'native' practices into their local communities. *Chevrot* (congregations held in homes or workshops) were popular amongst immigrants. A large number of these congregations were started in cities with high numbers of Jewish immigrants prior to the First World War, in particular London, Liverpool, Manchester, Leeds and Glasgow. It is estimated that around half of the newcomers belonged to one of these groups.[19] The presence of these large, rowdy congregations concerned the native population who believed the *Chevrot* promoted the image of the immigrant Jew as alien to British culture. As Gartner notes,

---

17   Endelman, *The Jews of Britain*, p. 145.
18   Ibid.
19   Lloyd P. Gartner, *The Jewish Immigrant in England 1870–1914* (London: Vallentine Mitchell, 1960), p. 192.

'[t]he immigrant *Chevrot* commenced and usually remained small, clangorous and often dirty. The passion, length, noise and frequency of the services held there were quite incomprehensible to Englishmen and to most English Jews.'[20] The *Chevrot* added to fears voiced in the press that the immigrant population posed a sanitation risk due to the cramped conditions in which the immigrants operated and 'came to be seen as a direct threat to the stability of the native Jewish population.'[21] The *Chevrot* became symbolic of all of the negative aspects of immigrant culture that the elite felt had no place in British society. For Anglo-Jewry, the promotion of acceptable and more restrained religion was important in the preservation of their own image. Elite Jews had a clear goal when promoting Anglicized religion to the immigrant populations: to make it feel less threatening and alien in order to encourage the immigrant Jews to worship in an acceptable British way. The *Chevrot* had to be reformed, as did other immigrant religious practices and structures.

Education and the Clubs

The education of young immigrant Jews was a particular concern for Anglo-Jewry. *Chederim* were a common feature of immigrant childhood. These were small educational groups popular in Eastern Europe, which provided religious instruction and, like the *Chevrot*, were quickly established in Jewish communities following the influx of immigrants. The *Chederim* provided a type of religious education that was inherently gendered. It was common for sons of new arrivals to enrol at a *Cheder* after their arrival in the UK and it was estimated that by 1891 approximately 2,000 boys aged between

20 Ibid., p. 189.
21 Judy Glasman, 'Assimilation by Design: London Synagogues in the Nineteenth Century', in *The Jewish Heritage in British History: Englishness and Jewishness*, ed. by Tony Kushner (London: Frank Cass, 1992), pp. 171–209 (p. 173).

5 and 15 were enrolled in such classes.[22] In these establishments, boys were likely to be engaged in a variety of classes, ranging from Hebrew education to the study of the Pentateuch and Rabbinical commentaries.[23] Girls were not provided with equivalent classes. The *Talmud Torah*, a less controversial educational establishment, provided similar classes for boys who, in the case of students at the Manchester *Talmud Torah*, would engage in 19 hours of study in addition to formal schooling.[24] The amount and quality of education provided for boys contrasted with the minimal religious education given to girls. By the time a boy reached 13, the age of his *Bar Mitzvah*, he had received a comprehensive, if not inspiring, religious education. For girls, who at this time had no similar ritual within Orthodox Judaism, religious education was less structured and often provided by the mother.

The *Cheder* provided a Jewish education with which immigrant families were familiar. Native Jewry viewed the *Chederim* with the same distrust with which they viewed the *Chevrot*. The *Jewish Chronicle*, the organ of the Anglo-Jewish middle-classes and elite, commented that the *Chederim* should be shut down as the conditions in which they operated were appalling.[25] Many children were crammed into one room and classes perceived as 'un-British', were carried out in Yiddish.

Settled Anglo-Jewry viewed the *Chederim*, along with the *Chevrot*, with contempt as their origins and the way in which they operated were unacceptable British social and educational traditions.[26] As a result, young immigrant Jews were placed under scrutiny and seen to be in need of reform as much as (if not more than) adults. Providing a formal British education for young immigrants was seen as one of the most effective ways to Anglicize immigrants and counter the threat that the immigrant population posed to the position of Anglo-Jewry. Through education, it was hoped that immigrant children would be exposed to an Anglicizing influence and that they would pressure their parents into conforming. A more

---

22   Endelman, *Jewish of Britain*, p. 146.
23   Gartner, *The Jewish Immigrant*, p. 232.
24   Ibid., p. 235.
25   See *Jewish Chronicle* (hereafter *JC*), 18 December 1891.
26   Black, *Social Politics*, p. 126.

acceptable alternative to the *Chederim* was the Jewish schools operated by the Anglo-Jewish community and the board schools, which had predominantly Jewish students. The 1870 Education Act and the introduction of the Cowper-Temple Clause, which stated that instruction in Christianity was not compulsory and that parents could withdraw their children from religion classes, certainly altered the ways in which Jewish children received their education. Large numbers of Jewish children began to attend Jewish 'Board Schools'. Approximately 85 per cent of immigrant children attended these schools, which employed large numbers of Jewish staff members and observed the Jewish calendar.[27]

The Board Schools, as well as the large community-run Jews' Free School (JFS), were crucial organizations in exerting control over their pupils. Black has argued they were able to 'shape and cultivate youth in a mode and image that both Jews and Britons would applaud'.[28] The JFS encouraged Anglicization amongst its pupils by stressing the importance of speaking English and promoting traditionally 'British' manners. During the 1905 prize giving service, the head teacher, Louis B. Abrahams, adjured parents to help with the Anglicization process by encouraging them to keep children off the streets, to move to the suburbs and to stop the use of Yiddish in the home.[29] The JFS attempted to reform children's outward appearance as well and provided its male pupils with a full suit of clothing once a year and provided girls with clothing even more frequently.[30] This provided a way to counter the image of immigrant Jews as poor and needy. For immigrant families, the idea that one could feel both a national and religious identity would have been a novelty, as in their home countries, Jews were often excluded from the 'nation' through their religion as non-Christians. By combining nationalistic and patriotic influences with its Jewish elements, the JFS was able to provide proof that notions of Jewishness and Britishness were not mutually exclusive; rather, both identities could work together in harmony.

27   Ibid., p. 116.
28   Ibid., p. 105.
29   Ibid., p. 110.
30   Gartner, *The Jewish Immigrant*, p. 222.

Education was seen as a powerful tool to combat the negative reputation of newly-arrived immigrant Jews. Through education and indoctrination the schools were able to provide guidance to immigrant families on the acceptable ways in which to conduct themselves. Education, however, had its limits. Once a student left school and began work, often at the age of 14, he or she was subject to both the positive and negative influences of British society. Some discredited both themselves and the Jewish community as a whole by engaging in prostitution, visiting music halls, being a visible presence on the streets and participating in other 'unwholesome' activities. The renowned performer and comedian Bud Flanagan, who took part in shows at music halls across London, exemplified this.[31] Youth clubs for young people run by wealthy Anglo-Jewry attempted to maintain some control over young people once they had left school and entered into the work force. The primary aims of these groups were twofold. First, and most obvious, was the desire to Anglicize their members by introducing them to behaviour necessary to adapt to British society, including sportsmanship for boys and etiquette for girls. Second, the clubs sought to exert influence over the religious observances of their members, encouraging club members to remain Jewish. The primary way in which the clubs combined these two goals was through the introduction of an Anglicized form of Judaism. As noted, immigrant families perceived Judaism practiced in Britain as alien to them. The clubs worked to break down that image. Club members were encouraged to attend the synagogue for the Sabbath services and on festivals. This had the result of introducing the members to Anglo-Judaism at the same time as drawing them away from the despised *Chevrot*. Through services and meetings, members were introduced to distinguished figures in Anglo-Judaism, such as the Chief Rabbi, in a setting that was familiar to them, helping the members to view the Rabbi in a positive light.[32] As a result, clubs were seen by established Anglo-Jewry as an important element of the continuing education of Jewish youth.

31   Bud Flanagan, *My Crazy Life* (London: Frederick Muller, 1961), pp. 22–5.
32   For an account on this type of work, see Tower Hamlets Local History Archive (hereafter THLA), LP 2254, 360.1, *How a Jewish working boys' club is run: An account of the Stepney Jewish Lads' Club*, 1914, pp. 14–17.

The majority of Jewish youth clubs catered to young people aged 14–18, which was viewed as the time when young people were most 'at-risk' to harmful influences. The clubs organized by both Orthodox and Liberal Jewish groups and for both boys and girls, operated for this age group. In some instances when the club had been successful, it was expanded to include an 'old boys/girls' section for those above the age of 18 and a junior club for those aged 11 and older. This was particularly true for the clubs that grew into settlements, namely the Stepney Lads' Club, the Brady Boys' Club, the Oxford and St George's Lads' Club and the West Central Girls' Club. The Jewish Lads' Brigade and the Scouts and Guides targeted different age groups. They began for younger members aged 11–15 and then expanded to include senior groups (up to 18) and, in the case of the Scouts and Guides, included a younger section. The differing age ranges had an impact on the activities the clubs included as the groups catering for younger members were targeting a less independent age group.

The largest numbers of clubs were located in London, particularly the East End, where the largest numbers of Jews lived. Provincial cities including Manchester, Liverpool, Bristol and Nottingham had smaller populations and as a result had fewer clubs. These cities typically had one girls' club and troops of Jewish Scouts and Guides and a Jewish Lads' Brigade (JLB) company. As a result, girls' clubs in the provinces had less competition for members, leaders and funders. This created clubs that were more able than their London counterparts to engage the whole community and could take into account local issues and communal traditions. For boys in the provincial cities their option was to join Scouts or the Jewish Lads' Brigade, as with the exception of Manchester, no non-uniformed Jewish boys' club existed outside of London. Thus, for boys, youth experiences were less localized and more national as the JLB and Scouts followed a national programme.

Within the historiography of late nineteenth and early twentieth-century youth culture, there has been a greater focus on non-Jewish youth clubs, particularly the Scouts and Guides. Notions of citizenship education have been addressed by Beavan, Warren, Springhall, Proctor and Rosenthal who have considered the way this has encouraged young people to conform to upper-class adult expectations of behaviour.[33] Rosenthal, for example, argued that the Scouts' ideology was 'firmly rooted in the ideology of the upper class' and based on 'unquestioning acceptance of social positions'.[34] This analysis is too narrow, particularly when Jewish groups are considered. In this respect, Proctor's study on uniforms within youth movements opens up some interesting points. Whilst discussing uniforms she noted that 'although designed by adults to reinforce social control and conformity, uniforms often allow[ed] youth to fashion their own meanings and identities apart from their elders'.[35] This view of uniforms can be applied to the Jewish Scout and Guide groups as well as to the Jewish Lads' Brigade as Jewish leaders were able to adapt the national programme to suit their specific needs and the needs of their members in the same way that young people were able to adapt their uniforms to denote their own code of belonging. Indeed, Proctor mentions that the experiences of Scouting have been assumed to correspond to the ideals set by the national leadership but that this 'simplifies the complex processes involved in the shaping of identity'.[36] More recently this view has been taken up by Mills in her work on the Scouting movement.[37] The perspectives of Proctor and

---

33   See for example Tammy Proctor, '(Uni)Forming Youth: Girl Guides and Boy Scouts in Britain 1908–1939', *History Workshop Journal*, 45 (1998), pp. 103–34; Michael Rosenthal, *The Character Factory: Baden-Powell and the Origins of the Scout Movement* (London: Collins, 1986); Brad Beaven, *Leisure, Citizenship and Working-Class Men in Britain 1850–1945* (Manchester: Manchester University Press, 2005); John Springhall, *Youth, Empire and Society: British Youth Movements 1883–1940* (London: Croom Helm, 1977); Alan Warren, 'Sir Robert Baden Powell, The Scout Movement and Citizen Training in Great Britain, 1900–1920', *English Historical Review*, 101 (1986), pp. 376–98.

34   Rosenthal, *The Character Factory*, p. 7.

35   Proctor, '(Uni)Forming Youth', p. 116.

36   Ibid., p. 103.

37   See Sarah Mills, '"An Instruction in Good Citizenship": Scouting and the Historical Geographies of Citizenship Education', *Transactions of the Institute of British Geographers*, 38 (2012), pp. 412–23; Sarah Mills, 'Duty to God/my Dharma/Allah/ Waheguru: Diverse Youthful Religiosities and the Politics and Performance of Informal Worship', *Social and Cultural Geography*, 13 (2012), pp. 481–99; and Sarah Mills, 'Scouting for Girls? Gender and the Scout Movement in Britain', *Gender, Place and Culture*, 18 (2011), pp. 537–56.

Mills will be kept in mind when looking both at individual members of the uniformed Jewish groups as well as when looking at the groups as a whole as this helps us to understand the influences the clubs exerted over individuals. It raises questions about the extent and forms of control the Jewish community exercised over their own group, which I will look at with particular regard to religious education.

Previous analysis of Jewish youth groups have examined the clubs' Anglicizing methods with minimal focus on the role of the development of religious identities. Kadish, for example, in her work for the Jewish Lads' Brigade centenary, only mentions religion in passing.[38] Other scholarly attention on Jewish youth groups has been provided by Tananbaum, Dee and, to a lesser extent, Livshin. Tananbaum, in her work on Jewish youth groups, has focused on the Anglicizing elements of club life. Although she mentions religious programming it is not, following Kadish, the primary focus of her work.[39] In a recent study Dee has looked at the sporting element, again with little focus on religion in its own right.[40] Livshin, rather than ignore the religious element, instead stated that religious education played such a minor role in club life that a religious revival in the interwar period was needed to counter the lack of religiosity amongst youth.[41] There is, it will be argued, a major lacuna in the existing historiography. Whilst this study in no way wishes to minimize the importance of Anglicizing influences and leisure activities, it will show that religion was still a vital element of club life, one that worked towards the promotion of suitably

38   See Sharman Kadish, *A Good Jew and A Good Englishman: The Jewish Lads' and Girls' Brigade, 1895–1995* (London: Vallentine Mitchell, 1995).

39   See Susan L. Tananbaum, 'Biology and Community: The Duality of Jewish Mothering in East London, 1880–1939', in *Mothering: Ideology, Experience and Agency*, ed. by Evelyn Nakano Glenn, Grace Chang and Linda Rennie Forcey (London: Routledge, 1994), pp. 311–32; Susan Tananbaum, 'Ironing out the Ghetto Bend: Sports and the Making of British Jews', *Journal of Sport History*, 31 (2004), pp. 53–75; Susan L. Tananbaum, 'Philanthropy and Identity: Gender and Ethnicity in London', *Journal of Social Research*, 30 (1997), pp. 937–61; and Tananbaum, *Jewish Immigrants*.

40   See David Dee, 'Nothing Specifically Jewish in Athletics? Sport, Physical Recreation and the Jewish Youth Movement in London, 1895–1914', *London Journal*, 34 (2009), pp. 81–101.

41   See Livshin, 'Acculturation', pp. 76–96.

British identities. As Pieren noted, clubs used a variety of methods to achieve Anglicization and religion was no exception.[42] Whilst this religious element certainly worked to complement the Anglicizing elements of club work, it was also an important element in and of itself. Instead of providing religious activities that the immigrant members would have been familiar with, the clubs provided forms of worship that conformed to acceptable Anglo-Jewish traditions. As a result many immigrant families questioned the inclusion of religion, since familiar elements of observance were not present. Yet, in spite of this tension, religion *was* an important element of the clubs' activities.

I will neither attempt to examine the ways in which the clubs were successful in achieving their goals of Anglicization, nor dispute the importance that clubs placed on themselves as an agent of Anglicization; rather, I will analyse the religious provisions that clubs provided for their members and how religious activities conformed to traditions and gender expectations in British society. In boys' and girls' clubs, religious observance and education took on distinct, if gendered, patterns. Boys were encouraged to conform to British society through militarism, sportsmanship and outward displays of patriotism. The ways in which religion was included within boys' clubs naturally reflected these elements. For girls, where the emphasis was on integration through domesticity, manners and social interactions, religious programming likewise reflected these themes.[43] Gender expectations from the nineteenth century were well formed and clear. Ideal notions of masculinity and femininity governed all youth experiences, including club work. It is therefore important to establish the expectations for the ideal man and woman. Starting with masculinity, a largely ignored concept in historical research until recently, though one that has received a lot of attention of late, this introductory section will explore the accepted gender identities within British (and more generally Western) society.

42   Kathrin Pieren, 'Cultivating Jewish Britons in the Edwardian Period: Jewish Youth Work Between the Call to Empire and the Home Cinema', unpublished conference paper, *Cultivating Britons: Culture and Identity in Britain, 1901–1936*, Oxford University, 16 September 2008, p. 7.
43   See Tananbaum, *Jewish Immigrant*, p. 111, for more discussion on this.

Masculinity

The notions of 'becoming a man' played an important role in the experience of childhood for boys in the nineteenth and twentieth centuries and encouraging boys to 'become men' played a key role in the club movement. In contrast to girls, who were encouraged to follow their mothers' examples, boys required specific training in order to fulfil certain masculine qualities:

> Boys become men not just by growing up, but by acquiring a variety of manly qualities and manly competencies as part of a conscious process which has no close parallels in the traditional experience of young women.[44]

Whilst a boy could be said to have become a man once he had started full time work, the process of becoming 'manly' required the adoption of certain skills and traits. These were divided into two sections: first, physical qualities, which dictated that men should be built in a way to maximize strength and, second, mental and moral qualities, which glorified independence. Training for boys was focused on these two areas above all other elements, including academic study, and featured an emphasis on sports and team games. This focus is seen in clubs' activities, which prioritized sporting events and the creation of 'character'. It is important to mention here that although masculinity today refers to 'inner core of identity' this was not the case until after the Second World War. Instead, prior to this point, masculinity referred to the legal privileges of men.[45] 'Manhood' and 'manliness' were the more dominant terms associated with men, but referred mostly to their physical attributes. As I will look at masculine identities, rather than legal rights and privileges, I will be using the terms manliness, manhood and masculinity to refer to physical and mental attributes.

The Jewish faith often required men to take part in religious rituals that could be seen by some outside of Judaism as a feminine activity. An example of this is that boys and men were expected to conduct ceremonies within

---

44   John Tosh, *Manliness and Masculinities in Nineteenth Century Britain: Essays on Gender, Family and Empire* (Harlow: Pearson Education, 2005), p. 31.

45   Ibid., p. 24.

the home, something viewed as both more spiritual and domestic and thus more feminine by their Protestant peers. However this, as a religious obligation, was seen as acceptable within the Jewish community. For club leaders, for example, it was not viewed as deviating from gender boundaries. It is important to keep this in mind when looking at masculinity within Jewish clubs. Despite such blurring of gender boundaries within Judaism, the clubs continued to focus on developing manly attributes mentioned above as a way to establish acceptably 'English' men, in particular through advocating the games ethic.

Outward appearance was the most obvious expression of manhood and as a result clubs, both Jewish and non-Jewish, utilized the image of the perfect man in order to promote this idealized masculinity. The ideal image of a man from the late nineteenth century onwards took inspiration from notions of correct manly appearance that developed during the Enlightenment. During the eighteenth century, a man who was physically beautiful, was seen to have developed qualities including 'love of work, moderation and cleanliness'.[46] Throughout the twentieth century, as a greater emphasis was placed on physical beauty, the ideal image of the masculine body emerged which took inspiration from Greek sculptures. German art historian Johann Joachim Winckelmann led the study of Greek figures that resulted in the establishment of the Greek ideal for the truly masculine body. In Britain, the Greek model was influenced particularly by the Elgin Marbles. In 1867, Walter Pater, who contributed to the development of the bodily ideal in Britain, added that the 'beautiful male figures must show no anger, desire or surprise' and that they must exemplify 'rest in motion', something that was seen as vital in developing young men.[47]

With the establishment of a well-defined physical standard of beauty, it was necessary for men to be able to achieve this ideal – or at least to work towards attaining it. As early as the 1860s, the athlete was honoured

---

46   George L. Mosse, *The Image of Man: The Creation of Modern Masculinities* (Oxford: Oxford University Press, 1996), p. 26.

47   Mosse, *Image*, p. 37.

as a hero and considered to be 'the human form divine'.[48] It was not just athletes who were commended in their perfection of the body. Gymnastics was seen as 'a vital step in the perfection of the male stereotype'.[49] Many clubs offered gymnastics, athletics and other physical activities in order to promote the attainment of this physical ideal. The development of the idea of the physical superiority of the Greeks led to the promotion of a single type of perfection for men – one which offered an easily measurable quality in which to judge the 'masculinity' (or otherwise) of a male. Sports were seen as a way in which to attain the perfection of the Greeks and bring a man closer to perfection, something that was seen as a significant goal of club work as a whole.

The particular view that Jewish men were the antithesis to manhood had developed in Europe in the course of the nineteenth century. Jews were classified as ugly in contrast to carefully cultivated masculine beauty. Physical ugliness was perceived as easy to judge and relied heavily on traditional Jewish stereotypes.[50] In addition to depicting the 'Jewish nose' as anti-Greek (and as a result, unmanly) 'the flat feet, the waddling gait (opposed to the manly stride), the neckless body, the big ears, and the swarthy color' all helped to identify Jewish men and place them in stark opposition to masculine beauty.[51] It was thus important for Jewish organizations to promote manliness at the same time as distancing themselves from anti-manliness. Whilst Jewish men were expected to be part of domestic observances, boys' clubs gave little attention to activities that were seen as 'feminine', such as domestic

---

48   Roberta Park, 'Biological Thought, Athletics and the Formation of a 'Man Character': 1830–1900', in *Manliness and Morality: Middle Class Masculinity in Britain and America 1880–1940*, ed. by J. A. Mangan and James Walvin (Manchester: Manchester University Press, 1987), pp. 7–34 (p. 7).

49   Mosse, *Image*, p. 40.

50   It was not just Jewish men who were considered to be divergent from masculine norms; for example, gays were also seen as less than masculine, and Jewish men were often seen as linked to gays. However, I am concerned here with the way in which Jewish men, specifically, were defined outside of the traditional view of the male.

51   Mosse, *Image*, p. 64. See also Sander Gilman, *The Jew's Body* (New York: Routledge, 1991) for a discussion of Jewish bodily stereotypes.

obligations. That is not to say that these were not present, but rather that they were downplayed in order to emphasize sporting activities.

Understandably, Jewish men were keen to break away from the image of themselves as ugly. The development of muscular Judaism, promoted by Max Nordau, and the development of Zionism were important counter movements to the negative classification of Jewish men: 'Muscular Judaism was not about weight training or body building *per se*; rather, it was about the cultivation of certain corporeal and moral ideals such as discipline, agility and strength, which would help form a regenerated race of healthy, physically fit, nationally minded and militarily strong Jews.'[52] In short, muscular Judaism was created in order to develop Jewish men who would then fit firmly into the masculine ideals of society. Club leaders used the ideas of Nordau to promote physical fitness and moral qualities amongst Jewish men through sports and developing the ideals of manly characteristics. Jewish notions of manliness promoted by the muscular Judaism movement were influenced by non-Jewish, and at times anti-Semitic notions of the ideal man: 'the tough Jews go so far as to create an ideal Jewish body imagery that closely resembles the classical Greek and Roman bodily ideals of the anti-Semites themselves.'[53] Excluded from the dominant definitions of masculinity, Jews went to efforts to ensure that they could still achieve this masculine ideal. For the Jewish clubs, countering this image of Jews as opposite to men was a vital part of their work. This can be seen in Jewish clubs' emphasis on physical activities and drills, which were designed to minimize difference and help Jewish boys achieve the physically acceptable body and was a key part in the clubs' efforts to Anglicize their members.

The supposed ugliness of the Jews did not stop at physical characteristics as Jews were pictured as ugly in character as well. 'A person's disordered outward appearance signalled a mind that lacked control over the passions, where male honour had become cowardice, honesty was unknown, and

52 Todd Samuel Presner, *Muscular Judaism: The Jewish Body and the Politics of Regeneration* (London: Routledge, 2007), p. 2.
53 Daniel Boyarin, *Unheroic Conduct: The Rise of Homosexuality and the Invention of the Jewish Man* (London: University of California Press, 1997), p. 246.

lustfulness had taken the place of purity'.[54] These negative characteristics were not attributed solely to Jews – instead they were ascribed to all 'outsiders'. However, along with 'restlessness' and 'perpetual motion', such traits were firmly associated with Jewish men. Through stereotyping, Jews were pictured as opposed to ideal manliness both outwardly *and* inwardly.

Ugliness, for men, was not the only marker of being an 'outsider'. Those who did not meet the expectations of manhood were considered to be feminine and, for the Jewish man, this was no exception. Eastern European Jews had long been viewed as the opposite of the knight and were instead viewed as 'gentle, timid and studious'.[55] This image of Jews as the antithesis of manliness was developed in line with the adoption of the masculine ideal. Influenced in part by Freud's work on Jews and homosexuality, as well as the more formal understanding of masculine ideals, this led to an increased view of the Jews (and gays) as feminine. The Jewish clubs, utilizing muscular Jewish beliefs, worked to counter this view by developing moral qualities, based on religious principles, which were seen as vital for masculinity. Jews were seen as a third sex, prone to hysteria, which was viewed as a womanly affliction.[56] They were characterized as passive, cowardly, soft and devious, with a weak physical form.[57] In this case, the divergence of Jews from masculine norms was the chief reason for accusations of Jewish male effeminacy. 'Moral elements were given particular emphasis by the Victorian middle class and included absolute virtues like "frankness" and "purity" and their application in "self-government".'[58] The most desirable traits for masculinity were those that were needed for survival in the business and professional world, specifically 'courage, resolution, tenacity and self-government or "independence"'.[59] The development of independence was a factor in much of a boy's upbringing and in subsequent adulthood, from the time spent at public schools to finding their way in business. Within youth clubs this was seen through self-management and allowing the boys to take responsibility

54   Mosse, *Image*, p. 59.
55   Boyarin, *Unheroic*, p. 13.
56   Ibid., p. 210.
57   Mosse, *Image*, p. 69.
58   Tosh, *Manliness*, p. 136.
59   Tosh, *Manliness*, p. 110.

for their own clubs which can be seen in the number of 'councils' and court of honours held and through the emphasis on team sports.

The link between moral and physical masculinity was encapsulated in the 'games ethic', which gained ground in Britain from the 1860s and was found in schools and clubs. The notion of the games ethic was vital in the construction of the clubs and the formation of their activities. As defined by Mangan, the games ethic was 'the belief that important expressive and instrumental qualities [could] be promoted through team games (in particular loyalty, self-control, perseverance, fairness and courage, both moral and physical)'.[60] The games ethic was supported initially by public schools and then in state schools and clubs, and encouraged sports and games as a way for men to develop the characteristics required for manliness as seen by the upper-classes. Clubs used team sports as a way to attract young people, but also to develop their members' manliness. The playing field was seen by the upper and middle classes as 'a singularly male space in which to vent noise, enthusiasm and feeling', which enabled the full development of masculine qualities to occur.[61] Sport, as the domain of men, was a vital tool in developing both the physical traits associated with manhood, but also the moral qualities and as a result, was a focus for many clubs.

The most obvious benefit of sports to the development of masculine qualities related to the perfection of the male physique. Athletics, gymnastics and body building, which have already been touched upon, were popular throughout Europe as a way to develop physical strength. In contrast, field games, including football and rugby, were a particularly British way to achieve masculine qualities. Through sports and team games, attention was placed squarely on the male body. This contributed to the development of the ideal masculine body by placing greater emphasis on developing muscles. The focus on sports was key in maintaining a notion of physical perfection in Britain and certainly was vital in stressing the need for men to develop their bodies. Indeed, 'the games playing cult ... gave concrete – and spectacular – attention to action through the medium of the

---

60   J. A. Mangan, 'Grammar Schools and the Games Ethic in the Victorian and Edwardian Era', *Albion*, 15 (1983), 313–15 (p. 314).

61   Melanie Tebbutt, *Being Boys: Youth Leisure and Identity in the Inter-War Years* (Manchester: Manchester University Press, 2012), p. 262.

male body'.[62] The development of outward appearance that resulted from playing team games was clearly significant, particularly for Jewish groups who used sport to promote the masculine appearance of Jews and counter the stereotypical image of Jewish ugliness. The promotion of team games, rather than individual sporting pursuits, placed a considerable emphasis on the collective, something that clubs were keen to utilize. Even pursuits that were traditionally individual became attached to the 'team'. In athletics for example, 'running for "the school", "the college", "the club" was of greater importance than running for oneself'.[63] The emphasis placed on the 'the team' was particularly noteworthy in Britain and was tied to Britain's imperial ambitions and need to preserve the Empire: 'team sports trained boys to obey (and later to give) orders; they subordinated the individual to the team effort; and they instilled stoicism in the face of pain and discomfort'.[64] In developing proper conduct on the sports field, men were encouraged to develop not only their physical appearance, but also encouraged to develop skills that would ensure the success and well-being of the British Empire.

The games-playing cult was a British phenomenon, used in all youth clubs, that played an increasingly pivotal role not only in the development of a masculine physique and manly qualities, but also in the suppression of the feminine.

Femininity

In the late nineteenth and early twentieth century, the woman's suffrage movement and increased opportunities for women in work and education were significant developments. Despite this, *notions* of women's roles remained largely unchanged until after the Second World War. Such

62   Park, 'Biological Thought', p. 10.

63   John Lowerson, *Sport and the English Middle-Classes, 1870–1914* (Manchester: Manchester University Press, 1995), p. 65.

64   Tosh, *Manliness*, p. 198. The emphasis on sport can be seen in other cultures at this time, for example in the USA.

continuity is hardly surprising considering the view that women themselves were considered to be unchangeable as 'women stood for immutability rather than progress'.[65] The late Victorian era viewed women as a complement to men and believed that 'God and nature had imbued women with qualities of mind and body that destined her for specific tasks, such as being man's helpmate, nurturing his children, and protecting the sanctity of his home.'[66] The private roles of wife and mother were therefore central to a woman's role and consequently to her identity.

One of the key roles performed by girls' clubs was promoting purity and providing protection for girls from negative influences within working class society. Women needed to remain respectable, both morally and physically, in order to fulfil their roles within the home. Central to this was the idea that a woman needed to distance herself from character traits associated with men. 'A lady' was considered to be feminine and as a consequence delicate; in contrast, the rejection of femininity was associated with tomboyism, cockiness and fighting.[67] The promotion of the 'feminine' image was something that both Jewish and non-Jewish clubs stressed. There was less emphasis placed on the physical appearance of the ideal woman than on the ideal man, but changing fashions and conventions led to changing notions of respectability affecting the image of the perfect woman. In Victorian and Edwardian society for example, the fashion was for a rounded female figure, whereas in the 1920s the trends resulted in shorter, tighter dress and a slim boyish shape, which reflected a kind of 'boyish athleticism', something the clubs tolerated.[68] This 'boyishness', however, was imbued with feminine conventions and certainly only applied to outward appearance – the feminine ideal of wife and mother remained.

65   George L. Mosse, *Nationalism and Sexuality: Respectability and Abnormal Sexuality in Modern Europe* (New York: Howard Fertig, 1985), p. 23.

66   Kathleen McCrone, 'Play Up! Play Up! And Play the Game! Sport at the Late Victorian Girls' Public School', in *From Fair Sex to Feminism: Sport and the Socialization of Women in the Industrial and Post-Industrial Eras*, ed. by J. A. Mangan and Roberta Park (London: Frank Cass, 1987), pp. 97–129 (p. 99).

67   Judy Giles, *Women, Identity and Private Life in Britain, 1900–1950* (Basingstoke: MacMillan, 1995), p. 60.

68   Pamela Horn, *Women in the 1920s* (Stroud: Allan Sutton, 1995), p. 20.

In this section, the analysis will focus on the role of the woman in the private sphere (that is within the home) and show how education and leisure helped to promote this ideal. I shall also explore the moral obligations of women as the spiritual influence within their families and within society as a whole. I will not focus on the role of suffrage or on increased employment opportunities as such, as although this undoubtedly influenced women's lives, it had little effect on the notion of an ideal woman (particularly for working class women) until after 1945.

Women's lives, unlike those of men, were centred on the home, regardless of the high percentage of females in the workplace, and this was stressed in the clubs where domestic activities, including ritual competence, were central. The importance of the home in women's lives persisted after the Second World War, if not in an identical form. Women were, however, not just intrinsically linked to the home, they were seen 'as irrational and emotional beings ... *excluded* from culture, political power and public space'.[69] The presence of women in the home and exclusion from public life (the domain of men) is at the heart of the notion of 'separate spheres' and the public/private divide, a theory popularized by Davidoff and Hall.[70] The separation of men's and women's lives was justified as 'men were identified with reason, women with emotions; men were associated with action, women with passivity; and finally men exercised domination, while women experienced submission'.[71] In short, the character of women was unsuited to public life and needed to be confined. This understanding of the public/private divisions of women's and men's roles was something that was understood, and came from, the women themselves as they contributed to discussions on the correct behaviour and occupations of women.[72]

69   Sue Bruley, *Women in Britain since 1900* (Basingstoke: MacMillan, 1999), p. 13. Emphasis my own.

70   See Leonore Davidoff and Catherine Hall, *Family Fortunes: Men and Women of the English Middle Class, 1780–1850* (London: Routledge, 1987).

71   Ina Zweininger-Bargielowska, *Women in Twentieth Century Britain* (Harlow: Pearson, 2001), pp. 8–9.

72   Anne Summers, *Female Lives: Moral States* (Newbury: Threshold, 2000), p. 6.

There are, however, limits to the extent to which *all* women adhered to this divide. Many women, especially those in the working classes, maintained employment and adopted a more public life. For Jewish women this was also true. In her study of oral history testimony from Manchester, Burman has noted that the mothers of two-thirds of those interviewed were engaged in some kind of paid work.[73] Eastern European tradition stressed that women should take employment, in addition to household work, to enable men to engage in religious scholarship (albeit not fulltime study). As a result, 'the sharp demarcation between home and work did not apply, and it was not necessarily a matter of shame for a woman to engage in paid work'.[74] For immigrant Jewish women, whilst the role of wife and mother was emphasized, taking on work outside of the home was not out of the ordinary. It is therefore important to consider that Jewish women were not confined solely to the home, but circumstances required them to enter the public sphere. Club leaders, particularly those working in the more impoverished areas, were aware of this, but they continued to promote ideal femininity. Despite the blurring of boundaries between the public and private for many women, the bourgeois *ideal* placed a certain centrality to the separate spheres ideology.

Popular women's magazines including *Women's Own*, *Home Chat* and *Women's Weekly* underscored the centrality of the home within a woman's life. Articles and features supported the domestic role of women and placed an emphasis on the need for women to remain within the 'private sphere' and as such they 'played a significant role in disseminating images of women that linked them tightly to the home and their role therein as domestic managers (housewives)'.[75] The clubs also utilized these images and used classes and events to encourage girls to take on these ideal roles within their family. The First World War gave many women a chance to leave the home and take on a wider range of employment. At the end of the war, however,

73 Burman, Rickie 'Jewish Woman and the Household Economy in Manchester, c. 1890–1920', in *The Making of Modern Anglo-Jewry*, ed. by David Cesarani (Oxford: Blackwell, 1990), pp. 55–76 (p. 58).

74 Ibid., p. 61.

75 Giles, *Women*, p. 6.

women were strongly encouraged to leave their jobs to allow returning soldiers to resume work. Increased employment during the war did not seriously challenge the notion of 'private spheres'. Certainly some public places, such as trains and buses became less gendered after 1918,[76] but nevertheless, the image of the ideal woman as belonging in the home persisted, despite changes in the political status of women, the presence of female MPs and the engagement of women in a wider pattern of employment.

As part of modernizing trends in Britain, Jewish women were expected to participate in the 'public sphere' of religion through attendance at the synagogue, although they were seated separately. Within Judaism, women were often more outwardly observant than men, especially in assimilated families, illustrated by the wife and female children of Viscount Herbert Samuel who 'regularly attended Sabbath services, whereas he attended only on High Holy Days'.[77] The perceived propensity of women toward religious observance meant that women were charged with ensuring men attended the synagogue. Similarly, women were blamed for causing a decline in religious observance, illustrated by Ray Frank talking about American Jewry in 1893:

> Go to the synagogue on a Friday night; where are the people? Our men cannot attend, keen business competition will not permit them. Where are our women? Keener indulgence in pleasures will not permit them ... with whom lies the blame? Where are the wise mothers of Israel today? ... That we are now in the position of backsliding is owing to us women.[78]

The *Jewish Chronicle* also shared this belief, stating 'possibly there is no feature of the age more dangerous or more distressing than the growing irreligion of women'.[79] For contemporary critics it was women who were to blame for a declining religious observance. Here, there was an expectation

---

76   Ibid., p. 102.

77   Paula E. Hyman, *Gender and Assimilation in Modern Jewish History: The Roles and Representation of Women* (London: University of Washington Press, 1997), p. 23.

78   Ray Frank, 'Women in the Synagogue', in *Papers of the Jewish Women's Congress Held at Chicago, September 4, 5, 6 and 7 1893* (Philadelphia: Jewish Publication Society of America, 1894), pp. 52–65 (p. 64) *Internet Archive* <http://archive.org> [accessed 12 July 2013].

79   *JC*, 12 March 1875.

for women to enter the public eye in order to attend a public religious service. Many girls' clubs had similar expectations for girls and provided opportunities for Jewish girls to take part in religious worship, although this was less formal than that provided in boys' clubs. Within Judaism, especially in the nineteenth century, women were not only meant to be more capable of religious feeling than men, but were also responsible for the continuation of the Jewish religion.

The emphasis on the 'private' sphere of women complemented their roles as wives and mothers. The strength of feeling regarding motherhood and housewifery was intensified at periods of national crisis such as the Boer War and particularly the First World War as the need for an increased population and improved fitness intensified. As a consequence of the First World War, for example, the government focused on the health of mother and baby by creating maternity feeding centres in large cities.[80] This was supported by women's magazines which promoted motherhood and housewifery amongst their female readership, often in infantilizing terms, referring to women as 'little wives', 'little mothers' and their 'little homes'.[81] The promotion of women as wives and mothers continued throughout the 1920s and 1930s. In a 1929 article entitled 'The Best Job for a Woman', *Good Housekeeping* magazine stated that women and girls should:

> Keep the idea of getting married *in the front of her head*. No woman who has ever achieved success in a business career ever is happy. The feminine nature craves masculine love and affection. Buried somewhere in each woman's heart is the desire for a home of her own and for children ... No girls can take a course of life against nature and find happiness and contentment. The happiest women in the world are those who cheerfully fulfil their natural destiny and get husbands and homes of their own with children in them.[82]

A woman's role as wife and mother was not solely promoted through adult reading material. Compulsory elementary education introduced

---

80   Horn, *Women*, p. 12.
81   Giles, *Women*, p. 60.
82   *Good Housekeeping*, January 1929, 'The Best Job for a Girl'. Quoted in Horn, *Women*, p. 61.

in 1880 featured education for girls based upon their future domestic duties, including needlework, cookery and laundry lessons.[83] This domestic education was often seen in clubs where girls were given opportunities to attend classes in millinery, fancy needlework and plain needlework.[84] These classes allowed the clubs to contribute to the promotion of the ideal, domestic woman. Fears of degeneration in the early twentieth century led to the introduction of infant care classes. These classes encouraged girls to '"set a high value on the housewives position" on the grounds that national efficiency must inevitably depend upon a strong tradition of homelife'.[85] Being a wife and a mother was supposed to be central to a woman's role and to her identity and this persisted despite declining birth rates, the emancipation of women and improved education and work opportunities.

It is vital also to look at the roles and expectations of women from *within* Jewish culture. In addition to the emphasis placed on motherhood and housewifery in British society on the whole, for Jewish women, an additional emphasis was placed on these roles. 'Victorian society saw the woman as the … guardian of her home, a role enhanced for Jewish women by the domestic rituals expected of them by religious law.'[86] Summers adds to this, detailing the expectations of Jewish women to be involved in Jewish education: 'mothers were expected to impart initial religious instruction to their own children and were, of course, the first to be blamed if these departed from the straight and narrow'.[87] Keeping *kosher* was an additional responsibility of the Jewish woman, which emphasized the spiritual importance of woman as a housewife. The need for Judaism to be passed

83   Bruley, *Women*, p. 16.
84   The National Archives (hereafter TNA), ED 41/262 Beatrice Club Annual Reports 1919–1926.
85   Penny Tinkler, 'Girlhood and Growing Up', in *Women in Twentieth Century Britain*, ed. by Ina Zweininger-Bargielowska (Harlow: Pearson, 2001), pp. 35–50 (p. 37).
86   Francis Guy, *Women of Worth: Jewish Women in Britain* (Manchester: Manchester Jewish Museum, 1992), p. 3.
87   Anne Summers, 'Gender, Religion and an Immigrant Minority: Jewish Women and the Suffrage Movement in Britain c. 1900–1920', *Women's History Review*, 21 (2012), pp. 399–418 (p. 403).

to children via the mother placed a greater stress on the role of motherhood for the Jewish woman and their key role within the Jewish family further increased this responsibility. 'Three millennia of tradition glorified Jewish women in the roles of wife and mother because they were vital to the Jewish family which was perceived as the key to Jewish survival.'[88] For Jewish women, being a wife and mother was not only important for their identity as a woman, but for their communal identity as Jews. The clubs, therefore, emphasized the role of food and motherhood in the religious education of girl members.

For women defined as wives and mothers and confined to the home, their religious and spiritual character was emphasized: 'religiosity was considered to be a woman's innate gift and the inculcation of religion to her children was considered her most important task'.[89] Indeed, as Summers noted, with women's exclusion from political and economic life in the British tradition (although not to the same extent for immigrant women) the remaining area for women to play a role focussed on the moral and spiritual arenas.[90] In contrast to men, women were seen to have a greater capacity for religious knowledge as they were perceived as more emotional.[91] Within the Evangelical tradition, for example, 'girls were raised to believe that they had a particular religious obligation to help family and society'.[92] Contemporary Jewish ideals had absorbed these views. As mothers, and confined to the home, women of the middle and upper classes were expected to help educate their family: 'bourgeois division of labour between the sexes also conferred responsibility upon the woman for religiously based

88   Linda Gordon Kuzmack, *Woman's Cause: The Jewish Woman's Movement in England and the United States 1881–1933* (Columbus: Ohio State University Press, 1990), p. 9.
89   Michael Galchinsky, 'Engendering Liberal Jews: Jewish Women in Victorian England', in *Jewish Women in Historical Perspective*, ed. by Judith R. Baskin (Detroit, MI: Wayne State University Press, 1998), pp. 208–26 (p. 211).
90   Summers, *Female Lives*, p. 18.
91   Lily Montagu, 'The Role of Women In Religious Life', in *A Reader of Early Liberal Judaism: The Writings of Israel Abrahams, Claude Montefiore, Lily Montagu and Israel Mattuck*, ed. by Edward Kessler (London: Vallentine Mitchell, 2004), pp. 127–9 (p. 127).
92   Kuzmack, *Woman's Cause*, p. 14.

good works, including religious education of children'.[93] Religious education was considered an acceptable form of work for women, within the
confines of their knowledge. Spirituality and religion were considered
vital parts of the woman's role within the family and innately suited to a
woman's emotional and delicate nature.

As noted, many depictions of Jewish manliness were opposed to traditional depictions of the non-Jewish man. For Jewish women, however, this
relationship to concepts of femininity was more ambiguous. The Jewish
woman was often seen as both the ideal of womanhood and at the same time
the embodiment of dangerous sexualities. Their desirability, innocence and
abilities at mothering were emphasized in politics and in popular culture.
Within nineteenth-century non-Jewish writing, the male Jew was represented as primitive whilst the female Jew was 'spiritual, cultured, patriotic,
emotional and modern'.[94] Within Parliament, the Jewish mother was commended for her abilities. In the Royal Commission on Alien Immigration
it was reported that:

> in the care of their children the Jewish mothers are a pattern to their Gentile neigh-
> bours in the East End. Go and visit the schools in the East End and see the Jewish
> children. They stand out in marked contrast to the other children for brightness and
> healthy appearance. That is only due to the Jewish mothers.[95]

Jewish women were depicted as the epitome of femininity. Despite these
favourable depictions, the Jewish woman was also seen as a dangerous
temptress. Jewish prostitution was seen as an example of the dangerousness
of the Jewish woman's sexuality. Jewish women were seen as particularly
susceptible to prostitution and 'symbolized the social evils which were
undermining the strength of the family and the Empire'.[96] As the image of

---

93   Hyman, *Gender*, p. 26.

94   Nadia Valman, *The Jewess in Nineteenth Century British Literary Culture* (Cambridge:
      Cambridge University Press, 2007), p. 209.

95   *Parliamentary Papers*, Mr J. Prag, evidence to the Royal Commission on Alien
      Immigration, 1903, ix pt ii, minutes of evidence, Q17877.

96   Lara V. Marks, *Model Mothers: Jewish Mothers Maternity Provision in East London,
      1870–1939* (Oxford: Clarendon, 1994), p. 3.

the Jewish mother was used in defence of the Jews, the image of the Jewish prostitute was often evoked in anti-alien debates. The Jewish woman was thus depicted in two strikingly contrasting ways: first, as the embodiment of femininity and, second, as the antithesis to the ideal woman. This affected clubs, which saw the maintenance of purity as one of their key concerns. Institutions, such as the Jewish Association for the Protection of Girls and Women and the girls' clubs worked to prevent women from succumbing to negative influences and thus contributing to the negative image of Jewish women in British society.

Jewish women held roles as wives and mothers similar to those of their non-Jewish counterparts, but with added responsibilities attached to Jewish religious observances and the need to preserve the Jewish faith. Activities within the clubs emphasized ideal notions of femininity, especially domesticity and purity. They also faced the burden of societal attitudes, which lauded them as wives and mothers but at the same time vilified their sexuality. For Jewish men, traditionally excluded from the manly ideal, Jews promoted their own notions of masculinity in the form of muscular Judaism, reflecting trends within non-Jewish society. For both Jews and non-Jews, masculinity was strongly dependent on the cultivation of the physique and on the development of moral code, which encouraged independence.

The ideal roles of men and women were clearly differentiated, for both Jews and non-Jews alike. Whilst boys were expected to play sports and develop independence, girls were encouraged to develop skills to help them become good wives and mothers. For the Jewish community, the need to adhere to these gender roles was especially important in order to dispel myths of the 'scandalous' Jewish woman and the 'feminine' Jewish man. Within Jewish schools and clubs, gendered education was crucial in promoting an acceptably British image that was a credit to the Jewish community as a whole. As this book contends, the religious programming of Jewish youth clubs played a key role in promoting acceptably gendered identities.

The Clubs

Religious activities were manifest in all of the Jewish clubs regardless of denomination. As will become apparent, in some clubs, such as the Oxford and St George's Jewish Lads' Club and the West Central Jewish Girls' Club they took on a more central role. For others, including the Brady Boys' Club, religion was less prominent as a response to their identity as a Jewish, but not religious, club. Even so, all Jewish youth clubs taught aspects of religiosity relevant to the distinct perceived needs of boys and girls. This study will look at the way in which these religious activities were able to promote gendered British identities, particularly examining the ways in which religious content made use of (or ignored) accepted gender norms within the UK.

What follows is not a narrow *political* history of youth or religious education. As a consequence I will not look at educational reforms or the impact that this had on Jewish communities, nor will I look at the formal schooling, except briefly in order to contextualize informal education. Rather, I will approach the study of religion and gender from a social history viewpoint, which will utilize both religious and gender studies. As a result, the analysis will focus on the impact that religious programming had on the social and cultural conditioning of young people and on the social conditions that resulted in such religious education.

This study will use primary documentation to analyse the clubs' activities. Annual reports produced by the clubs themselves, official club records, including minutes and correspondence, and club magazines will provide the basis for this study. These sources provide an organizational narrative on club activities which, whilst an invaluable source of evidence, needs to be dealt with critically. A number of these documents, particularly annual reports, were produced to publicize the clubs' achievements to investors, supporters and potential investors. As a result, these documents need to be read with the understanding that the information provided was designed to present each club in the best possible way. To some extent this is also true of club magazines as these, like the annual reports, were distributed to investors and the Jewish press. The youth involvement in producing the magazines, however, means that these documents are more complex. Unlike annual reports, which were produced solely by adult members, magazines were often edited, produced and written by the young people themselves. Yet, the use of these documents as a publicity tool does mean that it was likely that the production of these documents was overseen by a leader in order to present an acceptable image of the group. Club magazines were more popular amongst boys' clubs than girls'. At some point prior to 1939 all boys' clubs produced magazines, however, the runs were limited with many stopping when no-one could be found to take them over. Whereas annual reports and minutes can still be found for most clubs, there are fewer surviving magazines. Particularly useful collections of these are copies of the *Stepnian* from 1917 to 1922, the *Notting Hill Club Magazine* (1911–14), the '*Hutch*' (1912–15) and copies of various incarnations of the Jewish Lads' Brigade Magazines from 1910 to 1939.[97]

Public representations of the clubs will be explored through the press, both Jewish and non-Jewish to help supplement material generated by the clubs themselves. In particular, the *Jewish Chronicle, Jewish World, Jewish Guardian and Jewish Echo* will be used. It is important to note that the *Jewish Chronicle* and *Jewish World* papers were sympathetic to Orthodox Judaism whereas the *Jewish Guardian* took a more liberal outlook. This is particularly important to consider when looking at the Liberal Jewish Clubs. The *Jewish Echo* dealt with Scottish, and to a lesser extent, northern communities and thus represented a more localized view. Many of the articles within these papers were based on information submitted by the clubs directly to the newspapers as printed requests stated that: 'We shall be pleased to receive information from the secretaries of the various lads' and girls' clubs brief reports for insertion into this [the young Jewry] column.'[98] In these cases submissions were printed as submitted with identical (or near identical) reports featuring across multiple papers. These articles thus represent an ideal public image of clubs' activities, similar to that found

97   *The Stepnian* – London Library M395, University of Southampton Archives (hereafter SUA), MS172, *Notting Hill Club Magazine* SUA MS116, *The Hutch* Jewish Museum London (hereafter JML), 1991.30.1 and JLB magazines, SUA MS244.
98   *Jewish World* (hereafter *JW*), 29 September 1920.

in annual reports. In some instances journalists engaged in dialogue with the clubs, using their columns to respond to and at times challenge club work. This is particularly true of 'the Young Judean', a columnist in the *Jewish World*. He frequently reviewed submissions from the clubs, including annual reports and magazines, and added his opinion. In many cases, such as following his attack on the Hutchison House Club, the leaders responded to the criticism and offered counter arguments, which were then further analysed by the 'Young Judean'.[99] These 'conversations', as well as those found in the letters sections of papers add contemporary criticism to our understanding of clubs and thus provide a vital counter to official club reports. These discussions also present an idea of the circulation of ideas within the Jewish community, highlighting the importance of the Jewish press in disseminating information.

The 'top-down' nature of these sources is problematic. There are a limited number of oral history accounts available from former members and a handful of contemporary accounts of club activities from members. Such accounts can be found to a limited extent in club magazines, but also within larger collections such as a boy's report of a Jewish Lads' Brigade camp, written on his return found within the larger collection.[100] The scarcity of accounts from club members, rather than the leaders, will prove a challenge, as there is a tendency to report on idealized versions of club activities. Additionally, the nature of oral history testimony will also prove challenging. The construction of memory in relation to oral histories has been explored by many scholars. One of the most obvious challenges is that memory changes over time and is influenced by public understanding of events. It is thus important to bear this in mind when using oral history testimonies. An additional challenge can be found particularly in the case of accounts that were recorded in the 1990s and conducted by other historians which, as 'oral history is a dialogic discourse' naturally records memories that were geared to the interviewers' interests, rather than my own.[101] These include

---

99   See *JW*, 2 October 1930 to 6 November 1930.
100   SUA MS 244 and 233.
101   Alessandro Portelli, 'Oral History as Genre', in *Narrative and Genre*, ed. by Mary Chamberlain and Paul Thompson (London: Routledge, 1998), pp. 23–45 (p. 23).

the London Museum of Jewish Life oral history interviews, the Millennium Memory Bank collection, the Living Memory of the Jewish Community recordings and the collections held at Manchester Jewish Museum.[102] The analysis will thus take interviewers' motivations into account when using their interviews. The book will therefore make use of the limited number of accounts from young people in order to present a multi-layered approach from the bottom-up, as well as the top-down and one that does not rely solely on the 'official' point of view. In all cases, the varied evidence will be contextualized, allowing for a critical study of the subject matter.

It should also be noted that fuller records survive relating to boys' clubs, particularly from the Jewish Lads' Brigade, compared to those from girls' clubs. Whilst there are surviving records relating to girls' clubs, with the exception of the West Central Jewish Girls' Club, these records do not present a full picture of the clubs activities. Instead, they focus only on activities that were noteworthy enough to appear in annual reports. In these instances, newspaper reports will help to further elaborate on the clubs' activities. These newspaper reports are of particular value when looking at British Jewish identities in this period, as 'one important source for the construction and consolidation of [community] identities is doubtless the Jewish press'.[103] It has to be considered, however, that the newspaper resources utilized in this book present, as noted, an idealized image of how the clubs contributed to the formation of British Jewish identities – however useful they are in reconstructing their detailed activities.

The primary material examined covers a number of Jewish clubs across the UK rather than focusing exclusively on London-based organizations. Indeed, this is a limitation of much of the existing historiography. It is important to consider these provincial clubs in order to add depth to our understanding of Jewish youth groups. In some areas, the original documentation is rich, for example the Scottish Jewish Archives hold considerable information on Jewish Guides in Glasgow and the Liverpool Records

---

102   See MJM, JML and BL for copies of these collections.
103   Jonathan Webber, 'Introduction', in *Jewish Identities in the New Europe*, ed. by Jonathan Webber (London: Littman Library of Jewish Civilisation, 1994), pp. 1–32 (p. 24).

Office hold detailed accounts on the Liverpool Jewish Girls' Club. In others, however, evidence is scarce; information relating to the Nottingham Jewish Girls' Club, for instance, is limited to just three documents.[104] As the clubs looked at include not only groups within England, but also within Scotland, Ireland and, to a lesser extent, Wales, it is important to clarify the terminology used to discuss nationality and belonging. Throughout the original material there are some inconsistencies with the terms 'British' and 'English'. Here, I will use the word English when looking at clubs that operated solely within England (and, by extension, 'Scottish' for those that operated in Scotland). The term 'British' will be used when discussing clubs which operated *across* the UK. This distinction will help to examine subtle differences between Scottish, English and British identities and aid in a clearer understanding of appropriate national (as well as gendered) identities.[105]

The study will analyse a number of Jewish clubs before 1939. A thematic, rather than chronological, approach will aid comparisons to be made with the different types of Jewish youth clubs, whilst providing context in time and place throughout. The first two chapters will look at Orthodox clubs for boys and for girls as these constituted the majority of the youth groups at this time. Girls' clubs will be looked at first as these were the first clubs to open and as a result boys' clubs often followed patterns laid out by their female counterparts. The next two chapters will examine the uniformed youth groups (the Jewish Lads' Brigade and the Scouts and Guides) as whilst these groups followed similar patterns to their non-uniformed counterparts there were significant deviations. The final two chapters will focus on the Liberal Jewish clubs (that is, those influenced by Liberal Judaism) as these groups differed greatly from the examples provided by their Orthodox counterparts. This structure will enable depth and nuance of the argument to gradually be developed, as the deviations from traditional gender norms become more evident as the chapters progress,

---

104 See, for example, SJAC, SOC SCO 0001–0004 and Liverpool Records Office (hereafter LRO), 296 JGC.

105 It should be added that some contemporary documents refer to England when in fact covering the whole of the United Kingdom. The contemporary usage will be maintained but it is a complication that has to be kept in mind.

since the clubs looked at in later chapters adopted a less Orthodox religious stance. By approaching the different categories of clubs in separate chapters, common themes will be easily identifiable within each chapter and differences between each type of club will also be noted. The clubs that will be examined can be seen as 'social clubs', rather than educational, political or cultural ones. As a result, Zionist groups are not included here; although these clubs did have a social aspect, this was not their primary goal.

The first two chapters will concentrate on groups in and out of London, firstly on girls' clubs, including the Beatrice Club and Butler Street Girls' Club and secondly on boys' clubs, including the Brady Street Club and Victoria Boys' Club. A large number of clubs began in the late nineteenth and early twentieth century in the East End. These clubs were often attached to Orthodox Judaism and were usually run by a group of volunteers headed by a well-known figure within Anglo-Jewry. In both instances, the book will discuss the extent to which religion was dominated by the need to promote gender norms and explore how religious programming reflected different expectations of girls and boys.

The third and fourth chapters will look at national, uniformed youth groups. The Jewish Lads' Brigade (JLB) was the largest of the specifically Jewish clubs to operate in the UK and had branches in London, Manchester and Glasgow as well as in cities with smaller Jewish populations. Even so, the companies were operated under a central committee and each area had its own character. Whilst both the JLB and the Scouts and Guides (all groups within these umbrella organizations adopted uniforms to some extent) were known for their abilities to 'uniform' the outward appearance of their members, this chapter will look at whether this 'uniforming' quality can be applied to their religious practices. These chapters will also look at the extent to which the members were able to adapt the programme to their own needs in the same way they were able to adapt the uniform to their own individual and economic circumstances.[106]

The final chapters will look at the West Central Girls' Club (WCGC) and the Oxford and St George's Club (OSGC), run by Lily Montagu and

---

106　See Proctor, '(Uni)Forming Youth'.

Basil Henriques – leading figures within Liberal Judaism. In both of these clubs religion played a large role, influenced by their founders' beliefs. These chapters will, in contrast to previous chapters, ask whether gendered religious identities were specific to Orthodox Judaism.

Through analysing these four groups of Jewish clubs, this study will ask how religious programming within clubs helped leaders to promote acceptably gendered British identities. More specifically, it will examine the extent to which the gendering of religion can be seen as a vital component of Jewish education between 1880 and 1939. The answers to these questions will shed light on the social conditioning of young Jews and will help to elaborate our understanding of the immigrant Jewish experience as a whole. It will place emphasis especially on the case of Jewish girls' clubs, to which little scholarly attention has been dedicated and to which the first chapter will focus to demonstrate that religious programming was designed to effect a girl's identity.

CHAPTER 1

Girls' Clubs, 1886–1939

At the end of the nineteenth and beginning of the twentieth century, many girls' clubs were founded, both in and out of London. A number of these clubs had a religious basis with large numbers underpinned by varieties of Christianity. In areas with a large Jewish population, such as the East End of London, a number of Jewish clubs also emerged. These last mentioned were fuelled by the wave of new immigration to the country and the crowded and insanitary conditions in which many of the immigrant Jews lived. The clubs were focused on improving the lives of the members, both as proto-English females *and* as Jewish girls. This section will focus on a number of Jewish clubs both in and out of London. Within London, I will look at Leman Street Club, the Beatrice Club and the Butler Street Club, as they were some of the largest girls' clubs during the early twentieth century. There were also a number of smaller groups, including the Stepney Girls' Club and the Kilburn Girls' Recreation Club and these will also be included in this section. Outside London, several cities with large Jewish populations had their own girls' clubs, including Bristol, Nottingham, Glasgow, Dublin,[1] Cardiff and Liverpool.

The period between 1880 and 1939 marked changes in wider society that saw an increase in general philanthropy amongst the privileged classes. In particular, women became involved with charitable causes. Within the context of youth club work generally, several prominent female youth workers emerged, including Christian youth workers Maude Stanley and Emmeline Pethick (later Pethick-Lawrence) who worked with Christian

---

1   Although the Irish Free State (including Dublin) broke away from the United Kingdom in 1922, the work of the Dublin Adelaide Girls' Friendly Club has been included in this study as it began its work as part of the United Kingdom and then followed similar patters after partition until 1939.

girls and boys in the more deprived parts of London. Stanley's Soho club established in 1880 had the vaguely religious aim of showing girls 'a higher life worth living for' which alluded to the club's wider goal of providing uplifting social, cultural and religious experiences.[2] It can therefore be seen to have an indirect religious basis, although it does not mention religion specifically in its aims. Stanley observed that one of the most common ways clubs began was by drawing members from a particular church or parish.[3] In this way, religion in Christian clubs was a common basis for the founding of such organizations. Emmeline Pethick, who with Mary Neal founded the Esperance Club in the 1890s, saw the religious guidance of her girls as part of the clubs' duties. She stated that 'the working girl has not yet realized the importance of getting her own soul saved!'[4] Whilst the club was most known for its role in employment reform, religion was an underlying part of the club's mission, which the club promoted during the course of its evening activities through prayers. For these clubs, and the others like them, the motivation behind the creation of girls' clubs lay in the ideal of keeping women off the streets and protecting their virtues. This can be seen in religious missions such as those stated above, as it shows teachings about morality played a key part in the initial rationale of girls' clubs.

For Jewish women the stimulus for the creation of clubs came from two angles. First, the foundation of the clubs was consistent in the wider context of Victorian philanthropy. In the Jewish context, girls were raised with the knowledge that:

> they had a particular religious obligation to help family and society particularly its weak and unprotected citizens, through public as well as private philanthropy. As women became active in charitable societies, many came to believe that a woman's vocation as moral protector of the family might take her outside of the home to care for others.[5]

2   Maude Stanley, *The Way to Start and Manage a Girls Club* (London: Macmillan and Co, 1890), p. 48.

3   Stanley, *Girls Club*, p. 16.

4   Emmeline Pethick, 'Working Girls' Clubs', in *University and Social Settlements*, ed. by W. Reason (London: Methuen, 1898), pp. 101–14 (p. 102).

5   Linda Gordon Kuzmack, *Woman's Cause: The Jewish Woman's Movement in England and the United States 1881–1933* (Columbus: Ohio State University Press, 1990, p. 14.

This is a key reason for the emergence of girls' clubs: several prominent members of the established Anglo-Jewry such as Lady Montagu, Lady Magnus and the Rothschilds began to see their obligation to impoverished, immigrant Jewish girls. Second, creating these clubs worked to address particularly Jewish concerns that were brought about by the societal changes of industrialization and increased leisure time and leisure possibilities. For many of the Orthodox synagogues in both the UK and beyond these changes were a major issue. Many felt that the combination of industrialization and increased leisure resulted in poor attendance at services and as seen earlier, many believed that women were to blame for the decline in religiosity. Combined with this, immigrant Orthodoxy often took on a distinct character that some Anglo-Jewry felt was out of place in the UK and certainly at odds with Anglo-Orthodoxy. For Jewish girls' clubs therefore it was particularly vital to instil a religious feeling amongst the girl members, not only for the future of Anglo-Jewry, but also for the validation of the club managers' own efforts with the Jewish poor.

This feeling of obligation and the need to further the religious observance of the Anglo-Jewish population explains, in part, the reason for the emergence of clubs. It was not, however, just the club leaders who held this view. Although there was a certain amount of indifference to religion amongst the Jewish poor there were also those who, following traditional views on the position of women with regard to religion, felt that it was their obligation to learn more about their religious heritage. A letter to The *Jewish Chronicle* by a member of one of the London Clubs agreed that the religious elements of club life helped to secure the future of Judaism. 'I think that the future of Jewry lies in the hands of its daughters, for how much Judaism can a mother, practically ignorant of the holy tongue, teach her child?'[6] The message that the young women were responsible for the future of Judaism was clearly apparent in the objects and aims of the club, and was heard and absorbed by club members, as is evident through letters written by club members to the Jewish press. The justification for the religious elements in the working of the clubs is clear: by improving each

6   *JC*, 20 March 1908.

girl spiritually, she would in turn, improve the young men and enable girls to have a successful Jewish family life in the future.

The primary Victorian Jewish attitude towards women was to see them as the future of Judaism, and as delicate people who needed clear and careful guidance. As Linda Kuzmack notes, 'traditional Judaism's attitudes toward sex-role differences profoundly affected all aspects of Jewish women's lives'.[7] In the construction of Jewish tradition, girls were seen as the flag-bearers for respectability, a view that was supported by mainstream Victorian traditions, as well as guardians of home life and associated rituals and with the maintenance of Jewish faith.[8] In the context of increased immigration and increasing concern about the threat that immigration posed to the emancipation achieved by British Jews, this view of women, as the role model for respectability encompassing general moral values, as well as religious values, provides a key explanation of why girls were such a target for philanthropy.

In terms of religious participation in the synagogue and in the home, women were also seen as the most important influence over the family. Not only were women expected to be religious on a personal level, both in belief and practice, but they were also expected to lead their family in following a devout life. This was a feature of emancipated and enlightened Western culture as a whole, and the Jewish population was certainly not exempt from these expectations. 'Christian women, spurred by the nineteenth-century Evangelical revival sweeping England and America, which urged a return to God and morality had begun attending worship services in increasing numbers, and Jewish women were beginning to emulate their example.'[9] 'Bourgeois culture thus expected women to be at least moderately religious,

---

7   Kuzmack, *Woman's Cause*, p. 4.
8   Nadia Valman, 'Jewish Girls and the Battle of Cable Street', in *Remembering Cable Street: Fascism and Anti-Fascism in British Society*, ed. by Tony Kushner and Nadia Valman (London: Vallentine Mitchell, 1999), pp. 181–94 (p. 182); Frances Guy, *Women of Worth: Jewish Women in Britain* (Manchester: Manchester Jewish Museum, 1992), p. 3; Paula E. Hyman, *Gender and Assimilation in Modern Jewish History: The Roles and Representation of Women* (London: University of Washington Press, 1997), p. 23.
9   Kuzmack, *Woman's Cause*, p. 9.

certainly more religious than men.'[10] It is this viewpoint of the traditional Jewish woman's role that can explain the emergence of specifically Jewish *girls'* clubs in the decade prior to the emergence of clubs for Jewish boys. Combined with the view that it was women who had the greatest religious responsibility, these arguments proved a powerful force in the creation and defence of girls' clubs.

These beliefs can also explain not only the clubs' focus on the moral and social position of young women, but also the sheer quantity of clubs that were available for them. The formation of clubs for vulnerable Jewish girls provided native Jewry with 'an opportunity to display British Jews as staunchly moral, prepared to discharge unpleasant civic duties, standing as peers with the leaders of other religious denominations.'[11] Girls' clubs, therefore, provided a twofold benefit: firstly to help with the continuation of the Jewish faith and secondly to help preserve the position of Jews within English society as a whole. It is important to remember that the opening of girls' clubs was not unique to the Jewish community. Jewish clubs mirrored the general trends of the time. Nonetheless, many of the motivating factors behind the work of Jewish clubs were unique in the way that they were responding to specifically Jewish concerns and a specifically Jewish set of circumstances.

The Jewish Girls' Club was established in 1886 by Lady Magnus (1844–1924), noted philanthropist and daughter of Portsmouth's first Jewish Mayor who was connected to a number of charitable causes, including the Jewish Association for the Protection of Girls and Women.[12] The group was founded as a small, bi-weekly, sewing circle for girls aged 14 and over is often cited as the first girls' club for young Jewish women. The Club retained its core leaders throughout its early history, after it moved to new premises in Leman Street in 1903 the club was often referred to as the Leman Street Girls' Club. More importantly, the group retained the same purpose, working toward

10   Hyman, *Gender*, p. 26.
11   Valman, 'Jewish Girls', p. 187.
12   Sharman Kadish, 'Katie Magnus', *Oxford Dictionary of National Biography* (Oxford: Oxford University Press, 2004), <http://www.oxforddnb.com/view/article/55630> [accessed 2 February 2015].

the 'formation of character'.[13] Like many of the Jewish girls' clubs that began during this time, the club was Orthodox in character. Certainly, there were Liberal clubs and these will be looked at in a separate chapter.

Background and Ethos

The mission statement of each of the girls' clubs, although varying in some ways in their wording and geographical sensitivities, were largely similar. The Jewish Girls' Club drew its initial members from the Hanway Sabbath Class. The object was 'to improve and to refine, to consolidate and to develop the proper rearing of Jewish girls'.[14] This aim was clarified in 1903 when the girls were told that 'Jewish girls must be religious minded, modest, well mannered, good sisters, daughters and wives, and old fashioned enough to believe that marriage was the finishing touch and the best touch at all'.[15] For the Jewish Girls' Club, religious education was a vital step in creating good Jewish wives and mothers. The Beatrice Street Club, at its opening in 1901, stated that:

> its objects in the first place are social, to provide some break in the dull monotony of the life of the working girls of the Notting Hill district, and to supply for the girls a rendezvous, where, after the day's work they meet and spend the evening in music, physical recreation, or reading according to the bent of their various tastes. In addition it is hoped to give an educational side to the club by establishing classes for wood carving, choral singing, religion and Hebrew.[16]

The aims of the Beatrice Club can then be seen as both recreational and as educational, the latter including religious education. At the opening of the Club, Samuel Montagu appealed to the girls that they would:

13   *JC*, 1 May 1903.
14   *JC*, 26 December 1890.
15   *JC*, 11 May 1903.
16   *JC*, 29 March 1901.

not forget when they belonged to the club that there was a synagogue next door, and that its galleries were not always filled with young girls or even with older people. He thought that once the young girls went to the synagogue the young men would also go.[17]

The girls were encouraged to attend services, not just for themselves, but also for the good of the young men and the Jewish population as a whole, reinforcing the idea that women were responsible for the lack of religiosity amongst the Jewish community. At the Annual General Meeting of the Beatrice club in 1913, the chairman stated that the 'real object of the club was not so much for the social function of the classes, but for the purpose of enabling members to obtain comfort, advices and help so that they in turn could carry on the good work and know that Jewish girls could be good Jewesses and thus good citizens'.[18]

The Bristol Girls' Club began in the early twentieth century with the aim to

> help girls when they left school to go on trying to improve themselves both in mind and body ... one needed to be always trying to learn how to make full use of those wonderful gifts of God, our bodies and our minds and in doing so, we could best show our loving gratitude to God for His gifts.[19]

Here, the rationale for the club was largely similar to those found within London, emphasizing the need for girls to be engaged in continual improvement. The religious element was explicit and it is clear from this statement that the club believed that all of their actions were, in some sense, religious, thus religion was the key reason for its existence. It is clear from these examples that women were seen as an important tool for influencing young men, as they were generally during this period. It is therefore not surprising that the girls' clubs saw religion as a vital element of their programme, and also as a way to ensure wider religious participation within the Jewish community as a whole. This is particularly true of clubs that began prior

17 *JC*, 29 March 1901.
18 *JC*, 24 March 1913.
19 *JC*, 20 March 1903.

to 1914; however, clubs that were founded after the First World War had an additional reason for promoting religion.

In the 1920s, the Deborah Wenter Girls' Club was founded by the Chief Rabbi with a similar religious aim to older groups. Unlike clubs that had begun prior to the First World War, the aim of the group was not simply to prevent girls from losing their religion. The club operated in the same area as the Liberal-affiliated West Central Jewish Girls' Club and was specifically designed to keep young girls away from the perceived dangers of Liberal Judaism. In 1928 the group stated that 'affiliated as it was to the Orthodox congregation in Soho, it was founded primarily to provide a centre of recreation for the children of that congregation with the advantage of a religious atmosphere'.[20] During the club's early years, the link to Orthodoxy was frequently highlighted. For the Deborah Wenter Club – in addition to the aims of creating good Jewish wives and mothers that it had in common with other girls' clubs – it also had the additional aim of ensuring that the girls were adhering to the 'correct' or more specifically, Orthodox form of Judaism.

Once the clubs had been established, they needed to reinforce their religious position in order to justify their 'Jewishness' to the wider Jewish community. The clubs frequently asserted their religious outlook, especially during key points in the clubs' calendar such as at annual displays, prize-givings and in annual reports. Each year, at the Annual Display (the showcase of a club's work presented to its investors and members' parents) the Jewish Girls' Club at Leman Street publicly clarified that their religious position remained the same as it had been when the club was founded.[21] In 1911 the club stated that 'the three 'R's, Religion, Refinement and Recreation … are still our standard aims and personal service'.[22] For them, religion was the first item mentioned in their aims, therefore giving prominence to their religious obligations, stressing its importance over and above the other elements of club work. In the 1920s, the club continued to emphasize the continuity in its religious policy. In the annual report of the group in

20   *Jewish Guardian* (hereafter *JG*), 9 March 1928.
21   *JC*, 17 February 1911, *JG*, 7 April 1922 and 18 May 1928.
22   *JC*, 17 February 1911.

1922, it stated that 'we try to keep the club essentially Jewish as it always has been. We follow the lines set up by the Lady Magnus and teach our girls to know the beauty of their faith and the history of their own race and therefore care for both.'[23] Similarly, in 1928, the club emphasized the continuity in its religious policies: 'our aims and ideals … are the same set out for us by our late dear foundress Lady Magnus – that our girls shall be better, as well as happier, for being members of the club, and that they shall know and therefore care for their fine old religion, and its age-long hero-ic history'.[24] Throughout the history of the Leman Street Club, the religious ideal remained remarkably similar to that laid out at its founding. The club continued to stress the importance of the religious element of club work and frequently religion was mentioned *first* among the club's aims. This demonstrates that the club believed their religion to be key to its ethos, the foundation from which its social activities could flourish.

In partial contrast, the Beatrice Girls' Club had less explicit religious aims than the Leman Street Club. They stated that 'the real object of the club was not so much for the social function of the classes, but for the purpose of enabling members to obtain comfort, advice and help so that they in turn could carry on the good work and know that Jewish girls could be good Jews and thus good citizens',[25] noting religious priority in their aims. Whilst there was no overt mention of their religious practices, the club viewed part of its obligation to make the girls become 'good Jews'. A number of the clubs' activities, including evening prayer and Sabbath services (which will be looked at later) as well as the presence of the Chief Rabbi at a number of club events, demonstrate that religion *was* included, and that a religious element formed a large part of the club's responsibilities. In 1928, the chairman of the annual display recorded that 'the religious aspect … of the club was very valuable for in a Jewish club they must … inculcate loyalty to their religion'.[26] In this instance religion within the Beatrice Club was mentioned much more specifically than it had been

23   *JG*, 7 April 1922.
24   *JG*, 18 May 1928.
25   *JC*, 14 March 1913.
26   *JG*, 23 March 1928.

fifteen years earlier, likely as a response to fears within the wider Jewish community of the growing irreligiosity of young Jews. The chairman referred to the work done by the group as 'valuable' indicating that the club had managed to include religious events that had made an impact on the girls' religious lives.

Not all clubs maintained a positive attitude to their religious work. The Butler Street club recognized that their religious programming was lacking and in their second annual report gave an honest appraisal of their religious influence: 'so far no specifically religious work has been undertaken at the club with the exception of talks and lectures on Jewish history and the Scripture class ... each meeting however, is always closed by a short service'.[27] For many boys' clubs, occasional classes and sporadic synagogue parades were considered to be sufficient. In the Butler Street Club, however, there was a need to go beyond classes and evening services. Within the Leman Street and Butler Clubs as well, religious activities were seen to need more than just classes and a prayer services. As girls were expected to be more spiritual and had a duty to continue the Jewish faith amongst their families to an extent not expected for boys, the outlook of these clubs reflected this imperative. An element of continuity is evident in this outlook, as throughout this period the clubs remained concerned with providing religious education for the girls.

Having established their religious position, it was important for clubs to show that whilst they created good Jews, they also produced good citizens. Within boys' clubs, military style activities and patriotic parades formed an ideal platform for proving loyalty to Britain. These, however, were not seen as suitable activities for girls. Instead, girls' clubs emphasized their loyalty and indebtedness to the crown during key events and emphasized the link between religion and patriotism as seen in the Butler Street Club annual display in 1906:

> We cannot be sufficiently grateful to our countrymen for their sympathetic and friendly feeling. Our religion does not prevent us from being loyally English: God is within us everywhere; we will find Him if we seek Him and remain faithful to our

27   JML, 1993/79/1/2, Second Annual Report of the Butler Street Girls' Club, 1904.

principles and beliefs. Let us live up to our ideals and to be good and patient and worthy of God's use, and my earnest wish is that you should be fortified by that idea which will guard you against temptation and so your lives will ever make us proud of you, both as Jews and as English Girls.[28]

Whilst they remained loyal to their religion, the club could also be loyal to the country, which was particularly important with the passing of the 1905 Aliens Act, designed to restrict Jewish entry into the country. By referring to loyalty, the Butler Street Club aimed to promote the image of Jews as patriotic Britons in an atmosphere of intense anti-alienism. Girls' clubs, including the Butler Street Club, attempted to link the two identities of Britishness and Jewishness together to counter anti-immigrant sentiment. This, as will be seen in later chapters, was a method adopted by many clubs.

Religious Activities

Once the clubs had established their religious positions, it was important for them to include activities that reflected this essential feature. In girls' clubs, evening prayers were an important expression of religion. Unlike in boys' clubs, girls were encouraged at the end of each club evening to take part in a prayer service. From the outset, the Butler Street Club included such a prayer. The constitution of the club stated that 'everybody present at The Club is expected to attend the service which is held at the conclusion of each evening session'. In laying down the expectation that every member attend, the club was able to show its commitment to helping girls experience religion. The first annual report gave details on the service stating that 'the *Shema* is recited in Hebrew, a Psalm is read in English and the little service concludes with the singing of a Psalm or Hymn'.[29]

28   *JW*, 1 March 1906.
29   JML, 1993/79/1/1, Butler Street Girls' Club, First Annual Report, 1903.

With the recitation of the *Shema* (the prayer affirming essential tenets of Jewish belief), the service was explicitly Jewish. Even so, it avoided activities associated with Eastern European Jewish traditions such as lengthy, Yiddish services. Through the inclusion of English, rather than only Hebrew, the service served to introduce the girls to acceptable forms of English religion. In keeping the service simple, with familiar prayers and readings the club was showing the girls that they were able to conduct a similar service themselves in their own home. The service had the support of the local Jewish community and the Chief Rabbi expressed his approval at the prayers: 'He was glad to know that the members did not separate without a few words of prayer. All the girls, he hoped, would realize the purport of those prayers.'[30] Prayers at the Butler Street Club were therefore a significant part of club life that had the support of the Orthodox authorities. There were similar services held in the Liberal Jewish clubs, which tended to exclude more formal elements of worship. These will be looked at in Chapters 5 and 6.

These services were not unique to the Butler Street Club. Throughout the first decades of the twentieth century, most Jewish girls' clubs held a similar ritual at the end of each evening. In 1923, the Beatrice Club reported that 'the religious side of club life has been stimulated by prayers said at the end of each evening' and in 1935 the Bethnal Green Jewish Girls' Club stated that 'club evenings are always concluded with a prayer'.[31] No details were given for the content of these services, but it seems reasonable to assume that they were similar to the services in the Butler Street Club and therefore provided a simple, Anglicized service with a number of prayers and readings. In holding these prayer services, club leaders not only gave members an opportunity to explore their own religion, albeit in a limited fashion, but also provided them with skills that they would need to bring religion into their own future homes.

Alongside prayer, Sabbath services were an overt display of religion within the club setting. Not all girls' clubs were open on Friday evenings for the Sabbath, however, for those that were open, the Sabbath service

30   *JW*, 28 February 1908.
31   *JG*, 9 March 1923 and *JC*, 29 March 1935.

was the sole activity provided on that evening. Within girls' clubs, these services were not as formal as they were within boys' clubs and instead were more intimate gatherings, stressing the domestic elements of observance found within Friday evening traditions. For the Leman Street Club, the Sabbath service played a vital role in the club's activities. A key part of the service was the appearance of the room, which was described in detail by the Jewish press:

> a few pictures adorn the walls, some autumnal chrysanthemums grace the tables. Here too are the white table cloths, emblematic of Sabbath Purity, a pair of candles serve to assist in the illumination and some drawing room games and books and magazines give an air of refinement and quiet occupation to the apartment.[32]

Here, the emphasis of the service and the rituals was placed firmly on the domestic element. The club was able to emphasize the importance of maintaining domestic religion as an element of observance and in doing so reiterated to the girls the importance of developing these skills for use in their future homes. Four years later, in 1890, the *Jewish Chronicle* again reported on the club's Sabbath service:

> The ancient, pretty customs of the Orthodox Jewish Friday night were as far as possible maintained. The white cloth was spread, four candles lighted, a little nose gay lent its fragrance to the assembly. The arrangement of the evening consisted in reading the Sabbath Evening Prayers in turn. Then followed conversation, singing and reciting, with a glance at the Jewish papers; and a cup of coffee and a piece of the plainest cake or a roll finished the entertainment. The rent of the room and the light meal were paid for by Mrs Flower.[33]

Once again, the emphasis was placed on the domestic element of Sabbath observance. In providing only a small, simple meal, the club was demonstrating that the financial conditions of the girls should be no barrier to creating a suitable Sabbath ritual. The girls were encouraged to take part in the service by reading the Sabbath prayers and were introduced to acceptable 'English' Jewish traditions. For the Jewish Girls' Club, Sabbath services

32   *JC*, 24 September 1886.
33   *JC*, 26 December 1890.

were vital in establishing a sense of English, domestic observance that both emphasized Jewish traditions as well as domesticated gender roles.

There was, however, some formality within some of the girls' club services. When clubs began, particularly when they were formed close to a synagogue, the local Rabbis sought to establish a close relationship between the two. When the Kilburn Girls' Recreation Club began in 1907 the members were addressed by the members of the local community and the Rev. Lazurus 'expressed his pleasure at being able to welcome the club in the precincts of the synagogue, which he thought should be the centre of all sorts of Jewish activity'.[34] Unlike boys' clubs, girls did not attend the regular Sabbath services at the local synagogue and instead, special services were held for them in the afternoons such as the service held by the Beatrice Club. In 1913, it was reported that the girls attended a 'small service on Saturday afternoons' and in 1923 this service continued where girls attended 'the Sabbath afternoon service held at the New West End Synagogue'.[35] These services were small and informal, abbreviated from traditional services and lacked the grandeur associated with the synagogue parades (where groups would march through the local streets to the synagogue service) that were a feature of the activities in boys' clubs. In addition to feminine settings emphasizing intimacy, the contents and descriptions of services in girls' clubs frequently commented on the more feminine traits of 'beauty'. The 1919 Annual report of the Beatrice Club commented that 'our members continue to appreciate the beautiful Sabbath afternoon services at the New West End Synagogue'.[36] The focus on the beauty of the services was something that was only apparent in girls' clubs; within boys' clubs services were described as 'stirring' or 'appropriate'. Services in girls' clubs were therefore more informal than for their male counterparts. The events were smaller in scale and concentrated on 'feminine' traits rather than appear as regimented as was common amongst boys' club services.

34   *JC*, 12 June 1907.
35   *JC*, 14 March 1913; and TNA, ED 41/262, Beatrice Girls' Club Annual Report, 1923.
36   TNA ED 41/262, Nineteenth Annual Report of the Beatrice Girls' Club, Year Ending December 1919.

In addition to Sabbath services, girls' clubs also held services on Holy Days. The Chief Rabbi at the 1906 anniversary gathering of the Beatrice Girls' Club was 'especially glad to learn that on the New Year and the Day of Atonement services had been organized at the club. Not, of course because they were the only days on which they ought to pray, but because on these days it was extremely difficult to find seats in the synagogue.'[37] For the Beatrice Club, providing opportunities for worship on these days enabled the leaders to ensure that the members were able to attend a service, rather than be turned away from a full synagogue. These services therefore helped to ensure that girls were experiencing religiously significant events. Nearly thirty years later, The Bethnal Green Jewish Girls' Club reported in 1933 that 'High Holy Day services have been held at Adler Hall and at Camperdown House (for senior members). There were good attendances at both places.'[38] As significant days in the religious calendar, it is unsurprising that services were held on these days for club members and demonstrated that the clubs were sensitive of their need to provide for the religious needs of its members during High Holy Days.

Chanucah was a frequently celebrated holiday and as with the Sabbath services the focus for girls' club celebrations of the festival was on developing feminine traits and learning skills that would be useful in their future homes. A common feature of these celebrations was committee members providing a tea for members. In 1914 'the *Chanucah* party had that year been entirely managed by the members themselves and most of the toys that the children had received had been handmade'.[39] Allowing the members to plan the event themselves and develop their childcare skills provided vital training for the girls' roles as future wives and mothers and develop their leadership and hosting skills. By providing this opportunity in line with a Jewish festival, the club leaders emphasized the need for the girls to remain Jewish as well as to adhere to English gender norms. In 1929, the Leman Street Club held an event for members where 'a *Chanukah* tea was

37 *JC*, 30 March 1906.
38 BL)=, ORB 40/771 (8) Bethnal Green Jewish Girls' Club, Fifth Annual Report, Year Ending 31 December 1933.
39 *JC*, 15 May 1914.

provided at the club by the ladies of the committee and a small bazaar was held'.[40] This informal event differed from those within boys' clubs where members typically attended formal services before attending a 'tea'. Here, by placing the emphasis on the tea, the girls were encouraged to focus on the domestic elements of observance and to develop high standards of manners which were viewed as essential in the development of femininity, although it was not greatly linked to religion, the *Chanucah* justification allowed clubs to make *some* links with religion.[41] On some occasions club members were encouraged to take a more central role in planning the celebrations.

In Dublin, the Adelaide Girls' Friendly Club was involved with the *Chanucah* celebrations in the synagogue. In 1900, the newly formed club held their first concert for *Chanucah* and a year later the club, along with boys and girls from the Congregational School, chanted the *Chanucah* hymn (*Moaz Tzur*).[42] This formalized link to the synagogue was unusual for girls' clubs in London, which tended not to participate in official events at the synagogue and instead took part in more intimate services. It also demonstrates the club's commitment to the wider Jewish world as the young people were being encouraged to take part in the local religious community. It is possible that the remoteness of the Dublin Jewish community allowed for this unusual participatory equality: girls were not usually allowed to sing in synagogue services. It does demonstrate that the club was providing for the religious needs of the girls. In Bristol, the girls were not involved with religion in the synagogue, but they were still part of the religious community. During *Chanucah* in 1903, the girls held a gathering at the club premises and sang the 'historical hymn' before entertaining the community with recitations and plays.[43] The Nottingham Jewish Girls' Club ran a similar event in 1915, which began with the lighting

40   JML, T293, Annual Report for the Leman Street Girls Club, April 1929.

41   Susan L. Tananbaum, *The Jewish Immigrant in London 1880–1939* (London: Pickering and Chatto, 2014), p. 116.

42   *JC*, 28 December 1900 and 13 December 1901.

43   *JC*, 2 January 1903.

of the *Menorah* and the girls' rendition of *Moaz Tsur*.[44] On both of these occasions, the clubs remained outside of the synagogue in a non-religious building, observing traditional gendered separation within Orthodoxy, which goes some way to explain why the girls sang at the club rather than at the synagogue. Even so, the girls still engaged with traditional elements of *Chanucah* observance.

Purim was also celebrated by girls' clubs. This festival was observed in much the same way as *Chanucah*, with an emphasis on promoting acceptable gender roles, and, in comparison to London clubs, again on community. One of the earliest *Purim* events was held in Liverpool in 1896. Here the girls had 'a very enjoyable evening through the kindness of Mrs L. S. Cohen [where] an excellent magic lantern exhibit was provided and was followed by light refreshments'.[45] The committee, through the work of Mrs L. S. Cohen, was key in coordinating this small event. Committee members maintained involvement in many of the clubs' activities, such as in the Bristol Jewish Girls' Club, where the *Purim* entertainment 'consisted of several musical items rendered by some of the committee ladies'.[46] Here the committee was involved not just in the organization of the event, but in providing the entertainment, emphasizing the community element of club work, which was less commonly found in the London clubs. There was greater young member involvement in the celebrations in Birmingham in the same year where the *Purim* concert consisted of 'various items … mainly contributed by the members of the classes'.[47] Despite this, the event itself was led by adults and performed for members from the local community. Events such as these continued throughout the 1920s and 1930s, where club leaders and committee members continued to organize, participate in, and fund the events themselves, such as the *Purim* balls held yearly in Liverpool, where adults planned the event for the young people and

---

44   University College London Archives (hereafter UCLA) Programme Notting Jewish Girls' Club Chanucah Display, 1915, GASTER/NOT/A/NOT/1.
45   *JC*, 6 March 1896.
46   *JC*, 20 March 1920.
47   Ibid.

participated in the celebration with the girls.[48] London clubs used adults to teach, organize, influence – though often bemoaned the difficulty of attracting adult participants.

The clubs promoted acceptable gender roles during these events. The 'fancy dress' element of *Purim* celebrations provided the leaders with an opportunity to reward members' who had successfully mastered traditional feminine skills: 'Prizes for the cheapest costumes were awarded to 'What is it?' and 'influenza', for the prettiest costume to 'the park', 'a fairy-like being in green' and to 'A Hawaian [sic] Girl.' The most original costumes were 'the order of the bath' (i.e. the common everyday *bath*) and 'put and take'.[49] These costumes illustrate the 'light-hearted' nature of *Purim* and emphasized the club's adherence to a tradition associated with this religious festival. It is interesting to note that the costumes chosen for awards, however, were not religious, which although typical of *Purim* costume parties at the time, does show that religious background of the festival was not a major factor in the celebration of the day. The decision to award prizes to those who excelled in certain categories, instead emphasizes the club's desire to promote gender roles. The emphasis of awarding prizes to costumes was placed on domestic skills in particular dress-making, creativity and thriftiness as well as on feminine traits of beauty. By linking these skills with *Purim*, the club leaders were able to tie religious observation to national gender roles, thus proving the compatibility of national and religious identities. For girls' clubs, *Purim* provided an opportunity for members to take part in a religious activity that, like *Chanucah*, emphasized suitably feminine pastimes, as well as religious obligations.

In addition to Holy Days and Sabbath Services, religion was also evident at special events. At the opening of a new club or the opening of an existing club's new premises, prayer always formed a central part of the celebration. Often services would be attended by a senior religious figure, in many cases the Chief Rabbi, who would lead the club and the attendees in prayer. At the 1901 opening of the Beatrice Club for Working Girls, the

---

48   See, LRO, Liverpool Jewish Girls' Club Annual Report 1926–1927, 1936–1937 and
      1938–1939, 296/JCG/1–4.
49   *JG*, 24 March 1922.

Chief Rabbi led a consecration service which consisted of a Psalm and appropriate scripture passages. He also led the attendees in a prayer which asked 'may these maidens devote some of the hours they spend here to a loving and intelligent study of thy word in that it may be a lamp unto their feet and a light unto their path'.[50] Here the prayer, made relevant to the club members, could have helped to foster some interest in religion focusing on communal priorities (and perhaps the Chief Rabbi's priorities as well), which may not have been found through a generic prayer. Additionally, the prayer encouraged the members to continue to seek religious improvement throughout their time in the club. This prayer was not unique to this occasion. The Chief Rabbi, at the opening of the Butler Street Girls' Club in 1901, conducted a similar prayer and service. The prayer read on this occasion was almost identical to that read at the opening of the Beatrice Club. It appealed to members to 'enjoy friendly converse, the delight of reading and the joy of song, where their powers of body and of mind will be braced for further healthful effort'.[51] Once again, the prayer was targeted specifically at the club members requesting they make further study and improve themselves both spiritually and physically.

At the opening of The Jewish Girls' Club's new premises in 1903, again the Chief Rabbi read a similar prayer. This time he asked that:

> May, through the holy influence of kindly sympathy, the members become wiser and happier, feeling it their duty as Jewesses to be an example to those about them of stainless purity and perfect truthfulness, patterns of industry at their work and of womanly helpfulness in their homes.[52]

Here the expectation of the club members was not just that they improve their own spiritual and physical wellbeing, but that in so doing they would improve that of those around them. By laying out the need of the girls to continue their own education and to work to improve their relationship with God, the Chief Rabbi was clearly stating the importance of this work

---

50   *JC*, 29 March 1901.
51   *JC*, 19 December 1902.
52   *JC*, 1 May 1903.

in the clubs' life and encouraging the club leaders to provide facilities for the girls to learn as well as to attend classes.

Whilst religion was included in the clubs' annual calendar through special events and Holy Days, religious classes formed a part of the weekly programme in most girls' clubs. There was less opportunity for girls to attend formal religious education than for boys. In Glasgow, for example, it was estimated that only a third of Jewish girls in 1916 were receiving any kind of religious instruction and it seems reasonable to assume that this figure was similar throughout Britain.[53] Religious education within the club provided an important opportunity for the club leaders to educate the young women. Scripture and Hebrew classes were common features in many clubs: in the Kilburn Recreation and the Bethnal Green Clubs; Hebrew language classes were held; in Leman Street; classes were held in Scripture and Jewish history; and in the Butler Street Club; classes and lectures were held on Jewish history and Hebrew.[54] In 1907, a report of the Butler street club mentioned that the 'course of lectures on Biblical and post-Biblical history ... have been much appreciated by the girls. It seems a pity that more cannot be done in this respect in the boys' clubs.'[55] The lack of classes within boys' clubs had therefore been noted.

The prevalence of religious classes within girls' club can be attributed in part to the scarcity of formal education for girls. In providing classes for the young members, club leaders hoped to educate girls in religious matters and ensure the continuation of the Jewish faith in the face of the lack of opportunities for girls to attend classes at the synagogue or at the *Talmud Torah*, and the limited opportunities provided by the board schools and through the Jewish Religious Education Board. Within the Beatrice Club, the confirmation and Bible class was given importance amongst its other activities. The confirmation class had been publicized in the 1923 annual report, at the annual display and in the Jewish press. Additionally, the amount spent on the class was high in comparison to other activities

---

53   Kenneth Collins, *Aspects of Scottish Jewry* (Glasgow: Glasgow Jewish Representative Council, 1987), p. 31.
54   *JW*, 18 January 1907.
55   Ibid.

provided by the club. In 1923, the first year the class was run, for example, the expenditure for this class alone was £9. In comparison, the club spent 2/– on drilling, 8/6 on English classes, £1 5s 1d on tennis and £1 12s on prizes. The club spent more money on only one class that year, which was the singing class which cost £9 8s.[56] The amount of money spent on the combined confirmation and religion class demonstrates that the club viewed the class as important and recognized the need for the members to be educated in religious matters.

As in the London-based groups, classes formed a part of religious education in girls' clubs outside of the capital. In 1927 in Liverpool, the girls' club reported that 'classes have been held in drill, folk-dancing, recitation, Hebrew and Scripture, embroidery, dressmaking, plain sewing, knitting, millinery, singing, drawing, first aid and home nursing'.[57] The club offered a variety of classes, mostly developing practical household skills associated with a 'woman's role' in the home, as well as drill, which was likely to have been a more gymnastics-based class than the purely military drill found within boys' clubs. Even so, religious classes were still held. These classes were not only offered to the members, but were given some element of priority by the club leaders, based on their prominence within Annual Reports and in other club publicity. It is possible that this priority was given as the reports went out to subscribers and the Jewish community and that the leaders hoped to present a suitably religious character to these populations, rather than that girls signed up in large numbers. This would, however, still indicate that the clubs saw the role of these classes in creating suitably Jewish members as key in maintaining public support. Members from the Hebrew class performed at the club's annual displays each year, presenting Biblical stories in Hebrew. In 1923, the annual display 'included Biblical scenes enacted in Hebrew. The first set represented Joseph and his brethren, the second Ahab and Micaiah. The Hebrew was most excellently rendered by the girls and gave particular pleasure to the audience.'[58] Presenting results of the class at the annual display demonstrated that the

---

56   TNA ED 41/262 Beatrice Girls' Club Record of Expenditure for 1923.
57   LRO 363/CHC/98 Annual Report for the Liverpool Jewish Girls' Club 1926–1927.
58   *JG*, 6 April 1923.

club took their religious obligations seriously and was able to show its commitment to Jewish education.

Often the religious classes were not successful in attracting large attendance, however. Even so, they still continued, although there is limited evidence to suggest that the clubs strived to make them more interesting or appealing to members. At the Leman Street Club, the classes met every week and attracted a small number of club members in comparison with other activities. The class was, however, considered a success and in 1927 it was noted that 'considering that it had met regularly during the last six years, it was manifestly popular and had captured the imagination of the girls'.[59] Religion classes faced a number of difficulties within girls' clubs, not only the problem of attracting members. Leaders in the Leman Street Club commented that religion 'is always a subject a little difficult to teach and needs to be at once something more and something less than a lesson'.[60] This difficulty was often seen as a barrier in boys' clubs with many male club leaders refusing to teach religious classes as the leaders did not feel qualified to teach them. This was not the case within girls' clubs. Whilst several of these had visiting staff to teach religious classes, others had their own leaders teach religion. Despite difficulties faced by the groups in finding qualified staff and the insecurities of leaders in teaching religion, girls' clubs continued to provide classes to their members.

Summer Holidays

Outside the weekly schedule, summer holidays formed a key part of the club calendar. These trips were often subsidized, allowing more members to attend, lasted one or two weeks and took place near the sea or in the country. Within girls' clubs, these were uncommon prior to the 1920s and when they did happen the majority of girls' clubs stayed in a hostel or

59   *JG*, 9 December 1927.
60   JML, Annual Report, Jewish Girls' Club, April 1929.

other indoor venues unlike the outdoor camps held in boys' clubs. From the 1920s onwards, as more adventurous pursuits became acceptable for women, most clubs planned holidays, many of which were under canvas. These events provided leaders with an opportunity to expose the girls to a greater number of religious activities than they could within the rest of the year. Early girls' club holidays were often small and informal. Many of these events took place within a small Jewish community that allowed the girls' to be involved within local religious events and with local families. In 1889 at one of the earliest girls' club holidays, the members of the Leman Street Club formed a relationship with a 'respected resident' of Gravesend (the area in which they were staying). The girls were involved within the community and the local family showed their support for the girls by 'inviting them to tea and in lending them books and sending them little delicacies and "surprises" on the Sabbath'.[61]

This sense of family was a vital part of the early club holiday experience and helped to emphasize the domestic element to the Sabbath, although these experiences with local families only appear to have occurred where the numbers attending events were small. By becoming involved with a local family and visiting their house, the feminine obligations of the Sabbath were stressed and opportunities were provided for girls to mix with socially acceptable Anglo-Jewry and witness their religious observations. Later, as camps and holidays became more common, religious observance became more structured. At the North London Jewish Girls' Club camps in the 1930s, services were held on both the Friday evening and Saturday morning at the campground and led by the camp commandant.[62] There were no visitors or visiting Rabbis attending the clubs' camps who were able to conduct the services, as were common in boys' clubs' camps, but instead were led by those with a closer relationship to the club itself. The same can be seen at the 1937 camp of the Brady Girls' Club where 'services conducted by Miss Moses on Friday evenings and Saturday mornings were much appreciated by the girls'.[63] Whilst these services were more traditional than those held

61   *JC*, 25 October 1889.
62   *JC*, 31 August 1934 and 21 August 1936.
63   *JC*, 27 August 1937.

prior to the First World War, they were still relatively informal, especially when compared to the large scale and traditional services held at boys' club camps. Once again, the stress for girls' clubs was on less masculine and formal forms of religious observance and instead focused on a more informal and feminine religious experience.

The aim of the clubs can thus be seen as securing the future of the Jewish faith and enabling each girl to take a full part within the Jewish community as a whole, whether in religious or secular terms. For the Butler Street club a particular success story could be seen in the case of Florrie Passman, East End resident and daughter of an immigrant tailor.[64] She became a club member in 1903 at the age of 13, defying the rules stating members of the club should be at least 14 years old. She devoted her life to helping others in the club setting, initially within the Butler Street club, but when this closed, she worked with the Stepney Girls' Club. She continued this work until her death at age 98 and was awarded an MBE in 1976 for her services. In 1976 she spoke to the *Jewish Chronicle* about her time in the club and she recalled the religious elements of club life, in which she took part as a young girl:

> She clearly remembers a weekly Shabbat afternoon tea at the home of Dr Hermann Adler (Chief Rabbi 1891–1911), whose daughter Henrietta was a Butler Street Club manager. 'We looked forward to these visits and to the religious discussions that usually took place. Naturally I have many memories of my days as a Butler Street girl. But the things that remain clearest in my mind are the Jewish discussions and lectures from people like Lady Magnus, and how we regularly observed the festivals.'[65]

It is significant that Passman's recollections of her time in the club focus on the religious aspects of the club work. The club worked to instil a sense of religious observance and pride amongst its girl members.

Religion in Jewish girls' clubs was thus present throughout the clubs' histories. Starting with a religious element to their aims and objects, they

---

64   Iris Dove, 'Sisterhood or Surveillance? The Development of Working Girls' Clubs in London, 1880–1939', unpublished doctoral thesis, University of Greenwich, 1996, p. 135.

65   *JC*, 22 November 1976.

promoted religion through classes, services and prayer. Religious activities in girls' clubs were often informal in nature. Rather than emphasize the role of the synagogue and the ceremonial elements of religious observance, girls' clubs stressed the simplicity of religion through evening prayer services and small-scale Sabbath services. These small, informal services had the additional effect of reinforcing English gender norms. Sabbath services stressed the importance of domesticity; *Chanucah* celebrations focused on providing entertainment for younger children and evening prayers encouraged young women to learn a simple service, which they could take into their own future families. The domestic and feminine elements of religion within London's Jewish girls' clubs provided the greatest contrast between religion provided in boys' clubs and girls' clubs, respectively.

Conclusion: Girls' Clubs and Religion

In 1905, the *Jewish Chronicle* reported that religion in girls' clubs was much more evident than religion in boys' clubs. They stated that 'perhaps one reason why [religion] appears to flourish better in girls' clubs is the fact that women are less shy than men of talking to one another about religion.'[66] Indeed, Victorian culture as a whole, often saw women as more innately spiritual than men. Whilst, religion *was* more evident in girls' clubs, the reason given by the *Jewish Chronicle* cannot fully explain this. The specifically Jewish dependence on women as carriers of faith as well as the more general notion of religion and spirituality as a woman's role provide a more thorough interpretation of why religion was more predominant in girls' clubs than in their male counterparts.

Religion in girls' clubs was much less formal in character than that in boys' clubs. There was less emphasis on attending the synagogue and a greater emphasis on promoting more simple and domestic forms of

66   *JC*, 31 March 1905.

religious observance, integral to Jewish traditions. Within the clubs, girls were encouraged to take part in evening prayers, organize festival celebrations and obtain a (limited) Jewish education. Where more formal observance did occur, girls' clubs placed a greater emphasis on women as leaders amongst women, for example within Sabbath services led by club leaders. This helped to reinforce the religious separations between men and women, as well as establish informal religion, as opposed to formal displays or religiosity, as the concern of women.

In addition, religion helped to stress the role of women as wives and mothers. Clubs frequently incorporated domestic elements into religious observance and placed a large emphasis on Sabbath food. This underscored the importance of domesticity within both Jewish traditions and within British society. The notion of beauty as a feminine trait was also stressed with religious practices and within Sabbath meals. The frequent repetition of this quality within religious practices helped to establish beauty as a concern for girls, stressing beauty as a quality needed to demonstrate appropriate femininity within Judaism and within Britain.

In addition to the promotion of domesticity and traits perceived to be important for femininity, religion frequently underscored the significance of women in maintaining the Jewish faith. Within celebrations, the young members were encouraged to take a leading role, helping them to prepare for their future roles as guardians of the Jewish faith within their families. The clubs provided girls with experiences of pvractical religion, such as simplified and easy to recreate prayers, which helped to give the girls skills that they would need in order to maintain a religious household. In boys' clubs, excluding the Liberal Oxford and St George's Jewish Lads' Club, however, religion followed strict patterns and templates found within Orthodoxy and only minimal attempts were made to demonstrate that the boys could take religion from the club into their homes. This demonstrates a key difference between the roles of girls and boys and the training offered to young people in their future roles. Girls' clubs, through the domestication of their religious programming for girls, adhered to British gender norms and promoted the spiritual element of girls' responsibilities.

CHAPTER 2

Boys' Clubs, 1896–1939

A particular cause for concern within late nineteenth-century fears of the declining standards of British youth was the behaviour and appearance of teenage boys. The increased urbanization of the country, the perceived decline in the physical fitness of military recruits at the time of the Boer War and increased leisure time and expendable income created alarm that the country's male youth was degenerating. As Brad Beavan has highlighted, these fears were linked with juvenile bad behaviour: 'During the late nineteenth century youth delinquency became associated with wider anxieties related to increased urbanization, changes in work and leisure patterns and fears of imperial decline.'[1] Many middle-class philanthropists believed that organized leisure was the way to counter these threats and clubs for boys over the age of 14 (the school leaving age) were established. Youth worker Charles Russell's 1908 text, *Working Lads' Clubs*, was seen as the definitive guide on how to run a group for young boys. He stated that these associations were founded with three objects, which were designed to counter the perceived threats: recreation, education and religion.[2] This model, based on the successful working men's club movement, was seen as key to regenerating British youth and improving the physical and mental fitness of young men.

As a result of such concerns, clubs were particularly located in areas with a large working-class population. London, for example, was home to many working boys' clubs. As with girls' clubs, many of these groups had a Christian basis. A number of these groups began, however, within

---

1   Brad Beavan, *Leisure, Citizenship and Working-Class Men in Britain 1850–1945* (Manchester: Manchester University Press, 2005), p. 88.

2   Ibid., p. 92.

the Jewish community and were highly successful in their recruitment. A survey conducted by the Chief Rabbi's office in 1914 estimated that the twelve Jewish boys' clubs in the capital had a combined membership of approximately 2,750, which was just under half of all the eligible males aged between 14 and 18.[3] Many clubs began 'old boys' sections for former members to join once they had reached 18 and were no longer eligible for membership in the main club. These older groups were run on similar lines to the clubs for 14- to 18-year-olds and occasionally held activities together such as camps and holidays. The Victoria Club, for example, held camps for both the older and younger age groups at the same site.

Jewish youth workers adapted Christian models of youth work and emphasized similar priorities, which Susan Tananbaum suggested was a sign that 'middle class Jews had absorbed values that were essentially non-Jewish'.[4] This was not necessarily the case. Many of these standards, rather than being explicitly non-Jewish, were in fact secular principles not attached to any faith. There is no evidence that any of the clubs took in Christian elements into their club activities, but instead combined Jewish practices with English secular values. Much of the criticism placed on the clubs was based on the fact that these secular values formed a much greater role in Jewish clubs than in Christian ones. As a result of this emphasis, as will be demonstrated, the religious element within the Jewish clubs was much less defined than within their Christian counterparts. This chapter will look at a number of London's Jewish boys' clubs, as there were few clubs located outside of the capital. Whereas girls' clubs operated across the UK, boys in cities with smaller Jewish populations instead attended the Jewish Lads' Brigade, which will be looked at in a later chapter. As a result, I will use the term 'English' rather than British when talking about national identity as this provides a more accurate definition of the boys' club members.

The privilege afforded to British societal values has been noted in recent historiography on Jewish youth. In David Dee's work on sport and Jews,

---

3   David Dee, *Sport and British Jewry: Integration, Ethnicity and Anti-Semitism, 1890–1970* (Manchester: Manchester University Press, 2013), p. 22.

4   Susan Tananbaum, 'Ironing Out the Ghetto Bend: Sports and the Making of British Jews', *Journal of Sport History*, 31 (2004), 53–75 (p. 56).

he states that 'most organizations privileged sports and athleticism – all aspects of Britishness – and saw Jewish identity as essential, but arguably secondary'.[5] For Jewish boys' clubs, sporting activities were certainly the primary concern. Clubs emphasized the qualities of good sportsmanship and the physical improvements brought on by sports and linked participation in sporting activities with being British. This emphasis on sports certainly overshadowed the clubs' religious activities: 'When it came to a choice between Jewishness and sport, sport clearly won, but not at the risk of causing problems with the local non-Jewish population.'[6] For example, holding sporting events on Sundays was often abandoned by Jewish clubs for fear of antagonizing the local authorities. Indeed, Jewish clubs were sensitive to the demands of Christian religious needs often to a greater extent than they were to criticism from their own community.

Almost from the beginning of the clubs' existence, disapproval from the Jewish community surfaced regarding the religious side of club work. A 1905 article in the *Jewish Chronicle* stated that 'the religious element is less pronounced in boys' clubs [than in girls' clubs] if we except Stepney, where prayers are read at the termination of each club evening'.[7] Moreover, the opinion that boys' clubs failed to do enough towards the religious side of club work did not disappear after the 1900s. Indeed, throughout subsequent decades, criticism of the lack of religion in the clubs increased. A discussion in 1913 on religion in the Brady Street Club attracted a number of letters from within the community. British Zionist, Howard Sacher wrote that 'I will not, I hope be accused of exaggeration if I suggest that a single lecture by a non-Jew is hardly adequate to redeem the Jewish nature of this club'. Another anonymous correspondent, writing under the pseudonym 'A Club Manager', wrote that 'one misses ... any reference in [the club leaders'] account of the clubs' work to any specifically Jewish interests and ... the word "Jew" is not even contained in the [clubs'] title'.[8] An article on the Jewish clubs in London a year later commented that 'the feeling is largely

5   Dee, *Sport and British Jewry*, pp. 105–6.
6   Ibid., p. 108.
7   *JC*, 31 March 1905.
8   *JC*, 5 December 1913.

held, if not general, that though Jewish in name and composition, nothing is done in our clubs, which are maintained entirely by Jewish subscribers, that … makes the club in fact Jewish in any sense'.[9] Even after the First World War and as late as 1930, the same criticism was still directed at a number of the Jewish clubs. A reporter for the *Jewish World* newspaper wrote of the Hutchison House Club that 'by not a single word in the report can one gather that the club is a Jewish one … I am credibly informed that there is not one single non-Jewish member … unless it comes out clearly and unequivocally as a Jewish club – which in intent it is – the "Hutch" is lacking in its duty to the community'.[10] The amount and frequency of criticism levelled against the clubs can lead to the conclusion that the groups did nothing towards including a religious element within their activities. Indeed, Lady Janner of the Brady Club recalled that 'when [the club] first started in 1896, the idea was to make good little Jews into good Englishmen – this turned right round – to make good little Englishmen into good little Jews'.[11] Janner's memory of policy here is clearly simplified and does not do justice to the nuances of club work, which were present at the time. As this chapter will show, religion *was* evident in boys' clubs, although religion was used not simply for its own sake, but in order to promote secular English values at the same time as promoting Judaism.

Many of the groups included religious figures in their organization, ran services for Holy Days and the Sabbath and promoted Jewish values through classes. This chapter will look at the way in which Jewish boys' clubs, that is to say clubs that consisted of overwhelmingly Jewish boys, entirely Jewish leadership and were funded from the Jewish community, were able to include religion within their activities, through prayers, sermons and classes. It will explore the ways in which religion was promoted as 'manly' and analyse the language used to describe sermons. Additionally, this chapter will look at the content of religious worship to show that, when religion was included, it promoted the wider aims of the club such as promoting gender roles and encouraging the assimilation of the largely immigrant members into

9   *JC*, 9 January 1914.
10   *JW*, 2 October 1930.
11   JML, Tape 74, Interview with Lady Janner by Susan Tananbaum, 13 May 1986.

English society. During the annual summer camps especially, the content of religious programming was evidence of that which was included during the rest of the year. They provided an opportunity for the religious lessons that began during evening meetings to continue and be reinforced to the boys.

Background and Ethos

Jewish boys' clubs fell into two categories. First, those that viewed themselves as undenominational, but were still seen as Jewish on account of their membership and funding sources, and second, those that identified as 'Jewish' and took the title seriously. In no instances were boys' clubs started with the sole purpose of furthering religion. Instead, the clubs focused on recreation and aiding the assimilation of young immigrants into English society. Whilst accepting that religion was *not* the most important factor in the creation of the groups it was, however, one of a number of motivations behind the formation of clubs. The way in which the clubs viewed themselves (whether denominational or undenominational) had an impact on the inclusion of religious activities. It is therefore important to examine the rationale behind the creation of individual clubs to establish whether they viewed themselves explicitly Jewish, and if so, how this was made manifest.

A number of the clubs, especially in the early years, technically considered themselves to be open to all, regardless of religion. The Victoria Lads' Club, which began in 1901, claimed to be undenominational, yet from its outset it maintained a relationship with the Chief Rabbi and it was claimed in the *Jewish Chronicle* that the club 'owe[d] its origins largely to the Chief Rabbi and Mrs Adler'.[12] Certainly, the connection of the Chief Rabbi with the group helped to create a more religious tone in club events and went some way to allay fears that the club was not 'Jewish'. The Victoria Club did not face as much criticism as some undenominational clubs. This was

---

12   *JC*, 29 November 1901.

possibly due to the relationship of the group with the most high profile figure in Anglo-Judaism, which gave the impression that the club was more explicitly religious than others in spite of its claim to religious 'neutrality'.

Similarly, the Brady Boys' Club prior to 1918 viewed itself as undenominational. In the pre-war period the club was said to have:

> a threefold advantage. It helped them [the boys] in the first instance to make a success of their own lives, secondly it made them good and patriotic citizens and thirdly, it was to make a success for them in their race and in their community for honest dealing, by wise doing and by right living.[13]

Whilst it did not explicitly refer to religion, the third claim can be seen to apply to a limited extent to Jewishness – as members of the Jewish community, within both the religious and secular spheres. In particular, the claim that the club would help with 'right living' certainly alludes to a moral, and perhaps religious, aspect. Despite this allusion, there was no explicit reference to Judaism in club activities or descriptions prior to 1918. This undenominational aspect was heightened during the First World War and by 1914 the club claimed that they were *unable* to include a religious aspect in their work, and nor would they want to as the boys 'would resent a spiritual, meaning a religious, side in the club work and they do not want the managers to interfere in a matter regarding the private concerns of themselves'.[14] This indicates a certain resistance on the part of the members and also demonstrates that the leaders were unwilling to make attempts in this area. It also highlights a gendered approach to religion. As spirituality was not seen as a key concern for boys, club members and leaders exhibited a reluctance to engage with religious activities, which were frequently seen as un-masculine.

By far the most controversial organization with regard to its religious outlook was the Hutchison House Club. The group, founded in 1905, provides an ideal example of the lack of religious basis in the clubs as it claimed that 'by the constitution, the Hutchison House Club is undenominational,

---

13   *JW*, 8 March 1907.
14   *JC*, 9 January 1914.

nevertheless it caters more particularly for the needs of Jewish youth in East London'.[15] Despite its declaration that the club had no religious ties, both the boys and the adult leaders were 'wholly Jewish'.[16] The club viewed itself as undenominational, although there was a clear Jewishness in terms of membership. There were, however, no overtly religious activities and the managers had gone so far as to ban debates and lectures on Jewish subjects.[17] This opened the club for significant criticism from the press, who noted the apparent contradictions between the rejection of overtly religious activities at the same time as claiming to cater for the needs of Jewish boys. It will be shown later that despite the claim that the group was 'undenominational', there was a (limited) Jewish element to its activities, although not to an extent that was able to quiet the club's critics.

Whilst Hutchison House faced the most vitriolic attention, all of the clubs that viewed themselves as undenominational came in for criticism from the Jewish press as well as amongst the Jewish community. The key to this was that, although the clubs did not use the word Jewish in their title, the membership was overwhelmingly Jewish, was supported by an entirely Jewish leadership and funded from entirely Jewish sources. These clubs tended to place a much greater emphasis on leisure and sport than their explicitly 'Jewish' counterparts and as a consequence, the religious activities were a less significant part of the programme. Many of the community noted the contradictions between the 'undenominational' claim and the entirely Jewish membership and believed that more should be done in the clubs to contribute to the development of the religious identities of the young people. Whilst some of the most well-known (and certainly most criticized) clubs were 'undenominational', there were those that specifically addressed the Jewish element in their work. The openly 'Jewish' clubs came in for less negative attention in the Jewish press as they tended to focus more on religious aspects.

The Stepney Jewish Lads' Club was the most high profile of the explicitly Jewish clubs and from the outset included a number of religious activities

---

15   *JC*, 11 November 1927.
16   *JW*, 14 February 1929.
17   Ibid.

including nightly prayers and Sabbath services. The Reverend Stern at an event in 1903 claimed that the club was 'Jewish in deeds as well as in words' – a stark contrast to the criticisms levelled against the undenominational clubs which emphasized the lack of Jewish actions.[18] That a religious figure was able to note the Jewishness of the club demonstrates that the club was significantly Jewish in a way that could be appreciated amongst the whole Jewish community and not just in comparison to other youth groups. A similar attitude was clear within the Notting Hill Jewish Lads' Club which, in its 1911 magazine, stated explicitly that 'we at this club are glad to include the word Jewish in our title and try by our thought and actions to justify this qualification'.[19] It is possible that this declaration of pride was partly for publicity as club magazines were circulated amongst the wider Jewish community, including to the press. The public nature of these documents therefore needs to be considered when looking at articles published in the magazines, as the clubs were presenting what they perceived as the best image of themselves. In stating that the club was proud to be Jewish in a magazine circulated in the public domain, the club was aiming in part to dispel criticism and encourage the community to view the efforts of the Notting Hill Club positively as well as suggesting that the club was comfortable with openly Jewish identification. Unlike the undenominational clubs, these two groups not only included the word Jewish in their clubs' name, but also included Jewish elements in their programme in order to justify including the word 'Jewish' in their title.

In the interwar period the newly formed Cambridge and Bethnal Green Jewish Boys' Club adopted a religious attitude through their motto *'Serva Corpus, Cole Mentem, Animum Cura'* (Preserve the body, cultivate the mind, care for the spirit).[20] The reference to the spirit in this instance is distinctly religious and the use of this reference in the motto contrasts with the strictly recreational aims of other undenominational clubs. It is interesting to note that during the 1930s the Cambridge and Bethnal Green Club rejected its Jewish affiliation and opened its membership to Christian

18   *JW*, 16 January 1903.
19   SUA, MS116/121 AJ301 *Notting Hill Jewish Lads' Club Magazine*, April 1911.
20   *JG*, 14 November 1924, translated by Rebecca Holdorph.

boys as much as to Jewish ones. During the 1920s, however, the club can be seen as Jewish due to its identification as such and the inclusion of prayers and religious activities into its programme.

During the interwar years many within the Jewish community rethought their outlook on religion believing that Anglicizing efforts prior to 1914 had had a detrimental effect on Jewish piety amongst the immigrant community. Communal institutions increased the emphasis placed on religious activities as they 'searched for means to "re-Judaize" the East End young and stem their drift towards hedonism and materialism'.[21] The club movement was no different. This change ties in with the recollection of Lady Janner that the Brady Club changed its focus from Anglicizing members to making good Jews, and it fits in with wider concerns in the Jewish community that immigrant Jews had been so thoroughly Anglicized that they had lost their Jewish identity. The Brady Club, which, as seen earlier, initially considered itself to be undenominational, adapted its stance in light of wider changes in society which began to emphasize religious traditions in the face of perceived secularization. As the club grew and incorporated a girls' club, a junior club and a settlement (a University-style collection of facilities and services for a particular group of people), the attitude to religion changed, reflecting both the change in demographics of the club and the changes within British Jewry. In contrast to the previous declaration that the club was unable to include a religious element, in the 1930s it claimed that one of its objects was 'the promotion of the spiritual, educational, physical and social well-being of the local residents and the inculcation of a higher standard of living'.[22] This reflected a significant departure for the club, which had previously stated that it would not introduce a spiritual side to the activities and marked changes in the community as a whole. Whilst this change in policy had much to do with the growth of the Brady settlement, it provides an example of the way in which clubs evolved in line with wider concerns regarding the decline of religious observance.

21 Todd M. Endelman, *Jews in Britain, 1656–2000* (London: University of California Press, 2002), p. 206.
22 THLA, *Constitution – Brady Clubs and Settlement*, n.d 1930s.

The clear division between denominational and undenominational clubs is one that can *only* be found within boys' clubs. Girls were seen as spiritual and thus responsible for the diffusion of morality. Religion therefore formed a key part of their informal education.[23] Indeed, all Orthodox Jewish girls' clubs included an element of religious awareness within their mottos and objectives. For boys, however, this was not the case. Many of the clubs neglected the religious element in favour of developing 'manly' attributes, which tended to minimize spiritual and overtly religious concerns in favour of developing independence, sportsmanship and self-restraint. The presence of undenominational clubs thus marks a way in which religion in girls' and boys' clubs reflected gender norms in society as a whole and within British Jewry, more specifically.

Religious Activities

The inclusion of a prayer service was the major marker of difference between the types of Jewish boys' clubs. It was particularly pronounced prior to 1914 where only the clubs with the most explicitly Jewish ethos went to efforts to include a prayer service. When this was included, the clubs frequently faced difficulties in establishing the events within their routines and encountered opposition from members. An interview with a boy from an unknown club (though most likely the Brady Boys' Club) revealed some of the difficulties faced by club leaders in introducing prayers. When asked about how he would feel if a five minute prayer service was included at club meetings the boy remarked that:

> we would walk out in a body if such services were forced upon us or are ever introduced. We would either come late or late enough to know that if an opening prayer

---

23   Paula E. Hyman, *Gender and Assimilation in Modern Jewish History: The Roles and Representation of Women* (London: University of Washington Press, 1997), p. 25.

did take place it would be over, while we would find the means of escaping attending a prayer at the close of the evening.[24]

Despite the antipathy revealed by this testimony, some clubs were able to hold prayer services at the end of the evening – although there is no evidence of this in the undenominational Hutchison House Club or in the Victoria Club.

It was the Stepney Club that had the most success with formal prayers at the end of the evening. 'The service includes a short address, followed by a prayer in English, the singing of well-known hymns or Psalms and lasts between five and ten minutes. Attendance is voluntary and it is very gratifying to find that some forty or fifty lads are present each evening and their demeanour is most devout.'[25] Such initial high attendance can be attributed to Denzil Myer, the club worker who developed the service and was deeply involved with the club and its religious activities. He was instrumental in starting the service and his enthusiasm for this helped to increase attendances at the end of the evening. His role in instigating and promoting prayers was mentioned in the special memorial issue of the club magazine published after his death during the First World War. Reverend Stern stated that Myer:

> was very keen on starting the nightly prayers at the club following the example of the Oxford and St George's Jewish Boys' Club. His addresses at these prayers were always very simple and practical. He would try to impress upon the boys sound ethical views, purity in thought and deed, and a solid, clear idea of God ... He wanted boys to discover the truths of our religion for themselves. He never pressed the boys to attend prayers, though he used all his influence to attract them voluntarily.[26]

Indeed, Myer's biggest legacy to the club's religious life was the club prayer, which he wrote prior to the outbreak of war:

> Almighty God! we earnestly and sincerely pray to thee for courage to do what we know to be right. We ask for thy guidance when in doubt, and for thy forgiveness when we do wrong. Grant us strength to resist temptation and the sense to avoid it.

24   *JC*, 9 January 1914.
25   SUA MS172 AJ250, Folder 8, *Stepney Club Annual Report, June 1915*.
26   The London Library (hereafter LL) M395, *The Stepnian*, Memorial Number 1917.

> Give us wisdom in the choice of our friends, and gentle hearts to pity and help those weaker than ourselves. Keep Us, O. Lord, in health and strength, and let us always be a source of pride and satisfaction to our parents and to all whom we love and protect. Let our homes be free from care and our club a house of happiness. Amen.[27]

This was remarkably similar to the 'Lord's Prayer' found within Christian traditions, emphasizing the assimilation or acculturation elements present in the club. It was also designed to be relevant to the boys and drew on themes that would have been familiar to a young audience. The language used in the prayer was clearly accessible to young people, and made relevant to boys' lives by referring to friends, parents and the club. The prayer aimed to encourage young people to make wise choices and to live up to high moral standards set forward by both the club specifically and by Judaism more generally.

Myer added to the club prayer and produced a prayer book for use in the service. The book included both traditional Jewish elements including the *Shema*, *Kaddish* and Maimonides' articles of faith as well as English and secular elements through the National Anthem and the hymn 'O God Our Help in Ages Past'.[28] It also included a specially constructed war prayer:

> We earnestly pray to Thee, O. God, on behalf of our Club mates, our relatives and our friends, who are in the midst of danger, doing their duty to their Country and their King. Guard and protect them from all sorrow, pain and hurt, and bring them back to us in health and safety. We know that we must bear our share of the terrible losses by land and sea. Strengthen our faith in Thee so that we may bear our sorrows with stout hearts and with humility. Grant a speedy recovery to the wounded and ease their pain. Into Thy hand we commit the spirit of the dead, in the firm conviction that they will awake in the fullness of Thy light, in a happier and better world. Amen[29]

27   LL, M397, *Prayers: Stepney Jewish Lads' Club* (London: Eyre and Spottiswoode, 1915).

28   Ibid. 'O God our Help in Ages Past' is a traditional Christian Hymn written by Isaac Watts (a hymn writer and member of the Congregational Church in Southampton) based on Psalm 90. Whilst the inclusion of a Christian hymn is certainly noteworthy, the fact that the words were based on a Psalm meant that the inclusion of this song within a Jewish context was not necessarily a contradiction. Additionally, the very British association of the hymn certainly contributed to its inclusion.

29   Ibid.

This prayer was able to incorporate traditional Jewish elements as well as demonstrate loyalty to the King and to the national cause. This would have been significant, as it made clear to the wider British community that Judaism was compatible with commitment to a sense of national belonging: the emphasis placed on serving king and country helped to reinforce national loyalty and the use of phrases such as 'our share' and 'our sorrows' reinforced the idea that the Jewish population was part of the nation as a whole. This link between religion and war was common in society during the First World War, even by the non-religious.[30] The use of the war prayer by the Stepney Club thus reflects the increasing reliance on religious justification for war more generally. This combination of Jewish and national elements underscored both elements of club work, demonstrating that both Jewishness and Englishness could sit side by side compatibly. The use of the club prayer book continued until after the Second World War, and as a result the dual themes of religious and national identity were presented to a large number of Jewish boys.

Yet, with the exception of Stepney, prior to the Second World War there were few attempts at holding a prayer service at the end of boys' clubs meetings. This contrasted with girls' clubs, where the expectation of religiosity in young women ensured that most clubs held a short end of evening service. When services did occur within boys' clubs, the emphasis was placed on loyalty to the nation. This was particularly the case from 1914 to 1918 as can be seen in Stepney's war prayer, which drew strong links between Judaism and Englishness. This reflected the needs of the wider Jewish community, who felt they needed to prove their national loyalty when this was called into question, especially in immigrant areas. At the same time it also reflected masculine expectations which emphasized patriotism as well as a sense of renewed youthful religiosity, something that was common in both Jewish and non-Jewish communities during the First World War.[31]

30   Annette Becker, 'Faith, Ideologies and the "Cultures of War"', in *A Companion to World War One*, ed. by John Horne (Oxford: Wiley-Blackwell, 2010), pp. 234–47 (p. 236).

31   Rosie Kennedy, *The Children's War, Britain 1914–1918* (Basingstoke: Palgrave MacMillan, 2014), p. 3.

In the interwar period, however, there were a number of changes in the frequency of prayer services. Within the Stepney club, prayers continued to be held at the end of the evening and the influence of Myer continued to be felt in the club after his death. It was customary for the club to hold a *yahrzeit* service, which differed from the usual service: 'Included in this service was the club prayer, which [Myer] had specifically composed for the club, as well as the memorial prayer for the dead.'[32] This service followed Jewish traditions of mourning and placed importance on following Jewish rituals, something which would have been seen as key to developing the members as Jews. Myer's prayer book continued to be used by the club after his death and in the 1930s attempts were made to modernize the book, although the idea was not implemented. The prayer service likewise continued throughout the period, but by the 1930s both attendance and the behaviour of the members had declined. An article in the club magazine from correspondent 'DM' – probably D. Mendoza, the manager in charge – lamented the poor conduct of boys during the service. He asked:

> Does 'prayer time' at night attended by a dozen or so boys constitute club prayers? ... to come to club prayers with a handkerchief or even more unseemly objects upon one's head is surely a profanation of a Holy service. Club prayers should be treated with reverence, and not be a subterfuge for a late night game of ping-pong.[33]

This article, by presenting the criticism from an unidentified set of initials rather than a well-known manager, allowed the press to believe that club members were concerned with the lack of religion and that they wanted more solemnity with regards to religious observance, although it is possible that some within the community would have made the link between the initials and the club leader. Whilst the managers were concerned with the poor behaviour of members during the service, the boys had also noticed the growing indifference to prayers. A new member to the club in 1938 reported on his first evening: 'Just then a bell rang an [sic] everybody rushed for the door. I asked somebody whether it was the fire drill bell but

---

32   *JG*, 23 February 1923.
33   SUA MS172 AJ250 *Stepnian*, October 1934.

he told me that it was the bell for prayers. I went into the library and said prayers with the rest (three boys and a manager – the rest had gone home).'[34] These accounts indicate that throughout the 1930s attendance at the service had declined and that people were actively trying to avoid attending. It marked a departure from the behaviour first mentioned in 1915 when boys were considered to be 'most devout'. This changing attitude to prayers reflected a decline of enthusiasm in Judaism found where 'children of the immigrants were drawn to popular culture of the non-Jewish population over that of the Old World culture of their parents'.[35] The club prayers at Stepney therefore were more successful during their early years with the direct influence of Denzil Myer and with greater levels of religiosity at home, than they were after Myer's death. Even so, the club persisted in holding the service, indicating the club still valued this element of religious observance, although the young members did not.

Other clubs during the 1920s and 1930s began to hold prayer services, despite the difficulties seen at the Stepney club in this period. At the Cambridge and Bethnal Green Club a similar service to that provided in Stepney was held:

> [S]everal managers had been responsible for conducting weekday services which had been held regularly two or three times a week at the close of the evening. Attendances whilst not yet as large as they would have liked them to be nevertheless tended to increase and the results on the whole were fairly promising.[36]

During the 1930s, the previously undenominational Brady club began its own service. This coincided with the change in its religious policy and encapsulates the general shift towards religion in wider Jewish society where the religious culture of the interwar years has been described by Endelman as 'a shadow of its former self'.[37] Lady Janner recalled that in the 1930s the evening ended with an assembly, five-minute prayer and

---

34   SUA MS172 AJ250 *Stepnian*, November 1938.
35   Endelman, *The Jews in Britain*, p. 205.
36   *JG*, 4 May 1928.
37   Todd M. Endelman, *Radical Assimilation in English Jewish History 1656–1945* (Bloomington: Indiana University Press, 1990), p. 199.

announcements. The *Jewish Guardian* described this as 'a short voluntary service … at the close of every evening. Often the service closed with a short prayer by a manager.'[38] It is significant to note that these services, and the ones in Stepney, were voluntary, unlike in girls' clubs where attendance was expected from all members present during that evening. It further demonstrates that spirituality was not a great concern for boys' club leaders in line with gender expectations.

The prayer services at all of these clubs were short, simple and voluntary and there was evidence that they met with elements of success. The clubs which maintained themselves as undenominational revealed no evidence of a prayer service and it is likely that many of these organizations used the fact that they did not market themselves as Jewish as a reason not to attempt to include nightly prayers. For the Jewish clubs, however, prayer was included in their activities indicating that evening prayers were a significant factor in whether a club considered itself to be Jewish or not.

Sabbath services were a frequent part of both the Jewish and the undenominational clubs. These services helped to introduce the members to acceptable British forms of worship in a distinctly Jewish setting. Indeed, the question of whether or not to open on Friday nights was a matter of contention amongst many in the club community as well as in the wider Jewish society. A number of clubs opened on Fridays for a modified programme, which emphasized quiet activities.

Hutchison House Club, despite its undenominational outlook, liaised with the Chief Rabbi to provide an appropriate solution to the problem of whether to open on Friday nights. The leaders agreed with the Chief Rabbi that the club could be open on Friday nights and 'everybody was asked when he attended the club whether he spent Fridays at home. If he did he was forbidden to attend the club on these evenings. If he did not, they welcomed him at the club for quiet reading, games and conversation.'[39] Here, Hutchison House was showing adherence to Jewish customs by acknowledging the Sabbath (although it did not go to great lengths to include a service). This was justified by the club because of its undenominational

---

38   JML Tape 74, Interview with Lady Janner, May 13th 1986 and *JG*, 28 November 1930.
39   *JC*, 30 June 1905.

outlook – the club did not want to appear *too* Jewish and therefore hid behind this claim in order to avoid including a religious service. In the 1920s the Brady Club, in line with their change of religious outlook, went a step further than Hutchison House by including a service on Friday evenings. These began in 1926, and after a slow start, attendances increased to over 100 members each Friday. The managers cited the growth in attendance as proof that 'the members of the Brady Club always knew how to enjoy themselves and the fact that they maintained the Friday evening service proved that they were loyal to their faith'.[40] These services continued to grow and experienced continued success throughout the 1930s with a number of visiting religious ministers, including the Dayan Dr A. Feldman and Chief Rabbi, delivering addresses to the boys.[41] In providing a Friday night facility for the boys both the Hutchison House Club and the Brady Club showed an adherence to Judaism. The inclusion of a formal service within the Brady Club's programme in the 1920s further emphasizes the importance of formality within religion for boys and illustrates the club's shift from undenominational to Jewish.

Saturday afternoon services enabled the clubs to produce an even more structured event than those on Friday nights. They helped to promote gendered expectations of worship, establishing men as the public and formal front of Judaism, one which fitted with wider British expectations of the public/private divide between men and women as well as being 'institutionally central to religion'.[42] The Stepney Club ran Saturday services weekly at their club premises and it was reported that the events were well attended, although no specific numbers were given.[43] A letter from Denzil Myer encouraged boys to attend the services which he described as 'short and bright' and designed specifically for working boys who were obliged

40   *JG*, 11 February 1927.

41   See *JC*, 25 May 1934.

42   Lucy Delap and Sue Morgan, 'Introduction: Men, Masculinities and Religious Change in Post-Christian Britain', in *Men, Masculinities and Religious Change in Twentieth Century Britain*, ed. by Lucy Delap and Sue Morgan (Basingstoke: Palgrave Macmillan, 2013), pp. 1–29 (p. 2).

43   See *JW*, 16 January 1903.

to work on the Sabbath and therefore forget their religious identities. He closed the letter by making a plea to the members: 'I am sure that if you think the matter over, you will agree with me that there is something really missing from our lives if we are deprived of a pure and manly religious influence.'[44] It is interesting to note that Myer felt it necessary to promote 'manly' religion, which speaks to the need for the clubs actively to promote religion as something gendered. This fits within the wider context of youth groups throughout Britain, for example, the Boys' Brigade (a uniformed youth movement founded in Glasgow by William Alexander Smith in 1883). This group emphasized military drill and religion and sought to show the boys the 'manliness of Christianity' through linking the two concepts together.[45] Moreover, it is likely that the services included elements of 'muscular Judaism', linking sport and physical fitness with religious obligations. It provided a stark contrast to emphases of love and beauty found within services in girls' clubs. The content as well as the structure of the services therefore endeavoured to emphasize masculine qualities within the religious context, helping to reinforce gender expectations amongst the boys. The services at Stepney were attended by members of the Brady Boys' Club, but attendance from the Brady Club was poor as 'little was done to promote the services except exhibiting on the club notice board the official weekly notice of the service and a stereotyped letter from Mr Denzil Myer'.[46] The relative failure of the Brady Club in attracting members to attend the service highlights the importance of a dedicated leader who was prepared to promote religious activities within the club. Where the Stepney Club had such a leader, the services were a success, contrasting to the absence of this in the Brady Club.

The notion of 'manly' religion, although rarely fully defined, was something that was evident in a number of boys' club sermons and religious events. At the memorial service for Gerald Samuel, a leader from the Brady

44   LL, *The Stepnian*, Memorial Issue, 1917, Letter reprinted from November 1913.
45   Kennedy, *Children's War*, p. 88 also Donald M. MacFarlane, *First For Boys: The Story of the Boys' Brigade, 1883–1993* (London: The Boys' Brigade, 1993), p. 6 <http://www.boys-brigade.org.uk/ffb.pdf> [accessed 2 April 2013].
46   *JC*, 2 January 1914.

Street Club who was killed in the First World War, a large number of club boys were in attendance. There was no sermon at the event, instead, a letter written by Samuel to be recited on occasion of his death was read to the congregation. The letter, written a year prior, was addressed directly to the club members:

> There is nothing of which we can be more proud than our race and religion. It is a great heritage and it is a duty for everyone of us to keep it pure and unaltered, and to hand it down to our descendants, as our ancestors have preserved it for us. If you will let me preach to you for a minute I should like to say that, to my mind, our pride should be not in our ancient ceremonial and customs, valuable and beautiful as they are, but in the great virtues of unselfishness, sincerity, purity in mind and body, of trust in God, faith in his goodness, the belief in a future life, which are the only solid foundations of our race.[47]

In this letter the 'manly' qualities of religion were emphasized through the emphasis on 'unselfishness', 'sincerity' and 'purity', which echo the ideals found in the British sporting ethic prevalent amongst the clubs and within wider society at this time. Whilst not a typical example of a Saturday service, the content of the memorial provides an insight into the content likely to have been included within regular Saturday services. It certainly reflects the importance of letters from the front in encouraging 'mental mobilization' and thus the inculcation of masculine qualities amongst youth at home.[48] This is a clear indication that clubs used religion to promote gendered expectations of manliness. It is also interesting to note that Samuel was making a clear appeal for Orthodox traditions encouraging the boys to avoid the reform movement, which was gaining in popularity at this time. Through this letter, Samuel was able to not only link gender roles with religion, but was also able to include a message that endeavoured to encourage the boys to remain within Orthodoxy.

Services within clubs continued through the interwar period. In the 1920s, the Notting Hill Club held Sabbath evening services at the New

47   LL, M395, *The Stepnian*, September 1917, p. 4.
48   For a detailed examination of the importance of letters to children in the First World War see Kennedy, *Children's War*, pp. 21–50.

West End Synagogue where members were encouraged to attend regularly.[49] The idea of holding a Sabbath afternoon service was picked up by the Central Council of Jewish Working Boys' Clubs and Young Men's Institutions, which discussed the introduction of a co-ordinated service. It would be 'of a modified Orthodox character, with a considerable portion of English'.[50] Ultimately the council decided to leave Sabbath services to individual clubs, rather than to arrange a central service. Even so, the discussion indicates that club leadership was aware of the importance and the need for Sabbath services within club life. The continued formality of these services underscored the consistency in expectations of men within Judaism. By providing opportunities for formal worship the clubs were showing their commitment to providing religious services that were deemed appropriate within Anglo-Jewish norms. The emphasis placed on Sabbath services was a vital link in maintaining religious traditions amongst the boys. The services provided the clubs with an ideal way to introduce religion into club life through child friendly, but still traditional, services and more importantly emphasized a highly Anglicized version of Judaism which promoted sporting and English values and which during the war contributed to the education of young boys in the importance of militarism. At the same time the services provided a way to introduce the boys to worship within acceptable Anglo-Jewish traditions rather than Eastern European traditions.

Formal synagogue worship was not just maintained for the Sabbath. Holy Days and Festivals gave clubs an additional way to promote a more formal and gendered religion. With emphasis placed on formality, naturally New Year and Day of Atonement played an important role in boys' clubs. Both Brady and Stepney held services for their club members on these days. This allowed the boys to secure a seat for a service – something that was difficult to get in a synagogue. At the same time, the boys were able to gain a foundation in understanding the formalities expected of British Jewish services, rather than services within the Eastern European style. In Stepney, the club emphasized formality as boys were asked 'if possible, to

49   *JW*, 10 November 1921.
50   *JG*, 2 April 1926.

bring a *Talith* and Singer's prayer book'.[51] The club thus demonstrated that it was adhering to Orthodox principles through the inclusion of the *Talith*, adding to the formal nature of the event. This also helped to promote gendered expectations of religion, as this was something that was unique to men. Within the Brady club, services were also held for these days. There were those, however, within the community who doubted the motives behind the services. A correspondent to the *Jewish Chronicle* wrote that 'Brady managers condone [the New Year and Day of Atonement] services as a necessary means of saving face before the religiously inclined of their supporters'.[52] Regardless of the motives behind the services, the leaders of the Brady club were still providing a formal religious experience for the boys, one that emphasized the structured elements of worship. In both of these instances the formality of worship was to the fore, keeping in line with masculine expectations of religious observance within Judaism, rather than stressing domestic elements of Judaism.

One of these domestic elements can be seen within Passover commemorations, which provided an opportunity for a more domestic religious observance not often seen within boys' clubs. In 1933, Brady reported that 'a *Seder* service was ... arranged for those boys who had no Passover service at home'.[53] This was an unusual form of observance for a boys' club as the focus was on the domestic element of religion, which although it was acceptable (and indeed encouraged) within Judaism, was not fully so within British gender norms. As a result, it was unusual for boys' clubs to hold events based on eating and, in doing so, the club was showing that religious obligations were more important than maintaining traditional, national gender roles that would have downplayed the role of the meal within the club. This is likely due to the centrality of the Passover *Seder* within Judaism, so its absence (both within the home and the club) would have been viewed with suspicion by the Jewish community. This event, through emphasizing the role of the man as the leader within the *Seder* service, and thus taking a place at the (traditionally feminine) kitchen table,

<hr>

51   SUA, MS172 AJ250 Folder 4, *Stepney Jewish Chronicle*, No. 7, September 1903.
52   *JC*, 2 January 1914.
53   THLA, 360.1, *Brady Associated Clubs Annual Report 1933*.

also reinforces the notion of domestic space as one of performance. Here, by conducting the service, the boys were encouraged, despite the obvious femininity of the space, to assert an element of patriarchal 'power' over the domestic sphere through the performance of religious rituals.[54] The *Seder* service, like the services held on Friday nights throughout the year, showed sensitivities to the role of the family within traditions, and allowed the boys to explore the more domestic element of Judaism; it ensured that boys who had these services within their home did not attend the *Seder* at the club. For the Brady Club, the *Seder* helped to fulfil their religious obligations to the boys and showed that the club was willing to, at least partly, transgress national, secular gender roles in order to provide this important element of the Jewish calendar and model how to correctly lead the *Seder*.

Additionally, in terms of festivals, *Chanucah* and *Purim* were especially popular within the clubs. This was due in part to the nature of the days as 'child friendly'. *Chanucah* provided an opportunity for the groups to hold parties and teas, thus making religion more enjoyable for the boys. Even in the Hutchison House club *Chanucah* was noted through holding a ball in aid of the day.[55] Whilst this event was not necessarily a specifically religious observance of the day, it still showed that the club was aware of religious festivals. As a result, the Club was able and willing to mark these in their activities and demonstrate an adherence to Jewish principles and traditions albeit in a secular context. In the 1930s the Brady Club offered a much more traditional event which included a religious service followed by a tea and social for both the girls' and boys' club.[56] These events promoted religion through the readings at *Chanucah* which emphasised masculinity within religious teaching. If the service in this instance was similar to that in other clubs, it is likely that it focused on the heroic nature of the *Chanucah* story, emphasizing the role of Judas Maccabaeus and therefore promoting qualities traditionally associated with muscular Judaism. The use of the *Chanucah*

---

54   Kate Barclay, 'Place and Power on Irish Farms at the End of the Nineteenth Century', *Women's History Review*, 21 (2012), pp. 571–88 (p. 579).

55   *JW*, 26 November 1919.

56   THLA 360.1 *Brady Associated Clubs Annual Report* 1933 and THLA S/BRA/1/1/1, *Minutes from the Brady Settlement House Committee*, 8 January 1936.

story and the centrality given to the festival within the clubs reflects trends in all youth clubs, as well as within religious associations. Influenced by the increased prominence given to muscular Christianity (and by extension muscular Judaism) groups and associations prior to the First World War made explicit references to military figures within religious traditions, such as Judas Maccabaeus and David.[57] After 1918, with the decline of militarism, the festival of *Chanucah* retained its importance by associating the day with less controversial qualities of courage and adventure.

Both the Stepney Club and the Victoria club marked *Purim* by holding events for younger Jewish children. In 1903, the Stepney Club wrote that '[t]he annual *Purim* treat given by members of the club to the school children took place on Sunday March 15th. There were 120 children present. The evening started with a piano solo by J. Waas. This was followed by songs and recitations.'[58] As with *Chanucah* there was nothing explicitly religious in these events, although the songs and recitations may well have been religious ones, the celebrations were keeping in tone with the spirit of the day and demonstrated an adherence to Jewish traditions.

In 1913 the Hutchison House newsletter featured a poem on the subject of *Purim*. This poem clearly referred to the religious history behind the festival and made links to the Biblical background as well as imploring the boys to remember their religious heritage:[59]

The years roll onward ever, / The Feast of Purim comes again / And with all its gaieties / Obscuring all its heritage of pain / How oft in present times that be / We Jews, still suffer Hamans / Whilst revering Mordecai

Purim!! The feast that teaches us / Remembrance of oppressions in the past / Reminds us also in our joyful hours / That the Almighty's love will ever last

---

57 Kennedy, *Children's War*, p. 87 and Lucy Delap, 'Be Strong and Play the Man: Anglican Masculinities in the Twentieth Century', in *Men, Masculinities and Religious Change in Twentieth Century Britain*, ed. by Lucy Delap and Sue Morgan (Basingstoke: Palgrave Macmillan, 2013), pp. 119–45 (p. 121).

58 SUA MS172 AJ250 Folder 4, *Stepney Jewish Club Chronicle*, No. 3, April 1903.

59 JML, 1990.2.3, *The Hutch*, March 1913.

God's chosen people!! What a noted name / Is held by every Jew throughout the Sphere / We hear it. Let us strive with might and main / To prove ourselves still worthy it to bear.[60]

This poem with its acknowledgement of the Biblical story of *Purim* is particularly significant within the Hutchison House Club as this group rarely referenced religion. The inclusion of an explicitly religious article within the newsletter, which was sent to members and the public, demonstrates that although the club played down the importance of religion, it was still conscious of its wider duty and its Biblical and religious heritage and wanted to ensure that those outside of the club itself still viewed the group as within the Jewish domain. *Purim* was also mentioned in the newsletter of the Notting Hill Club which reported on the special evening they held in honour of the festival where a visitor to the club explained the origins of the day and 'special delicacies were obtained from the bar'.[61] The emphasis on the 'special delicacies' demonstrates that the club was adhering to the spirit of *Purim* and also marked the day as special in contrast to normal evenings at the club.

In 1924, the *Jewish Guardian* reported that:

> 60 juniors were guests of their senior members of the Victoria Club and were entertained to a Tea, followed by a concert at which their hosts were present on Saturday last. The whole affair was voted a huge success. This tea was given by members of the club to their younger brothers and sisters in celebration of *Purim*.[62]

These events, which encouraged engagement with younger children, were unusual amongst boys' clubs. Here, the boys were given the opportunity to host and plan an event for younger children, a role that was placed firmly within the female sphere and indeed were frequent occurrences within girls' clubs which sought to develop skills for the girls' future success as mothers. That two different boys' clubs held similar events attests to the importance of religion, in particular enjoyable religion, which would have

60   JML, 1990.2.3, *The Hutch*, March 1913, p. 4.
61   SUA MS116/121 AJ301 *Notting Hill Jewish Lads' Club Magazine*, April 1911.
62   *JG*, 4 April 1924.

helped to encourage worship in future generations. These examples can be seen as a time when religious events took greater importance than preserving gender roles. Thus boys were allowed to move into the female sphere by planning an event in celebration of *Purim*.

Another way for clubs to introduce religion was by introducing religious figures into the group. This had the added advantage of familiarizing the largely immigrant members with figures in Anglo-Jewish practices, especially through the involvement of the Chief Rabbi, who as seen earlier, maintained a symbolic connection to a number of clubs. In 1914, the Stepney Club noted the value of including a minister within club life, claiming that the ideal way of introducing religion into the lives of working boys was to involve a 'minister-manager' to run the organization. In turn, this would lead to the boys happily attending synagogue.[63] The concept of a minister-manager was, however, ultimately impractical as in most cases religious figures were either unwilling or unable to devote regular time to the clubs. Nevertheless, religious figures frequently associated themselves with the work of a particular group. Within Stepney, for example, the Reverend Stern took on the presidency of the club in order to 'bring the club nearer to the synagogue'.[64]

The Chief Rabbi was present at a number of club events, especially at consecrations of buildings and prize-givings. He attended an event at the Victoria Club when the boys were '*en-fete*'. Here the Chief Rabbi was 'warmly received by the boys and gave a most entertaining little speech which was followed with evident keen pleasure by all the lads present, who thoroughly appreciated the anecdotes with which he enlivened his remarks'.[65] The presence of the Chief Rabbi helped to introduce boys to a key concept of Anglo-Judaism – the position of one Chief Rabbi for the entire country (and indeed the empire), rather than one for a small area as was traditional in Eastern Europe. Even the otherwise non-religious club, Hutchison House, included religious figures within their adult membership

---

63   THLA, LP 2254 (360.1) *How a Jewish Working Boys' Club is Run: An Account of the Stepney Jewish Lads' Club*, 1914, p. 15.

64   *JW*, 22 February 1907.

65   *JC*, 29 November 1901.

through the Reverend David Hirsch who served as a chaplain in the British Army during the First World War.[66] The inclusion of a former forces chaplain shows that, whilst the club was Jewish, it was also showing allegiance to the UK and maintaining an image of Britishness at the same time as linking the group with physical fitness and military prowess. Evidence of the practice of introducing religious figures can be seen in both the clubs that readily identified as Jewish, as well as those that were undenominational. This was therefore a key way in which groups could demonstrate their Jewishness and situate themselves as part of the Anglo-Jewish community without overtly preaching to the young members or including unpopular religious activities.

The opening of new premises provided an ideal opportunity for club leaders to include religion and religious figures. At the opening of the new club building for the West Central Jewish Lads' Club in 1900, the Chief Rabbi gave an address to the boys: 'vouchsafe to these lads a spirit of understanding and of Godly fear that they may not stain the hours given to recreation by words that debase and actions that degrade or by the sight that would profane Thy Holy Sabbath and appointed times'.[67] Dr Adler, the Chief Rabbi, also addressed the boys and added that he

> exhorted them to do honour to their faith and race by leading honourable lives. In the Psalm they had first sung which ushered in the close of the Sabbath their sons had been compared with plants … he hoped that they would grow up like tall plants full of manly vigour but manly in the highest sense of the word, chivalrous to women and the weak, truthful and honourable as they became Jews and Englishmen in all their actions.[68]

In these addresses, much like those given at weekly services, the boys were encouraged to be honourable and full of 'manly vigour'. The emphasis on qualities deemed to be of importance for men is significant, helping to promote masculinity as a religious obligation. Religion was used here as a way to promote these aims, thus linking Judaism and English gender

---

66   *JW*, 15 October 1919.
67   *JC*, 12 October 1900.
68   Ibid.

norms and promoting notions of manliness as a religious duty. Yet, five years later in the Hutchison House Club, the Chief Rabbi preached different themes: 'grant these lads a spirit of understanding and of reverence that they may never stain the hours given to labour or to rest by thoughts that debase, by sullied words or degrading actions. Inspire the lads with a thirst for knowledge, that they may give some of the hours they spend here to the loving study of the Holy word Thou hast taught us and of the glorious world Thou hast made.'[69] As in the West Central event, the boys were exhorted to spend their time wisely, but they were also encouraged to devote themselves to learning. In this instance, the qualities mentioned during the address were not specifically English gender norms as seen in the earlier service, but instead addressed concerns faced within Anglo-Jewry and within wider society, that young people were becoming distanced from religion and wasting their leisure time. This focus on religion and lack of attention afforded to militarism and masculinity was unusual for boys' clubs prior to 1918. The balance between Englishness and Judaism was a delicate one, requiring a subtle, sometimes contradictory reading of gender norms between the two.

These competing themes continued to be fought out after 1918. The prayers at the consecration of the new Brady Club premises in 1938 incorporated both Englishness and Jewishness. The congregation at the event sang a selection of Psalms which focused on salvation, the reading of the *Shema* and a collection of biblical verses as well as a prayer for the King, the national anthem and a reading from Eleazar of Worms which emphasized the need for struggle and 'being a man', rather than on pre-1918 militarism.[70] Here the service was used to encourage Englishness through the prayer for the Royal family at the same time as Jewishness through the *Shema*. The service also encouraged the promotion of traditional British gender norms, encouraging manliness through actions and struggle with an emphasis on 'manly character'. In this way, the club was able to combine accepted

---

69   *JC*, 30 June 1905.
70   THLA LP 5267 360.1 *Brady Boys' Club Consecration of New Club Building Monday 14 February 5698–1938.*

concepts of manliness with traditional Jewish practices, demonstrating continuity with 'manly' religion promoted before 1914.

Religion within special events was not just about the services themselves. Annual displays provided members a chance to demonstrate skills that they had developed within the club. At the Hutchison House Annual display in 1908 one boy chose a subject that was tied with his religious heritage: 'probably the most noteworthy exhibit was that of a deceased chicken, which lay in solitary splendour in order to display a lad's proficiency in attaching to its well-nourished body the seal of the Board of *Shechita*'.[71] This was a rather different expression of religion compared to that found within services, one that focused on the more practical rather than the spiritual elements of religion. The boy demonstrating his skill at creating *kosher* meat provided on one level a contrast to the other displays at the event, which focused on more secular skills including tailoring and shorthand. The decision to exhibit this skill was the boy's, demonstrating that he had chosen to display and develop his talents within a religiously significant act. The fact that the club accommodated and acknowledged his skill demonstrates that the group was aware of the religious needs of the boys and was happy to demonstrate this aspect of Jewishness and Jewish tradition in public despite its undenominational claim. However, the importance of this willingness should not be over-estimated. Although this display was clearly attached to Jewish customs and showed adherence to Jewish heritage, show-casing the skills of one member did not require others to be actively involved in this display of religion. Moreover, this was a technical skill, not on one level dissimilar from that of those involved in manufacture, thus the importance of this display as a consciously religious event should not be overestimated.

Events, whether annual displays, prize-givings or the consecration of new buildings can be seen as a way in which the clubs were able to display their religious basis to the public. During these events, sermons were made relevant to the club and demonstrated an adherence to Jewish traditions as well as to gender norms through their content and the trades demonstrated

---

71   *JC*, 24 January 1908. The Board of *Shechita* is the organization which oversees the production of *kosher* food.

by boys. At boy-led events, however, such as the annual display, religious activities should be viewed perhaps less as an expression of religion, and more as an opportunity for the boys to 'show off' their talents. Religious classes, on the other hand, demonstrate a conscious effort on behalf of the club managers and the boys attending the classes to engage with religion.

A number of boys' clubs acknowledged religion through including classes and lectures on Jewish subjects. Regular classes on religious topics provided an opportunity for club leadership to demonstrate that the club was concerned with the development of its members' Jewish identities. The Stepney Club reported that 'on Wednesday evenings from about 8–10pm there is a Jewish study circle under the direction of Mr Van Leer, and the great interest shown by the few who attend it, yes verily the few, as there are only four boys, proves that it must be, and is really, very absorbing'.[72] The Brady Club in 1907 held a weekly class on Jewish history and the North London Jewish Club in 1922 held 'lectures on Jewish history given on Thursday evenings by Rabbi Harris Cohen'.[73] In addition to regular classes, a number of the clubs ran occasional lectures on Jewish subjects and both the Brady Club and the Notting Hill Club included talks on Jewish history.[74]

The classes in these groups focused on Jewish history, however, rather than religion itself. This allowed club leaders to approach religion from an inoffensive standpoint, which would not put off members. The history classes allowed boys to explore both their religious and secular traditions and practices in what was to be considered a more 'manly' and appealing way, through the study of military victories and battles. There are no records relating to the content of these classes, although it seems that they focused as much on the secular as on the religious. A contemporary view held that *all* Jewish history, whether explicitly religious or not, contributed to the religious education of young Jews: 'instruction in Jewish history [throughout the ages] is then ... above all, instruction in the history

72   SUA, MS172 AJ250, Folder 4, *Stepney Jewish Club Chronicle*, No. 2, March 1903.
73   *JC*, 12 December 1902 and *JG*, 5 May 1922.
74   See *JG*, 5 May 1922, 30 November 1923 and 28 January 1927.

of Judaism and of Jewish religious life',[75] therefore to some contemporary standards, these classes were able, through an examination of history, to provide some element of religious education. Jewish history classes and lectures served as an ideal way to introduce a Jewish element that would not be seen by youth as something feminine or abstract, due to the concentration of the classes on military history, but would still enable them to develop in a spiritual way. The religious classes, combined with other elements of religious programming mentioned above, provided the basis for religious education within boys' clubs. Summer camps provided a perfect opportunity for the consolidation of the religious teachings begun during the year and provided an extended time period for the inclusion and promotion of religious practices.

Summer Camps

Annual summer camps gave a further opportunity to provide religious experiences for boys. These experiences ranged from simply providing *kosher* food to twice daily prayer services. Whilst the intensity of these events differed, they did provide a religious experience of some kind, which went further than the experience that clubs could provide of an evening. One of the simplest ways clubs could include a Jewish element was through providing *kosher* food. Many camps catered for this need and publicized their adherence to the law, such as the announcement from the Victoria club featured in the *Jewish Chronicle* in 1936 that at the club camp '*Kashrut* will be observed'.[76] This promoted the religious element to the Jewish community and helped to allay the community's fears that the clubs were not Jewish by demonstrating adherence to the most basic Jewish laws.

75   Morris Joseph, 'Jewish Religious Education', *Jewish Quarterly Review*, 9 (1897), pp. 631–68 (p. 653).
76   *JC*, 19 June 1936.

Camps were also organized for particular religious events. In the same year as the Victoria Club held a *kosher* event, the Stepney club went one further and held a weekend-long Passover Camp which was reviewed in the club magazine. 'A special *kosher* Passover camp was held at Stapleford Abbots during the Easter week-end. The main activity of the camp … was eating *Motzos* with snowballing and ice-hockey occupying a bad second place. No-one was allowed more than twenty-one blankets, the weather being considered sufficiently warm to make a larger number unnecessary.'[77] This review of the camp from one of the boys mentioned no specifically religious activities, other than eating *Motzos* though it seems reasonable to assume that some element of religious activity, possibly a *Seder* or a service such as that provided by the Brady Club in 1933 and discussed earlier, took place. The presence of an event devoted solely to Passover indicates that the managers were sufficiently aware of its religious identity and felt comfortable addressing this to the young members. This suggests that the club leaders were aware of the need to make religion more 'manly'. They did this through placing Passover festivities in the context of a camp, which was frequently seen as an enjoyable, masculine event, rather than the solely domestic *Seder* seen earlier in the Brady Club.

At all camps, whether specifically tied to a religious event or not, clubs held prayers in the morning and evening. This was an important expression of religious identity and provided a chance for the clubs to demonstrate their adherence to Judaism. There is evidence of these twice daily prayer services occurring in a number of clubs, including the Brady Club, the Stepney Club and the West Central Lads' Club and throughout a diverse time period – from the early 1900s until the outbreak of the Second World War. Most of these prayer services were very short – the Brady Club allowed just five minutes for this and the Victoria club allowed half an hour for prayers and lights out combined.[78] The short time allowance indicates that the clubs did not place a great deal of emphasis on these services. Whilst the inclusion of prayers does show that the clubs were aware of the need to include this element of observance, the lack of attention paid to them

77   SUA, MS172 AJ250, *Stepnian*, July 1936.
78   *JC*, 22 July 1938 and *JW*, 14 August 1908.

in the schedule shows that religion was seen as an additional component
of the activities, rather than something that was a key element of the camp.
In most groups, these prayer services were compulsory; however, in the
Notting Hill Club, the service was optional. The club hoped, even though
the service was voluntary, that all of the boys would feel the desire to participate in their Jewish faith and attend the services.[79] The voluntary nature
of the service shows that the managers trusted the boys to attend and
make their own choices with regard to how they observed religion. The
club also made efforts to adhere to Orthodox traditions: 'members desir-
ing to say *Kaddish* may rely on the regular attendance of *Minyan*'.[80] This
traditional prayer provision provides an indication that religious tradition
was important within the club, reflecting both the members' needs and
their parents' expectations, and in the case of the Notting Hill Club, this
position was linked to Orthodoxy. It is noteworthy that the club provided
opportunity for the young people to say *Kaddish*, the prayer of mourning, an obligation for those young people who had lost either a parent or
a sibling. It indicates that the club was aware that the background of the
young people was different from the background of 'native-born', middle-
class Anglo-Jewish youth, and was more likely to have lost close family
members whether as a result of conditions in their home country prior to
arrival in the UK or whether this was due to poverty and living conditions
in London. Its inclusion within the camp setting indicates that the club
leaders were sympathetic to the cultural and social differences of their club
members. In any case, however, prayer was not given a great role in terms
of time allowance, indicating that although it was valued, it was not seen
as something worthy enough (or indeed manly enough) to warrant a great
deal of attention.

Where prayers were often given only a small amount of attention
during the camps, the rituals associated with the Sabbath were treated as
an important part of the holiday experience. In girls' clubs, emphasis was

79   SUA, MS116/21 AJ301 *Notting Hill Jewish Lads' Club Magazine*, August 1911.
80   SUA, MS116/21 AJ301, *Notting Hill Jewish Lads Club Magazine*, June 1914. *Minyan*
      is the quorum of ten Jewish male adults needed for the fulfilment of certain religious
      obligations including the recitation of the *Kaddish*.

placed on the Sabbath meal on Friday evening. This was not the case with boys' clubs. There are no written accounts of the Sabbath meal in boys' camps (although this does not mean the event did not occur, just that it was not considered noteworthy). In contrast, the Passover *Seder* was observed.[81] The *Seder* followed Anglo-Jewish traditions with a white table cloth and more formal table settings than other meals held during camps and boys dressed in formal attire for the event, rather than in usual camp clothing.[82] This indicates that the event was given a sense of importance and was treated as such by the boys. It is important to note, however, that although the meal *was* a feature, there was little emphasis placed on it in official accounts. This lack of publicity demonstrates that for boys' clubs, the domestic elements of observance, which were stressed in girls' clubs, were considered less noteworthy than formal services, which frequently featured in such accounts. Even so, such involvement does not entirely transgress Jewish gender roles, indeed, men's participation in both Sabbath and Passover meals was a vital element of religious experience. The meals *did* challenge British gender norms, which placed attention to beauty and the domestic in the feminine sphere, and is likely the reason for the lack of attention given to the meals in club accounts.

The Sabbath services on camps, unlike the Sabbath meal, were given a special emphasis. Visitors to the site often delivered the sermons. For example, in the 1920s Reverend Polack, the Jewish master at Clifton College, visited camps held by the Stepney Club and the Victoria Club. This practice began during some of the first camps held at the beginning of the century and continued until the outbreak of the Second World War.[83] The services, given by someone who was largely unknown to the club, helped to add a sense of grandeur to the event. By including someone new, the services were emphasizing the formality of worship, and therefore emphasizing the link between masculinity and formal religious worship. The content

---

81   Whilst Passover is typically around April and summer camps are held in July/August, evidence suggests that there were Passover meals held at camp. The reason for this discrepancy in the dates is unclear.

82   JML 279.20, Victoria Boys' Club Camp, August 1922.

83   *JW*, 14 August 1908, 24 August 1921, 7 September 1922 and 2 September 1926.

of the sermons also helped to emphasize gender ideals. At the 1907 camp for the Victoria Club, 'Mr Polack, who was staying in camp … conducted the service, and addressed some stirring words to the lads on the value of modesty.'[84] This reinforced expectations that boys adhere to the public school sporting ethic, in particular the value of being a good winner and modesty in success. In this pre-First World War setting, the lack of attention given to promoting militarism indicates that masculinity prior to 1918 was not based solely on militarism, but rather on a combination of factors of which militarism was only one aspect. It is also significant that the sermons were described as 'stirring'. This language was restricted to boys' clubs as in girls' clubs services were commonly described as 'beautiful'. The use of the word stirring indicates that for boys religion needed to be both lively and exciting – a contrast to that expected of girls. The language used to describe services thus reinforced gender traditions.

In a sermon preached at the Stepney Club camp the boys were encouraged to see the 'the club as a training ground for life'.[85] During this service the boys were told to take the lessons of the sporting activities of the club into their future lives. Again, the service was described as 'inspiring', indicating that there was a certain element of engagement. The West Central Jewish Lads' Club service in 1937 featured a local Christian minister delivering the address on good fellowship.[86] The presence of a Christian minister is significant and it indicates a desire on the leaders' part to emphasize the need for good relations between Jews and the local population and forge links to combat the rise of anti-Semitism in Europe, and in Britain specifically with the rise of the British Union of Fascists (BUF), at this time.

As with services and prayers held in clubs during the year, there were mixed views of the boys' behaviour. In 1907, the Hutchison house club reported that during prayers and the Sabbath service 'the decorum of the lads and their participation and interest in the hymns and prayers were everything that could be desired'.[87] This indicates that the boys were well

84   *JW*, 16 August 1907.
85   SUA MS172 AJ250 *Stepnian*, July 1935.
86   *JC*, 27 August 1937.
87   *JW*, 16 August 1907.

behaved and joined in the service. However, as this account was written by one of the club leaders, this may have been over-stated. A lads' report of the West Central Lads, Club camp from 1903 gave perhaps a more realistic account of the Sabbath from the perspective of the members. In his diary he stated that on the 'First Saturday – being Sabbath did nothing all day, slept on floor as bed kept walking' and 'Second Saturday – same as last, but slept on bed.'[88] The overwhelming theme of his narrative is that of boredom and the boy mentions neither a service nor any other religious event. Indeed, it is difficult to assume from this that the boy enjoyed the Sabbath at camp or to assume that anything of significance to him had occurred. Its only redeeming feature from a religious perspective is that there was no evidence of Sabbath desecration.

Conclusion: Boys' Clubs and Religion

Through events during the year and at the annual summer camps it can be seen that religious elements were present in all clubs, despite contemporary criticism. Though, seemingly limited, those clubs that claimed to be Jewish naturally took a more proactive approach to the inclusion of religion than the clubs which viewed themselves as undenominational. In the clubs that included the word 'Jewish', evening prayers were often a feature, particularly in the Stepney Jewish Lads' Club where a prayer book formalized the event. Classes and lectures provided an opportunity for both 'Jewish' and undenominational clubs to explore religion through Jewish history classes, which were designed to appeal to the boys. Sabbath services, either on camp or throughout the year, were held by all groups. These services emphasized the sanctity of the Sabbath and set it apart from other days at the club or on camp. The subjects preached often drew on 'manly' subjects (although these manly subjects were seldom defined) and were used to emphasize the other

---

88   SUA, MS172 AJ250/4 *West Central Jewish Lads' Club Magazine*, No. 9, 8 August 1903.

aims of club life, especially Anglicization and the sporting ethic, helping to reiterate the main aims of the club. The inclusion of militarism within 'manly' religion reflected changes within society as a whole. Prior to 1918 religion in many instances for boys' clubs was based around the promotion of Jewish military heroes and on developing skills. After 1918, however, the focus of 'manly' religion was redefined in order to minimize the importance of militarism for the creation of masculine identities. Instead clubs chose to emphasize less controversial traits of courage and self-reliance, something that can be seen clearly in the changing emphasis in *Chanucah* sermons where the focus switched from military success prior to 1918 to stressing courage after the end of the First World War.

The structure of religion in the clubs is striking when compared to that seen in Girls' Clubs. Holy Day, Sabbath services and even prayers followed formal structures and emphasized masculine norms within Judaism. Through formality and masculine language, religion in boys' clubs clearly conformed to Anglo-Jewish gender norms. There is, however, some evidence that in developing religious aspects, boys' clubs worked outside of stereotypical gendered roles. The *Purim* parties run by boys broke gender boundaries and encouraged boys to become involved with hosting events for children – something traditionally feminine. The Sabbath meals at camp demonstrated an attention to feminine elements of Judaism. The relative lack of focus on these events in official accounts of the clubs shows that this was not considered to be a large part of the religious experience for boys, and certainly not one that needed emphasizing. Religion in boys' clubs was therefore present, despite the criticism the clubs faced, and focused on structured, formal observance setting up gendered expectations for the future.

CHAPTER 3

The Jewish Lads' Brigade, 1895–1939

Previous chapters have looked at Jewish youth clubs; however, the most well-known youth groups of this period can be categorized as a youth *movement*, or youth *organization*. According to Springhall, these organizations had

> a willingness to admit an unlimited number of children, adolescents and young adults with the aim of propagating some sort of code of living. It should also encourage the participation of its youthful members as leaders and organizers, allow for the possibility of competing for awards and badges, and provide them with an identity or status in the form of a uniform.[1]

Certainly, when looking at youth clubs, the most distinctive are groups that provided uniforms for their members as this provided a highly visible common identity amongst its members. The term 'uniformed youth group' utilizing the above definition will be employed as this is the most significant visual identifier of groups that fit within this broad characterization. This definition is useful in the context of Jewish youth groups as it isolates those with a similar purpose, namely the Jewish Lads' Brigade (JLB) and Jewish Scout and Guide groups. Within the Jewish context, these were the only groups to require members to wear a type of uniform, allowed for the completion of awards and encouraged their members to adopt a specific attitude to life. These clubs were also based around military models, although there has been some debate about the extent to which this was true within the Scout and Guide organizations.[2] This contrasts with other Jewish clubs, which, although requiring their members to take

---

1   John Springhall, *Youth, Empire and Society: British Youth Movements 1883–1940* (London: Croom Helm, 1977), p. 13.

2   See Alan Warren, 'Sir Robert Baden Powell, The Scout Movement and Citizen Training in Great Britain, 1900–1920', *English Historical Review*, 101 (1986), pp. 376–98;

care of their appearance, did not require them to wear a specific uniform and did not include awards or badges. There were, of course, aspects in common with *all* Jewish youth groups, uniformed and non-uniformed. Both types of groups encouraged members to participate in leadership roles and, more importantly, both aimed to encourage a specific 'code of living' amongst their members. It is due to these common features that I have included both groups in this study, which will be the focus for the next two chapters.

Tammy Proctor's study of Scouts and Guides and the construction of identities through uniform raises some important questions about the effectiveness of uniforms in providing a cohesive experience for *all* young people involved in the movement. In particular, she addresses the ways in which young people were able to adapt their own clothing to fit their socio-economic circumstances, for example, through purchasing the cheapest hat rather than the most expensive one, which allowed for members of poorer families to attend. She demonstrates that through this process, uniforms provided a way for the movement to reinforce social class and other societal divisions.[3] This is equally true of the Jewish uniformed groups. Jewish Scout and Guide groups, as well as the Jewish Lads' Brigade, aware of many members' poverty, offered low cost options to members. This can be seen in the case of the JLB, which, in its early years, provided a minimal uniform consisting of just a waistband, a haversack and a cap, but also offered a lower cost alternative of a less fashionable pillbox hat.[4] This gave young people an indication of those members who were poorer than others and thus the uniform served as a way to reinforce certain social divisions. The relevance of Proctor's argument extends beyond the use of uniform. It includes questions of how Jewish leaders were able to adapt the national programme for Scouts and Guides and for the JLB to fit their own religious

---

    and Michael Rosenthal, *The Character Factory: Baden-Powell and the Origins of the Scout Movement* (London: Collins, 1986).

3   Tammy Proctor, '(Uni)Forming Youth: Girl Guides and Boy Scouts in Britain, 1908–1939', *History Workshop Journal*, 45 (1998), pp. 103–34.

4   Sharman Kadish, *A Good Jew and a Good Englishman: The Jewish Lads' and Girls' Brigade 1895–1995* (London: Vallentine Mitchell & Co, 1995), pp. 62–4.

and community needs. The issue of similarities across the Jewish uniformed groups (as well as in comparison to non-Jewish groups) is thus an important factor to consider when looking at the 'uniformed' youth groups.

This chapter will look at the Jewish Lads' Brigade, the longest running such group. I will discuss how the groups utilized religion in their weekly routine through prayer and Sabbath services and explore how they used religion during special events including religious holidays and summer camps. This will add nuance to Kaddish's work on the JLB, which did not focus on the role of religion. I will also look at the more abstract ways they attempted to include religion, through their aims and objectives and the promotion of a 'Jewish' code of living. As the JLB organizations operated nationally I will use the term British when discussing the movement over-all; however, I will use the terms English or Scottish as appropriate when looking at individual groups.

The Jewish Lads' Brigade

The Jewish Lad's Brigade (JLB) was the most well-known of the Jewish youth clubs to emerge at the end of the nineteenth century. With a wide geographic spread and a large membership, the activities of the JLB came under great scrutiny from the Anglo-Jewish community, who were con-cerned about the upbringing of young Jews. The *Jewish Chronicle*, *Jewish Guardian* and *Jewish World* newspapers supported the activities of the JLB and its efforts to Anglicize the immigrant members and to 'iron out the ghetto bend'. The emergence of the JLB can be seen in this context of a more general trend of developing brigades for young men, which had begun to emerge toward the end of the nineteenth century. The first of these, the Boys' Brigade (a Christian group founded by William Alexander Smith in 1883) combined drill and religious instruction and owed is origins, like other non-uniformed groups, to fears of the degeneration of the British 'race'. Springhall viewed this model of drill and religion, created by Smith and later perpetuated by the Church Lads' Brigade as a sign that the subsequent brigades, including the JLB, revealed a lack of imagination.[5] Even so the JLB differed from the template of the other brigades. *The Daily Telegraph* reported that '[t]he only brigade of the five recognized ones which differs … is the JLB, where the religious element is in no sense obtruded, there being no religious instruction and but a few synagogue parades'.[6] The lack of a devotional element contrasts with non-Jewish groups and even contrasted with a number of Jewish clubs (and specifically those for girls) most of which adopted a more proactive attitude toward religion in the form of daily prayer, classes and services. This is not to say the JLB did not include a religious element within its programme, but the religious element included was less than that included within the Christian Brigades.

This section will discuss the elements of the Brigade programme, which included religious aspects. First, I will look at the ethos of the Brigade as well as the role religion played within the weekly programme, focusing on Friday evening services and synagogue parades. Second, I will examine religion at summer camps, through daily prayers and weekly services and discuss how the construction of religious spaces reinforced power roles. Finally, I will examine the role of the Brigade chaplain. In this thematic approach, it will become clear that religion, prior to the Second World War, was not the primary concern of the Brigade. Instead, the creation of British, masculine identities was the most important and religious aspects existed in order to complement this aim.

Background and Ethos

Albert E. W. Goldsmid, a former colonel in the British Army, founded the JLB in 1895. The first Company of the Brigade was started at the Jews' Free School, followed shortly by the formation of other groups around the capital. Unlike the Scout and Guide Association, the JLB was exclusively

---

5   Springhall, *Youth, Empire and Society*, p. 37.
6   *Daily Telegraph*, 24 August 1909. See also Kadish, *A Good Jew*, p. 12.

for Jews and drew its members and leaders from local Jewish populations. The first group outside London was formed in Liverpool, which affiliated with the JLB in January 1898.[7] This was followed by companies opening in Birmingham, Liverpool, Dublin, Manchester and Glasgow, the major urban centres for Jewish immigration before 1914, and in towns with smaller Jewish populations, such as Leeds and Hull.[8] The Brigade quickly adopted the aim 'to instil into the rising generation from its earliest youth, habits of orderliness, cleanliness and honour, so that in learning to respect themselves, they will do a credit to their community'.[9] This motto was particularly relevant in light of the arrival of Eastern European immigrants who were (in the minds of Anglo-Jewry) damaging the reputation of the Jewish community as a whole through their poverty and foreign behaviours. The JLB sought to downplay the notions of Jewish difference through, in part, the use of uniform which allowed Jewish boys to present a more ordered and acceptable appearance which fitted with notions of the Jewish muscular ideal and downplayed the Jews as effeminate and distinctive. It, however, was not the first attempt to establish a Jewish Brigade. In 1891 Francis Cohen contacted William Smith of the Boys' Brigade to ascertain whether a Jewish section could be included. The request was refused as the constitution of the Boys' Brigade meant that they 'could not enrol a Company on other than a Christian basis which is an essential feature of our organization'.[10] Cohen contacted the *Jewish Chronicle* with his intention to found an organization modelled on the Christian Brigades, which would 'aim at arousing and sustaining among [Jewish boys] a definitely *Jewish* spirit of manliness'.[11] His aim was thus to promote the notion of the 'muscle Jew', based on the Greek ideal of beauty – an image which often stood in opposition to Jewish stereotypes, which can be seen in the context of Max Nordau's ideas of muscular Judaism.[12] Cohen's plans seemed

7   Kadish, *A Good Jew*, p. 21.
8   Richard A. Voeltz, '"A Good Jew and a Good Englishman": The Jewish Lads' Brigade 1894–1922', *Journal of Contemporary History*, 23 (1988), pp. 119–27 (p. 120).
9   Kadish, *A Good Jew*, p. 12.
10   SUA, MS 244, AR1, JLB First Annual Report.
11   *JC*, 27 May 1892.
12   Presner, *Muscular Judaism*, p. 2.

to have gathered interest from the Jewish community, but he made little progress. Cohen was, nevertheless, one of the founding members of the Brigade and he served on the Executive committee and was the first Brigade chaplain. As a result, Cohen's ideals were, to a certain extent, evident in the formation of the JLB.

For Cohen, the idea of 'Jewish spirit', to set the Brigade apart from similar Christian groups, was something that should be encouraged amongst boys and certainly the JLB proclaimed to have this as an explicit aim. It stated in 1898 that:

> The Brigade is not a theological organization; it is in the highest sense of the word religious, for its aim is the physical inculcation of the moral laws on which Judaism is based, and no-one who has visited a camp can have failed to observe the inter-working of spiritual and temporal influence towards the common good of the lads. The aim of the Brigade, however, is not to impose theology upon them, but to teach them to walk as they profess – to clinch the words of religion by moral action.[13]

By stating that the Brigade was not concerned with theology it contrasted with the Christian brigades. The lack of theological concern did not, however, mean that the organization distanced itself from religion. The Brigade stated that it was concerned with the inclusion of a religious element, one that could be included through physical activities, placing it firmly within ideas of muscular Judaism. The inclusion of religion through physical activities, rather than through religious classes, can be seen in the description of the JLB as a purely social club, rather than as a social *and* educational one, as all other groups were listed in directories of youth organizations.[14] Whilst this description reflects the Brigade's aim of including religion within their additional activities, it is interesting to note that none of the

---

13   *JC*, 8 July 1898.

14   THLA, 360.1, *Stepney Juvenile Organisations Committee Handbook*, 1929. This is not the only source of this type. Records exist of these documents being produced from the 1920s onwards at yearly intervals. These directories indicated the location of clubs and societies for young people, included information about their structure and a brief summary of the purpose of each organization and whether it was 'educational' or 'social'.

Brigade's activities were classed as educational. Certainly, the JLB held no 'classes' at this time, instead focusing on drill, parades and social activities, but these activities were seen as educational in that they helped the young men to become British gentlemen, developing skills that would enable them to become a credit to their community.

In 1929, the Brigade again set out its religious position, this time in response to criticism from the Jewish press:

> As to Jewish influence and guidance I [Harold Lion, Commanding Officer of the 2nd London Battalion] need only say that a large number of officers are in continuous attendance supervising boys at their work and games and the building has never been so fully thronged by either managers or members as under the present regime. During the Holy Days arrangements were made for Passover food to be supplied in the Canteen, and the very large numbers present soon exhausted the stock in hand.[15]

The description of religious activities marked a clear shift from the statement made thirty years earlier which claimed that the Brigade was concerned with the 'physical inculcation of the moral laws' and the 'inter-working of spiritual and temporal influence'.[16] By 1929, the Brigade was providing directly religious activities through High Holy Day arrangements, something that had not been considered an element of the regular programme in 1898. Additionally, the Jewish influence in 1929 was considered to be as much a result of the identities of the officers as it was through the religious festivals. This change presented a contrast to Zionism, from which the Brigade wished to distance itself and marked an addition to Nordau's ideas of muscular Judaism – a concept which had become firmly associated with Zionism. In both cases, the religious element of the programme, although seen as present by the Brigade itself, was clearly not a major part of the Brigade's activities.

Despite the changes that occurred prior to the 1920s within the minutiae of the Brigade's religious policy, the JLB continued to identify as a Jewish group. As the Brigade had stated that it wished to foster a 'Jewish spirit', the question of who to admit as a member was something that

---

15   *JW*, 9 May 1929.
16   *JC*, 8 July 1898.

was given attention by the executive committee. In 1898, the committee received a letter from the Brady Street Company, asking permission to enrol a boy whose mother was Jewish but whose father was Protestant.[17] The executive agreed that the boy should be allowed to join the company. This incident demonstrates that the Brigade leaders were sensitive to the issue of Jewish lineage, and that membership was clearly restricted to those deemed to be of the faith. Later that year, the executive addressed the question of whether the adult volunteers needed to be Jewish. This decision limited the number of potential adult volunteer leaders at a time when adult membership was perpetually low. In this instance, the committee decided to 'admit only Israelites as officers except in the case of insuperable difficulty in forming a Company without the assistance of a non-Jew intimately connected with an association of a Company'.[18] Thus, despite the shortage of leaders, the Jewish identity of officers was seen as a vital qualification, except where a potential officer was already familiar with a group and presumably had shown himself to be both sensitive to and knowledgeable about Judaism, although it is unlikely that many non-Jewish adults sought to join. Such flexibility, although minor, was likely due to Jewish lineage being passed on by women – as the JLB consisted only of men, the Brigade could afford at times to be flexible. The Jewishness of the Brigade was placed above the ease of recruitment, showing that the JLB was aware of the need to demonstrate its commitment to Jewish ideals.

In addition to respecting the need to maintain a solely Jewish membership, sensitivity to restrictions on the Sabbath was shown by the Brigade. The JLB, like others, sought to emphasize Sabbath observance as a response to concerns over its correct observance within youth clubs, which were frequently voiced within the Jewish press. In 1902 a parade was held for members of all of the Brigades. As this was made up of predominantly Christian members, the parade was held on a Saturday. The Brigade sought the permission of the Chief Rabbi as to whether they were allowed to participate, and permission was granted for the boys to march as long as they

17   SUA MS244, Gen 78, Minutes, 5 April 1898.
18   SUA, MS244, Gen 80, Executive Committee Minutes, 1 July 1898.

did not carry colours.[19] Allowing the boys to march enabled the JLB to present its success in encouraging Jewish boys to present an idealized image of Britishness. By participating in a public display with the other, non-Jewish Brigades, the JLB engaged with a process in which the performance of the march contributed to the creation of an alternative image of Jewishness which emphasized the ideas of muscular Judaism rather than stereotypes of weak, ill-disciplined Jews.[20] After the outbreak of war in 1914, a London Company asked permission to conduct longer route marches on Saturdays in order to take part in extended drill; however, this request was declined as the committee felt that 'this proposal was considered inadvisable as likely to hurt the susceptibilities of strictly conforming Jews and was therefore not appropriate'.[21] By seeking permission, the Officer in Charge of the Company showed that he was aware of the need to keep the Sabbath, and the committee itself demonstrated the same concern. However, neither the Officer in Charge nor the committee agreed on a personal level with the need to ban marches on the Sabbath.[22] Instead, they were agreeing to protect the image of the Brigade as a religious organization and to show sensitivity to members and the public. The attitude of the committee members certainly sheds light on the religious attitude of the JLB as a whole. For them, religion was not something included for its own sake, but rather something that was included to protect the image of the Brigade within the Jewish community as a Jewish organization, rather than a secular one, and indeed indicates the leaders' desire to promote 'manly' and public activities over religious ones.

19   Ibid., 2 February 1902.
20   Karel Arnaut, 'Making Space for Performativity: Publics, Powers and Places in a Multi-Register Town Festival', in Bruno Boute and Thomas Småberg (eds), *Devising Order: Socio-Religious Models, Rituals and the Performativity of Practice* (Leiden: Brill Academic Publishing, 2012), pp. 81–102, p. 82.
21   SUA, MS244, Gen 84, Minutes, 19 November 1914.
22   Ibid.

Religious Activities

One of the most obvious ways in which clubs included a religious element within their programme was through religion classes. For boys' clubs as a whole, religious classes were less popular than within girls' clubs. Most boys' clubs shunned the notion of religious-based classes and the JLB was no exception. Additionally, the Brigade followed a prescribed national programme and a system of achievement like the Scouts and Guides, albeit one which could be adapted to suit local needs, and therefore relied less on the structure provided by classes than their non-uniformed counterparts. It was only in the 1920s that the Brigade instituted a handful of classes on religious matters. In 1921, the headquarters received a letter from Mr Joseph Cowen, who requested that 'the curriculum of the Brigade reflected the training of its members in matters Jewish, and suggesting the inclusion of lectures on Jewish history, etc.'.[23] Whilst secular (in the sense that the classes did not address matters related to religious practice) in nature these classes (as within boys' clubs) would have been viewed by contemporaries to contribute in some way to the religious education of the boys. The committee agreed to Cowen's request and made arrangements for 'a course of lectures on Jewish history and similar subjects'.[24] In Liverpool, the executive decided in 1925 to 'provide facilities at Harold House for the study of Jewish interest in Hebrew and English'.[25] The classes were held at 8pm on Friday evenings for the older boys in the Company. Even so, no provision was made for the younger boys to attend a religious class of any kind within the JLB. In Manchester, a Hebrew literature class was established in 1930. Although only a small number of members signed up, the inclusion of the class shows that the Manchester staff were aware of the need to provide instruction on Jewish subjects.[26] In these instances, the Brigade

---

23 SUA, MS244, Gen 86, Minutes, 25 April 1921.
24 Ibid.
25 *JG*, 6 November 1925.
26 Manchester County Records Office (hereafter MCRO), MS1320 2342, Minutes, 1 December 1930.

demonstrated that it was sympathetic to the need for a Jewish, although not specifically ritual, education. The inclusion of these classes within particular localities, rather than nationally, demonstrates one way in which the leaders were able to modify the JLB experience to suit their own community's needs. In this case, the leaders in Manchester and Liverpool highlighted a need for additional education, which was not identified by groups in other areas – for example Hull and Glasgow. It is significant that these classes emerged in the 1920s. Many of the boys in the interwar period would have lacked religious education from outside the JLB – a result of the general decline in religion within the UK as well as the impact of Anglicization within the Jewish community. It is also likely that the inclusion of Hebrew classes was a result of the growth of Zionist clubs and their emphasis on Hebrew as a living language. However, the classes and lectures provided by the Brigade were limited in their scope and would not have compensated for the general lack of formal religious education. Moreover, not all age groups within the Brigade were afforded the opportunity to attend religious classes, therefore limiting their scope and influence and these classes were not offered in all locations, which further limited their success. The JLB demonstrated an awareness of the need, but failed to provide classes to encompass all of its members and the central office had limited interest in dictating local classes. This calls into question the commitment of the Brigade to provide for the religious education of its members.

Unlike educational classes, which were uncommon in the JLB, synagogue parades were a frequent feature of the programme from its early history. Many companies attended a synagogue service a few times each year, with the primary aim of exhibiting the skills that had been learnt during drill classes. A typical Sabbath parade included a march to the local synagogue, a special service followed by a full company inspection and a tea or reception led by the synagogue staff. These parades had the added benefit of demonstrating an alternative view of Jews to the public – one that depicted Jewish boys as ideal British men. Through enacting the public performance of parading to the synagogue, the JLB was contributing to the promotion of this image within wider society.[27] The content of the sermons

27   Arnaut, 'Making Space', pp. 81–5.

was largely similar at all events, with the service based on military success
and the need for the boys to be patriotic, self-sufficient, clean and obedi-
ent, calling on Biblical images of Joshua, David and Judas Maccabaeus to
promote these ideals as inherently Jewish. At an 1898 parade to the New
West End Synagogue, the sermon was delivered by minister Reverend
Simeon Singer, who told the boys

> in plain and simple language of the moral discipline which lay behind the physical
> exercises to which they voluntarily submitted themselves. The lessons of courage
> and of self-restraint, taught by their warlike ancestors were brought home to them
> and they were shown how each of them was learning to become at the same time a
> gentleman and a servant of the state. Such are the lessons which they learn practi-
> cally week-by-week. [He] showed them the inner purposes of their practices and
> they cannot fail to return to their drill with an enlightened perception of the great
> moral purpose which inspires it.[28]

The content of this service illustrates the claim of the Brigade that the
religious element of their programme was achieved through physical exercise and demonstrates a level of comfort with the notion of militarism.
However, this sermon is significant in another way. This sermon certainly
helped to promote the main aim of the Brigade. Rather than interpreting
the service as a way in which the Brigade justified its physical work, it is
better seen as a way in which religion was used to promote the main aim
of the Brigade – to create orderly, well-behaved and distinctly British Jews
who encapsulated Victorian notions of masculinity through their strength,
stature, and courage. By referencing 'warlike ancestors', the JLB was able
to demonstrate that gender norms and religious obligations were firmly
linked and present throughout Jewish history.

Sermons were not only used to promote militarism and physical prowess, but also helped to increase a sense of patriotism amongst the largely
immigrant members. At a service in 1899, Reverend M. Hyamson delivered
an address on patriotism and the forces. Speaking from underneath a Union
Flag, he stated that 'patriotism should not be aroused in Jews by pride in their
country and by gratitude for the privileges enjoyed there. It is a religious duty

---

28   *JC*, 8 July 1898.

imposed upon them by their faith.'[29] Here the boys were encouraged to be patriotic as a requirement of Judaism – something that would have spoken to all members of the JLB, including those who had been born outside of the UK. By encouraging patriotism, the Brigade leaders were demonstrating the need for the Jewish population to show national loyalties. Again, this can be viewed as a way the brigade used religion to promote one of its main objects – creating good Englishmen of the 'Hebrew persuasion'. The early sermons were a way for the Brigade to promote the principal aims of the Brigade and the development of masculine young men, drawing heavily on militarism and patriotism in order to promote these qualities amongst the young members. The emphasis on military and patriotic qualities of Judaism allowed services to be more than simply an opportunity for worship; rather, they reflected the overall ethos of the Brigade.

Initially, the Brigade held regular synagogue parades in conjunction with parades on Jewish holidays. In contrast, after the First World War, the JLB provided parades solely on religiously significant days, due in part to the decline in popularity of militarism, which led to a reluctance to take part in frequent public parades. In particular, *Chanucah* was one of the most keenly anticipated events in the Brigade Calendar, and the commemoration of the festival took on a similar style to that of general synagogue parades. After the *Chanucah* sermon, the boys were invited to an elaborate tea, which was more likely to have drawn the boys' attendance than the sermon itself. A reporter giving the reasons for the popularity of *Chanucah* celebrations stated that the 'the natural pride which all Jews feel in commemorating the deeds of the Maccabees appeals with special force to the members of the Brigade who feel a sense of kinship with the warriors of old in their fight for the honour of the Jewish faith'.[30] The content of *Chanucah* sermons prior to the First World War was largely similar to that provided in regular Sabbath sermons. They drew on the story of Judas Maccabaeus to extol the virtues of Jewish militarism and physical fitness underscoring their importance in the creation of ideal Jewish men. In 1907, the Rev. Michael Adler, the Brigade chaplain, delivered an address focusing

29   *JC*, 23 June 1899.
30   *JG*, 6 January 1922.

on the strength Maccabaeus gained during his youth and his subsequent war successes. He stated that members of the Brigade 'could become a hero in their everyday life, even as the gallant Judas, if only they would strive to be "strong and mighty in their youth" and live up to the traditions of the Brigade'.[31] Sermons provided an additional opportunity for the Brigade to promote its own aims of improving the members' physical conditions, something that was particularly apt for *Chanucah*. During the First World War itself, the *Chanucah* sermons continued to promote militarism, and in addition to drawing on images of Maccabaeus, praised the number of managers and former members serving in the forces.[32] In promoting this military image, the Brigade was once again promoting an ideal of masculinity as well as national loyalty.

After the end of the war, in line with public opinion no longer glorifying the idea of battle, the services no longer focused purely on the military elements of *Chanucah*, but the event was no less popular for it. In 1920, the service encouraged the boys to 'have the courage to proclaim themselves Jews, and to be proud of their race and to do credit to their community'.[33] In the 1922 sermon, the congregation was told of a tale of the young boy who showed courage in affixing a flag to a ship being fired at during a war with the Dutch, placing an (albeit extremely tenuous) connection with the JLB – the name of the ship was *Camperdown* – the same as the Brigade's Headquarters.[34] In both instances, the sermons were drawing not on the *military* elements of the *Chanucah* story, but instead emphasized *courage* – a much less problematic topic in the interwar period.

Courage in the face of difficulty was a value that was seen as a particularly manly quality and in promoting this, the Brigade continued to show its adherence to British gender norms. In linking the address to courage, the Brigade was showing that, despite the decline in popularity of militarism, Judaism and in particular *Chanucah* could continue to promote a subtler form of masculine values. That the *Chanucah* service could be adapted to

31   *JC*, 29 November 1907.
32   See *JC*, 10 December 1915.
33   *JW*, 22 December 1920.
34   *JG*, 6 January 1922.

contemporary opinions shows that the popularity of the service was not solely based on its initial militarism. The service remained one of the most popular events in the JLB calendar, drawing hundreds of members from London, and on occasions from further afield, with provincial units holding their own events. The *Chanucah* services must therefore be seen as a way in which the Brigade was able to fulfil its religious duty to members. Additionally, the services were able to promote its wider aims of producing good citizens at the same time as appealing to shifts in British culture.

In addition to the *Chanucah* services, the Brigade celebrated and observed a number of additional Jewish Holy Days. *Purim* was, after *Chanucah*, the most frequently observed festival in the JLB calendar. The first all-Brigade parade was held at *Purim* in 1898 at which the Rev. Francis Cohen, Brigade chaplain, presided and a total of 275 members attended.[35] After this initial parade, *Purim* was not celebrated on a large scale. Instead, a number of companies chose to celebrate on their own, especially during the interwar period; both Sheffield and Manchester held *Purim* celebrations during the 1930s.[36] The Manchester Companies, in particular, observed *Purim* on a regular basis. These services began in 1933, as it was not possible to hold the regular *Chanucah* parade that year. In subsequent years the Battalion held parades on both *Chanucah* and *Purim*. It was reported that prior to the parade, 'attendance at drills for several weeks before *Purim* were noticed to have markedly improved'.[37] This should not, however, be taken as an indication that the religious service was a draw for Brigade members; instead it is likely that they were drawn in by the promise of a celebration tea and the opportunity to march through the streets. In addition to *Purim, Simchat Torah* was also observed by companies, who often attended a synagogue service and afterwards were entertained with a tea in the *Succah*. This event would have helped to underscore not only religious obligations, but through the use of the *Succah*, would have drawn on notions of adventure and outdoor survival that were associated with

---

35   SUA, MS244, AR1.
36   See for example SUA, MS244, AR1.and SUA, MS244, Adv 26, *The Advance*, May/ June 1933.
37   SUA, MS244, Adv 26, *The Advance*, May/June 1933.

masculinity and militarism. These three religious days, *Purim*, *Simchat Torah* and *Chanucah*, provided an opportunity for the Brigade to experience 'adventure' and fun, themes that the Brigade was keen to include within their programme whilst showing its allegiance to Judaism.

The JLB did not just celebrate the Holy Days associated with pleasure. In the early 1920s, the Brigade Bugle Band contributed to services at a number of synagogues around London, where they 'acted as *Baale Tekiah* [*Shofar* blower] at the services held on *Rosh Hashanah*'.[38] Whilst this was not specifically a Brigade activity, the Brigade had gone some way to show that it was associated with the activities of the buglers, emphasizing their religious sentiments and encouraged young members to take on a formal, public role in the synagogue – something that was expected of Jewish men. In the late 1930s, Camperdown House hosted religious services in conjunction with the United Synagogue for the High Holy Days and in Manchester similar services were held which had the added benefit of raising funds for the group.[39] These services certainly show that the Brigade was aware of its religious obligations, the observance of High Holy Days was in no way comparable to the scale and number of events that occurred for the more enjoyable religious holidays. In this sense, the Brigade was providing for the boys' religious needs, whilst maintaining *Chanucah*, *Purim* and *Simchat Torah* as grander events, as these festivals corresponded to some (or all) of the Brigade's main aims which emphasized militarism (prior to 1918), discipline and courage. Through this, it can be seen that religious activities which drew on concepts and traits associated with masculinity, were emphasized. Those that were more religiously significant, but contained little to emphasize masculine norms, were downplayed.

In 1923, the Brigade recognized that they needed to do more for the religious development of the members than holding synagogue parades and celebrating only certain days in the Jewish calendar. This coincided with an awareness in Anglo-Jewry of the growing secularization of society and increasing attempts to promote religiosity amongst the Jewish population.

---

38   *JW*, 29 September 1920.
39   See THLA 360.1, Association for Jewish Youth Annual Report 1938 and MCRO MS130, 2342.

JLB staff made arrangements with the United Synagogue to hold Friday evening services at Camperdown House, the Brigade's Headquarters, in order to 'deepen ... the love of the lads for their faith and enable ... many who are unable to attend a synagogue service to take part in public worship'.[40] The services began in November 1923, and although attendance was not as large as the committee had hoped, they appeared to be a success amongst those who did attend:

> The service conducted by the Rev. H. Mayerowitsch and D. Hirsch, with the Brigade Choir under Mr Alman was most impressive, and the interest of the boys was unmistakable. The attendance, slightly over 60, was disappointing, but as this increased on Friday last to over 90, it is hoped that in this new feature, the Brigade will be true to its motto, and go 'from strength to strength'.[41]

The following year, at the request of the United Synagogue, the services had moved from Camperdown House to the Great Synagogue. This emphasized the ritual of religious worship expected of men and went some way to encourage the development of religious gender divisions. Despite the promising start, the move to the Great Synagogue resulted in a decrease in numbers. The Brigade committee, which had opposed the move, viewed the services as 'a failure' and cancelled the programme.[42] The services were restarted in 1926 for members of the Brigade, as well as the other Jewish youth clubs in London, in the hope that this would increase attendance. Even so, this attempt was short lived and the services were cancelled shortly after. A final attempt to restart these services occurred in 1930 with the support of the Association for Jewish Youth (AJY). In May 1930, the committee agreed to work with the AJY and they believed that 'in conjunction with a suitable programme of recreation for the evening it might be possible to reintroduce these services successfully'.[43] The relative informality of these events reflects a change in the status of religion within society particularly with young people, rather than signifying a change to the way in which the Brigade viewed the importance of masculinity. On this

40   SUA, MS244, AR9, Annual Report, 1923.
41   *JG*, 30 November 1923.
42   SUA, MS244, Gen 86, Minutes, 2 December 1924.
43   SUA, MS244, Gen 87, Minutes, 5 May 1930.

occasion, the services proved more successful than in previous attempts, and they continued throughout the 1930s. From these attempts, it is clear that the committee was aware of the need to provide a regular religious event in the Brigade calendar, although they were unable to secure satisfactory attendance through solely religious elements. It was only when the services were combined with a social element that they were successful.

The Manchester Battalion of the Brigade held a service similar to those held in London from 1926, which unlike those held in London met with considerable success. The services consisted of a 10-minute address and featured singing in both Hebrew and English, with the address delivered by members of the Manchester Jewish Community. Attendances were initially small with thirty-five members present the first evening yet, by the end of 1927, each service attracted between eighty to one hundred members. The services took a one-year break in 1930, and then reappeared in 1931 with upwards of 100 members attending.[44] The importance of these services in providing for the religious life of the members was noted by one officer who claimed that 'in some cases it was the only Jewish contact they had because in the homes it was rare ... They found it at JLB.'[45] These services were thus perceived to be providing a vital function in the promotion of religion amongst the Brigade's members. The success of these events, in contrast with those held in London, can be attributed to the attitude of the respective committees. In London, the services were supported by the committee until they moved to the Great Synagogue, when numbers declined substantially; the services in Manchester received the full support of the committee. As a result, the Manchester services attracted larger numbers of members and adults who attended each evening. In London, therefore, the reluctance of the committee to support a religious emphasis resulted in the failure of the services, whereas in Manchester, the attitudes of the adults assisted with the success of this religious element. In both instances the services reflected a desire to institute a more formal and thus more gendered religion, one which was not present in girls' clubs.

44 MCRO, MS1230, 2342, Minutes (see minutes 6 September 1926–6 October 1931).
45 MJM, Oral History Recording J237.

Summer Camps

Evening meetings and synagogue parades formed the basis of the Brigade's activities but as in other youth clubs, the annual summer camp was the highpoint of their calendar. Camps would take place for one to two weeks at a rural site, often near the beach, and were open to any member of the Brigade. In most years, two camps were held, one for the provincial regiments – often held in North Wales – and one for the London regiments, usually held in Deal, Kent, and both events provided adult members a chance to increase the religious influence on the boys. The camp staff consisted of a chaplain, often the Brigade chaplain, or one of the local companies' or regiments' chaplain, who was responsible for running worship services and for the spiritual elements of the programme. The inclusion of morning and evening prayers was a key way for the boys to experience the daily application of religion, whereas Sabbath services (held on all Friday evenings and Saturday mornings during the camps) allowed for explicitly religious teachings – something that was not evident in many other Brigade activities. In addition to prayers and services, the camps were able to include religious elements through *kosher* provisions in both the pre-First World War period and the late 1930s, through abstaining from drill on the Sabbath, and through the inclusion of a quiet prayer tent for general use.

Sabbath services were held, weather permitting, in the open air, with the Brigade members assembling around a makeshift reading desk, formed of drums covered with a Union Flag (giving them the name 'drumhead service'). The presence of the Union Flag, particularly during the early years of the Brigade, when many of the members were immigrants or children of immigrants, served to emphasize the patriotism of the Brigade, both to its members, and to those outside of the organization who questioned the Britishness of the Jewish community. The services were led by the camp chaplain, and members of the public were invited to attend, ensuring that the wider Jewish community was aware that not only was the Brigade able to produce regimented and orderly boys, it promoted Jewish identities, as well.

At one of the earliest Brigade camps, in 1899, the service was held by Rev. Cohen, Brigade chaplain. Cohen 'presented a sermon from the tent taken from the *Sedrah* of the day "when thou goest forth in camp against thy enemies then keep thee from every evil thing" it is needless to say that the chaplain gave a very practical and forcible address from this appropriate text'.[46] The reading, taken from Deuteronomy 23:9, stresses the importance of cleanliness, in keeping with the aims of the Brigade set forth in the motto as well as the need for the Brigade to 'iron out the ghetto bend'. At the 1905 camp, the Rev. M. Adler, acting as camp chaplain, led the Saturday morning service, addressing the boys on the need for self-reliance, another vital trait in the creation of British masculinity. At the provincial camp of the same year, the sermon was delivered on the subject of 'work and play' imploring the boys to show interest in their work.[47] Similar themes were featured in camp services both before and after the First World War and certainly helped to promote the popular image of masculinity which valued both physical and mental health and hygiene.

In 1932, boys at the London regiments' camp were told to aim high in life, and to 'remember the lessons the brigade taught – self-restraint, discipline, strength of body and mind ... The training they [the members] received in the Brigade was very valuable. It gave them a sense of discipline and the ability to play the game'.[48] The idea of 'playing the game', a notion that developed in Victorian public schools, emphasised that through team games young people could develop their sense of loyalty, self-control, perseverance, fairness and courage.[49] The skills gained through encouraging sportsmanship were identical to those needed for masculinity, and the notion was therefore seized by the Brigade, as is evident in later sermons. In sermons encouraging health and sportsmanship, the Brigade's aims of instilling orderliness, cleanliness and honour, as well the need to become productive and loyal members of British society, were pushed to the forefront of the religious programming, both at camps and during the year.

46   *JC*, 25 August 1899.
47   *JC*, 4 August 1905.
48   *JC*, 12 August 1932.
49   J. A. Mangan, 'Grammar Schools and the Games Ethic in the Victorian and Edwardian Era', *Albion*, 15 (1983), 313–35 (p. 314).

Whilst the themes of self-reliance, hard-work and determination remained a feature of camp services after the First World War, those after 1918 referenced more explicitly the need to be a credit to the Jewish community, adhering to qualities of British 'gentlemen', and in doing so, avoid anti-Semitism. In 1924, boys at the provincial camp were urged to do their 'utmost to make the name of Jew clean and sweet wherever he went and whatever place in the world he occupied'.[50] In 1929, the boys were given a similar address at the London camp, in which they were told that in order to combat anti-Semitic feeling, they had to 'cultivate the spirit of playing the game, and to play for the honour of their people … to play their part as citizens, and to take their full share of the burdens of this country'.[51] Here the notion of fairness and decency was used, both to emphasize masculinity and to contrast anti-Semitic sentiments. All services, whether pre- or post-war reflected the wider aims of the JLB and showed its allegiance to British values of sportsmanship. In providing services the Brigade was able to show its support for religion, and through the content of the sermons was able to create good Englishmen, or indeed, good *British* men.

The camp Sabbath sermons remained largely similar in content and structure until 1937, when, at the request of Rabbi Gollop, then its chaplain, the Brigade purchased a marquee for use as a camp synagogue. The marquee was fully equipped as a synagogue with the funds provided by Gollop and the congregation of the Orthodox, but Anglicized, Hampstead Synagogue. The inclusion of a camp synagogue allowed for even more ritual and formality in Sabbath observances at camp. The presence of the Marquee created an 'absolute space', that is one that was defined by clearly defined boundaries – in this case the tent walls. This contrasted with previous Sabbath spaces, which lacked physical markers. The absolute space of the synagogue marquee allowed the Brigade Chaplain to exert greater control over the production and experience of religious practice at camp, thus controlling the members' exposure to more Orthodox religion.[52] At the consecration

---

50   *JG*, 8 August 1924.
51   *JW*, 22 August 1929.
52   David Harvey, 'Space as Keyword', in N. Castree and D. Gregory (eds), *David Harvey: A Critical Reader* (Oxford: Basil Blackwell, 2006), pp. 270–93 (p. 275).

service for members of the Brigade and outside guests, two *Sefarim* were borrowed from the Hampstead Synagogue and placed in the Ark, and, for the first time at a camp service, the perpetual lamp was lit. These elements of ritual marked an important departure from previous camp services, which concentrated on the importance of their surroundings and on the service itself, rather than on Orthodox elements of observance. Through the influence of Gollop, and despite the personal beliefs of members of the committee, the Brigade was showing its allegiance to Orthodoxy and the importance of correct observance of ceremonies and emphasising a deeper element of Jewish tradition. Despite the closer adherence to ritual practices, the Brigade's themes of orderliness and honour and the ideal of Britishness amongst its members continued to be promoted. Gollop especially stressed the importance of 'physical cleanliness – what a boy in the Brigade would call smartness ... [and] of holiness, purity and cleanliness.'[53] The addition of the camp synagogue, whilst not strictly necessary as the Brigade had been successfully including services prior to the introduction of the marquee, allowed for a closer allegiance to Orthodox practices as a result of the increased structure of the space, which allowed for increased structure to the service. It clearly placed the Brigade as a 'Jewish' camp, not just during the service itself, but throughout the holiday, as the synagogue marquee reminded visitors of the essential Jewishness of the Brigade. This combination of extreme formality and the continuing promotion of masculine themes resulted in a service which placed ideals of manliness and, in particular, correct muscular Judaism, even more centrally than it had previously.

Official accounts and press reports on the services stressed that behaviour during the services was good.[54] In reality, despite attempting to provide services that would appeal to boys, the conduct of the members during these services was far from the ideal promoted. The provincial camp inspector in 1932 complained that 'I should like to see more decorum at the services and more real harmonious worship. The audience does not pay sufficient attention.'[55] The inspector, however, did not offer any suggestions to gain

53   *JC*, 6 August 1937.
54   Ibid.
55   MCRO, MS130 2340 Minutes, Report on St Anne's Camp, 1932.

the audience's attention, and no changes were made to the services the following year. At the provincial camp, one member recalled an occasion where a minister walked into town with members who wanted to attend the service in Llandudno. He remembered:

> We wore all this Khaki and we walked to *Shul* and when we got to the *Shul* of course the officer saw that we all marched in, there was about 40–50 of us and a lot of the Birmingham boys had in mind once they got in the *Shul* and they started reading the *Torah* they would make an excuse like they were going to the toilet and they all disappeared, so when the service was over at about a quarter to twelve the officer says fall in and there's only about ten of us there.[56]

It is not entirely surprising that the Brigade was unable to retain the attention, or even the presence, of young boys during services. The behaviour of the boys certainly indicates that whilst the Brigade was happy to provide services, it remained unable, and perhaps unwilling, to devote attention to developing these services to engage the members or to ensure that they remained in the building, rather than to just preach at them.

Whilst Sabbath services occurred only twice a week at camp, prayer services were held twice *daily*, allowing for a more frequent form of religious observance. Prayers were held before breakfast and at the end of the day, and helped to create a culture in which daily religious practices were part of the routine. Regarding the Lytham camp in 1905, the *Jewish Chronicle* reported that:

> The chaplain then goes round on what is called prayer inspection to see that the devotions of Morning Prayer are not lightly cast aside. Hardly is this over when the Bugles sound the 'fall in', the markers hurry to their position, the companies take up their stations opposite their markers and the whole battalion moves as one machine.[57]

It is clear that morning prayer was taken seriously by the Brigade, and that attempts were made to ensure that the boys adhered correctly to their religious obligations. What is also striking about this report is the sense conveyed by the reporter that prayer was something to be taken care of as

---

56 MJM Oral History Collection, J142.
57 *JC*, 4 August 1939.

quickly as possible. One Manchester member recalled that 'Oh, I didn't like it. You'd start off in the morning there with prayer parade about an hour and a quarter … I used to go mad listening to it. Oh they stood there, an hour and a quarter.'[58] Although likely an exaggeration, there is an indication here that the hour-long prayer service was taken seriously by the leaders, but perhaps not by the members themselves, who viewed the prayer parade negatively. Whilst time was given over every day to prayer, it was not lengthy in comparison to other activities, indicating that prayer was seen as less important than, for example, drill. This is supported by notes from the Camp Sub-Committee meeting, which in 1905 changed the time table from 'Reveille 5.30, Parade for prayers 6.30, Breakfast 7.30' to 'Reveille 6, Parade for prayers 7, Breakfast 7.15.'[59] The time spent for prayers decreased from one hour to just fifteen minutes, which further indicates that the prayer was not seen as the most important part of the day.

The practice of laying *tephillin* (black boxes with leather straps Orthodox men wear during morning prayer) was an area with which both the London and the provincial camps struggled. Whilst boys were not required to bring *tephillin*, nor was any time built into the schedule to allow for their laying as morning prayers held at camp were typically less formal than standard morning prayer, members were not discouraged from doing so. In 1908, a boy asked to be excused from prayers in order to lay *tephillin*. His request, however, was denied and he was told that he could get up at 5.30 a.m. to do so.[60] Whilst it is likely the boy wished to be excused from prayers for fun, rather than for religious observances, this incident indicates that the camp timetable did not allow for boys to follow these religious requirements within the camp day. This situation had not changed by the 1930s and at the provincial camp in 1932, the camp inspector stated that 'a clear ruling on the laying of *tephillin* is desirable'.[61] Nothing had been done on this recommendation and in 1933 a similar recommendation was made. The lack of time given to laying *tephillin* indicates that

58   MJM, Oral History Recordings, J157.
59   SUA MS 244 Gen 79, Camp Sub- Committee Meetings, 7 September 1905.
60   *JW*, 31 July 1908.
61   MCRO, MS130 2340 Minutes, Report on St Anne's Camp, 1932.

whilst the Brigade was happy to include prayer within its programme, it was unwilling to devote any more time to religious, specifically Orthodox, observances than it already did – in essence, the bare minimum. Whilst adherence to Orthodox practices such as the laying of *tephillin* was, at times, minimal, the JLB maintained official links to Orthodoxy through the post of the chaplain.

The Chaplain

The position of camp chaplain was a key way to ensure that religious activities were included during the summer. During the year, the post of chaplain was a way for the Brigade to cater for the religious needs of its members and demonstrated a desire within the Brigade to maintain links with synagogues. One JLB officer stated that the Company's chaplain played a pivotal role in ensuring the group maintained a Jewish atmosphere.[62] Whilst the Scouts often had religious figures attached to certain troops, no other Jewish club had an official religious position within their organization; though several clubs did have religious figures associated with them, this was a less formal link. The individual JLB companies often had their own chaplains and the three Battalions had their own, in addition to the overall Brigade chaplain. Prior to the Second World War, there were three chaplains, the Reverend Francis Cohen (1897–1905), the Reverend Michael Adler (1906–35) and Rabbi Dayan Mark Gollop (1935–8). Both Cohen and Adler served as chaplain to the forces, underscoring the bond between the Brigade and the military. The chaplain's duties were minimal and largely confined to holding Sabbath service at camps and organizing the services at the annual Brigade Parade. The role of the chaplain was never formally defined; instead, it allowed for each chaplain to define the role for himself. Cohen, as one of the founder members of the JLB, served

62   MJM, Oral History Recordings, MJ 237.

on the executive committee but neither Adler nor Gollop were given this privilege. Moreover, the position of a Brigade chaplain helped to maintain the links with the United Synagogue, and thus maintain links with an acceptably English form of Orthodox Judaism.[63] It is significant that Gollop ended his association with the Brigade on religious grounds in 1938, calling into question the Brigade's commitment to the Jewish faith, more specifically Orthodox Judaism. Indeed, this departure can be seen as the Brigade marking a formal split from being seen officially as Orthodox, whilst still retaining an element of Judaism.

The presence of Cohen on the executive committee certainly reflected the centrality of the role of the chaplain within the JLB's early years. It also demonstrates a commitment to the early ideals of the Brigade, with regards to the relationship between the 'spiritual and temporal' elements of a boy's life. Goldsmid, the founder of the Brigade, as an Orthodox Jew, certainly viewed the role of chaplain as more important than later committee members, who harboured a desire to maintain distance from Orthodox practices. Cohen was, in addition to his role as chaplain, a founding member of the Brigade, which goes some way to explaining his presence on the committee, a role that cannot be entirely attributed to his position as chaplain. Relations between the Brigade and the first two chaplains were largely cordial, excluding a minor incident involving Cohen, in which he took offence at not being asked to officiate at a service. This was quickly smoothed out by Goldsmid, despite Cohen's resignation letter expressing his intention to 'relieve the executive from the incubus of my insignificant personality'.[64] In fact, Cohen continued with the Brigade until his immigration to Australia in 1905, and Adler continued in the role for nearly thirty years, and was the longest serving Brigade chaplain. The contribution of these two chaplains to Brigade life was minimal – particularly Adler, as towards the end of his tenure rather than attending events, he merely sent letters apologizing for his absence. Adler's lack of involvement coincided with a general slackening in religious observances. For example, it is during this period that camp

63   Kadish, *A Good Jew*, p. 110.
64   SUA, MS 244, Gen 78, Letter from Francis Cohen 16 June 1897 in minutes from meeting 20 July 1897.

food was no longer *Kosher*, something that reflected both general changes within ordinary society (rather than the religious elite) during the interwar years as well as the decline of the importance of the chaplain's (specifically Adler's) role in maintaining religious standards.

The appointment and resignation of Gollop, in contrast to the position of the previous chaplains, sheds light on the Brigade's lack of commitment to religious observance. As a member of the United Synagogue, and recently appointed *Dayan*, his role as chaplain indicates that the Brigade was concerned, as it had been previously, with maintaining links with Orthodox Judaism. From the outset, unlike his predecessors, Gollop was unhappy with religious activities provided by the JLB. In 1937, Gollop consecrated the new camp synagogue, which, as noted, enabled more Orthodox practices to be included within camp life. In 1938, he focused on adhering to the laws of *kashrut* within the camp setting; at his request, the committee agreed that 'camp should conform more closely to *Kashrus* by the provision of separate crockery and cutlery'.[65] The Brigade purchased the items required for this at a cost of £180, which was paid by Gollop himself. The following year, at the weekend camp held at Epping, the *Jewish Chronicle* reported that 'there were, of course, separate crockery and cutlery for milk and meat each clearly labelled on different shelves'.[66] It indicated that in respect to food, the Brigade was aware of, and responsive to, the need to remain in line with Orthodoxy.

The final disagreement between Gollop and the Brigade came in 1938 at a meal held in order to raise funds. Shortly before the event, Gollop withdrew as he discovered the meal was not *kosher*, which sparked his resignation from the Brigade. At an interview with Ernest Halstead of the Executive Committee in November, he laid out his reasons for his resignation, and the terms on which he could be induced to retain his association with the JLB. Gollop commented that it had been 'consistently the policy and practice of the Brigade to decide and act in religious matters without consulting me'.[67] The committee responded that it was not their policy, but

---

65   SUA, MS 244, Gen 67, Minutes, 4 July 1938.
66   *JC*, 7 July 1939.
67   SUA MS 244, Gen 67, Report on Interview 16 November 1938.

their practice, based on their previous chaplains, who had not wished to get involved in this way. Gollop's additional complaints were that where the committee had acted on his requests, he 'felt that this had been done merely to please him and that in fact he had been considered a nuisance for making complaints at all'.[68] He added that he needed to be part of the committee in order to 'give advice and assistance in all matters where religion and religious observance were concerned'.[69] Tellingly, Halstead made no comment on either of those final points, certainly indicating that Gollop was right in his assumption that he had indeed been viewed as a nuisance in requesting stricter religious conformity.

The committee's subsequent discussion on the resignation of the chaplain further illustrates the attitude of the committee members to religion within the Brigade. Of the eight members who participated in the discussions, five were in favour of accepting the resignation, with just three members proposing to make changes in order to encourage the continuation of Gollop's role as chaplain. Halstead (overall Brigade Commandant from 1929 to 1946), who had ties to the Orthodox New West End Synagogue, Bayswater (although it was likely this was maintained at the insistence of his wife) was sympathetic towards Liberal Judaism and advocated doing nothing.[70] He felt that to accede to Gollop's request and run the Brigade on the 'strictest of Orthodox measures' would lead to the alienation of those opposed to Orthodoxy, as well as increased disagreements on minutiae.[71] Mr Woolf, a member of the Brigade Council who supported Halstead's view, expressed similar concerns, adding that it went 'against all modern tendencies to do anything which would make the Brigade adhere more strictly to religious observances'.[72] In contrast, Mr Jacobi also a member of the Brigade Council 'expressed grave concern at the Brigades' tendency to increasingly ignore the religious and spiritual side of its work and he thought that the absence of an orthodox chaplain would have the most

68   Ibid.
69   Ibid.
70   Kadish, *A Good Jew*, p. 111.
71   SUA MS 244, Gen 67, Minutes, 5 December 1938.
72   Ibid.

unfortunate reaction on this side of the Brigade's activities'.[73] The contrasting views of the committee members illustrate not only religious sympathies of the adult members (largely progressive rather than Orthodox – a contrast to the largely Orthodox young members), but also the ambivalence of a number of the leaders to religious practices. In refusing to allow Gollop a role on the committee, they were in favour of very limited religious observance. Although concessions were made to include a low level of religious elements, Judaism itself was not a priority. Indeed, where religion did not directly promote the masculine aims of the Brigade, it was considered a nuisance. The acceptance of Gollop's resignation, and the disregard for the recommendation of the Chief Rabbi that Gollop remain in his post, indicate that the JLB felt comfortable in effecting a more formal split from Orthodoxy. Certainly the committee was aware of this. Following the interview conducted with Gollop in November, Halstead noted that 'This incident has, I think, made it difficult, if not impossible, for any Orthodox minister to accept the office of chaplain in the future, whatever his private opinions might be, a position which requires earnest consideration on our part.'[74] The committee decided that this was not an issue; indeed the Brigade did not appoint another chaplain until the end of the Second World War.

The incident with Gollop illustrates the decline of the acceptance of Orthodoxy within the Brigade. Gollop's departure also marks the Brigade's willingness to demonstrate publicly their lack of association with the United Synagogue; the JLB no longer needed to show the public their explicit ties with Orthodoxy. Whereas previously, as seen from the requests for concessions to be made on the Sabbath, the Brigade staff had been aware of the need to maintain ties and appear Orthodox, the position had changed, and headquarters' staff no longer felt the need to maintain such a link. Certainly, this incident says much about the religious background of the leaders and the need for the Brigade to remain affiliated with official religion. The departure of Gollop therefore demonstrated the executive committee's desire to maintain autonomy from Orthodoxy,

<hr>

73 Ibid.
74 SUA, MS 244, Gen 67, Report on Interview 16 November 1938.

rather than a decision at grassroots level, though it is unlikely that this would have affected local JLB Brigades, who would have retained their existing practices.

JLB and Religion

One of the most striking features of the religious elements included within the JLB was the manner in which religious activities were used as a platform for furthering the main, masculine, aims of the organization. Prior to the First World War, this can be seen through the promotion of militarism within sermons, in particular *Chanucah* services, which extolled the virtues of Biblical Jews as a warrior race and encouraged the boys to follow in the footsteps of figures such as Judas Maccabaeus. After the First World War, when militarism had become less acceptable, religious leaders within the programme chose to encourage cleanliness, manners, sportsmanship, and gentlemanly behaviour. Religion was thus not seen as important when compared to the other elements of the club. Clearly, the aim of the JLB was the primary concern of the group and religion was used to push this agenda, rather than seen as an important element in and of itself.[75] Whilst Judaism itself was by no means the primary aim of the Brigade, religious activities were included within the programme and boys were encouraged to take part in religious events – if less so than sports and drill which predominated. The chaplain informed the lads at the 1905 Lytham camp that 'almost the whole object of religion is to teach us to control our conduct'.[76] This phrase encapsulates the view of the JLB towards religion – that the object of religion was to improve the conduct of the members. It shows that whilst the JLB viewed itself as a religious organization and indeed was sensitive to its religious obligations, it still lacked religious activities included for their own sake, but instead was used to promote gender norms. The JLB can therefore

75   SUA MS 244 AR/2, First Annual Report of the Jewish Lads' Brigade.
76   *JW*, 5 August 1904.

be said to be seen as an organization which used religion to promote its own aims of ensuring that Jewish youth conformed to standards in terms of gender roles, behaviour and appearance, as well as allowing individual groups to adjust the programme to fit in with their own specific needs. For young people who felt that the JLB was not significantly 'British' enough, the Scout and Guide organizations provided an opportunity for members to proclaim their nationality and their religion. Jewish Scout and Guide groups, like JLB companies, were able to adapt the national programme to suit their own religious and communal requirements, albeit in a more obviously patriotic setting than the Brigade.

CHAPTER 4

Jewish Scout and Guide Groups, 1907–1939

In 1907, Mafeking veteran Robert Baden-Powell ran a camp on Brownsea Island with a small group of boys from London. A year later, drawing on his experience from the camp and in the army, he published a series of articles called 'Scouting for Boys', which provided various 'how-to' guides for boys to develop themselves into useful citizens. Before the series had been fully published, Scouting became immensely popular amongst boys, with troops forming all over the country and abroad. By 1909, The Scout Association had been officially formed. Individual troops were created across the country, often attached to existing youth groups (such as the Boys' Brigade) or to places of worship. A number of Jewish Troops emerged, attached to synagogues and various youth clubs.[1]

Shortly after the publication of *Scouting for Boys*, girls started to join troops in order to take part in traditionally adventurous and thus 'masculine' activities. At a gathering of Scouts in 1909, Baden-Powell decided that there was enough female interest in Scouting for an exclusively female organization to be created. This group was called the Girl Guides and was officially started in 1910. Both organizations were similar: Guides and Scouts worked towards badges, worked in patrols and focused on outdoors activities. There were, however, subtle and not so subtle differences. For the girls, badges focused on housework and first aid skills, and for boys, heroic acts and military skills. Scouts were organized into patrols of around six boys, each of which had a Patrol Leader. A Scout Troop consisted of one or more patrols grouped together with a Scoutmaster, sometimes called a Scouter

---

1   For a detailed history of the Scout and Guide movements see Michael Rosenthal, *The Character Factory: Baden Powell and the Origins of the Boy Scout Movement* (London: Collins, 1986); and Tammy M. Proctor, *On My Honour: Guides and Scouts in Interwar Britain* (Philadelphia: Transactions of the American Philosophical Society, 2002).

or Scout Leader, who was the adult in charge. Guide units were organized in similar ways, but instead of calling groups troops, groups of Guides were called Companies. Guide leaders were called Guiders or Captains, with the other leaders called lieutenants. Whilst both the Guides and the Scouts maintained a military influence in their names and awards, for the Guides, this was downplayed in order to concentrate on more feminine, domestic pursuits, helping to counter accusations of tomboyism that plagued the Guides during this period. Certainly this link with militarism for the Guides marks a distinction between them and non-uniformed groups. Whilst other Jewish girls' clubs distanced themselves entirely from anything that could be considered masculine in nature, such as the military, within the Guides this masculine link, although downplayed, was certainly present.

This section will look at Guide and Scout groups that identified themselves as Jewish, rather than those who had both Jewish and non-Jewish members. The ways in which various troops and companies included religion in their evening meetings, as well as on camps, on religious holidays and at the synagogue will be analysed. It will examine the work of the Council of Jewish Scouters formed in the 1920s and a group of Jewish women involved in Guiding to promote the inclusion of religious activities in Scouting and Guiding. I will show that both Jewish Scout Troops and Jewish Guide Groups were able to incorporate a large number of religious elements into their programming and, in contrast to members of other clubs, allowed the members to express themselves religiously and not necessarily in keeping within gender norms.

Background and Ethos

The Scout movement proved to be very popular with Jewish boys. Troops that were composed specifically of Jewish youth were in existence throughout the UK, with a concentration of groups in the East End. The earliest record of a Jewish troop officially linked with the movement was in 1909, and affiliated with the East London Synagogue, though there may have been unofficial troops before then.[2] Indeed, Selim Bernstein, a boy from the East End, attended Baden-Powell's Scout camp in 1909. This free camp was open to thirty boys from around the country and members had to be nominated by a friend as well as receive the most votes from fellow Boy Scouts in order to attend.[3] The fact that someone from a Jewish troop was successful in achieving the most votes from around the country suggests that there was quite a sizeable number of Jewish boys (or those willing to vote for a Jewish boy) in the organization by this time. The popularity of Scouts amongst Jewish boys is also evident in Scouting headquarters. The first council of the Scout movement in 1909 included a number of religious figureheads, including the Archbishops of Canterbury, York and Westminster, members of the Wesleyan, Presbyterian and Free Churches, as well as a representative from the Jewish Lads' Brigade (JLB), Sir Frederick Nathan.[4] The inclusion of a Jewish figure indicates that the number of Jewish Scouts was enough to warrant official representation. The popularity of Jewish Scout groups continued to grow and by 1939 there were troops in a number of areas around London, including Stepney, Hackney, Willesden and Finchley. Outside London, Jewish Scouts were more widespread than the Jewish Lads' Brigade with troops in Glasgow, Edinburgh, Dublin, Margate, Southend-on-Sea, Middlesbrough, Liverpool, Manchester, Hull and Nottingham among others. One possible reason for this large number of provincial troops is that Scouting provided a detailed and easy to follow programme, which was clearly British in its origins. The national framework provided an easily adapted model, which allowed leaders to work in the needs of their community, which was particularly important for Jewish troops, which extended across the county with groups existing as far apart as Portsmouth and Glasgow. Those in Liverpool were, for example, able to adapt their activities in order to promote interfaith relations as a response to similar gestures from other, Christian troops in the city.[5] This ability for each group to tailor their activities to their own circumstances indicates the

2   The Scout Association Archives (hereafter TSA) Vol. i/51.
3   *JC*, 3 September 1909.
4   TSA vol i/53.
5   TSA 263.

flexibility of Scouting and Guiding and suggests why these groups were so popular. Additionally, troops could be formed with numbers as small as six members and one troop leader, and required very little financial backing from the Scoutmaster. This contrasted with the JLB, which required adult volunteers to donate sizeable amounts of money each year to financially support the organization, as it did not receive the same funding the Scout organization did from the community.

The Guide movement also proved to be popular amongst the Jewish population. In 1913, the 1st Whitechapel Company was the first specifically Jewish Company to be formed, just three years after the Guide Movement began. During the 1920s, a large number of Jewish companies existed and by 1927 there were twenty-four groups registered in London alone. By 1939 there were an even greater number, both in and out of London.[6] The small numbers of companies registered in the first decade of the movement can be attributed to concerns that the Guides encouraged tomboyish and 'unladylike' behaviour amongst its members, something that Anglo-Jewry certainly would not wish to encourage amongst immigrant-origin Jews. During the 1920s, after repeated assertions from the Guide Movement and a growing presence of Guides nationally, this appears to have been less of a concern, and can account for the rapid growth of the movement in both Jewish and non-Jewish communities.

The popularity of both the Guides and the Scouts within the Jewish sphere can be attributed to two factors. First, unlike other Jewish youth groups, it was not dependent on one highly involved individual. Instead, the organization was conducted on a national level, although as mentioned they could be tailored to suit the needs of the local community, and Captains and Scout leaders changed on a regular basis. Second, and most important, Scouting and Guiding was an essentially British organization. Unlike the Jewish Lads' Brigade and other Jewish youth clubs, these two groups inculcated a sense of national pride and loyalty as its primary aim and were strongly associated with a quintessentially British hero. A sense of Jewishness could be added to a group, however, this did not take away from the sense of Britishness, and its affiliation with Baden-Powell – a

6   Guide Association Archives (hereafter GAA), Karen Stapley, List of Jewish Guide
     Companies in London.

nationally recognized war hero. This was a vital consideration for a community committed to proving its British loyalty. In Manchester, the Jewish Guide Company was formed in conjunction with the synagogue in 1927. The group was successful in attracting members, which the leaders felt was due to the association of the company with the synagogue.[7] In this instance, the group demonstrated both religious and national affiliations, which can account for its success, and something that can account for the successes of both Jewish Guides and Scouts nationally.

Unlike groups such as the Boys' Brigade that emerged during the end of the nineteenth and beginning of the twentieth century, the Boy Scouts were not formed in attachment to a specific religious group. In *Scouting for Boys*, Baden-Powell took a casual attitude towards religion and religious observance, stating that 'Religion is a very simple thing, 1st to believe in God, 2nd to do good to other people'[8] and that 'No man is much good unless he believes in God and obeys His laws. So every Scout should have a religion.'[9] At no point did Baden-Powell state that members should belong to one religion rather than another. In the early years of the movement, the religious policy of the organization was loosely defined, with Scoutmasters taking their guidance from *Scouting for Boys* and a book of instructions for Scouters which said that: '[a]n organization of this kind would fail in its object if it did not bring the members to a knowledge of religion'.[10] As the movement grew, it became clear that the Association would need to form an official policy regarding religion. This policy was adopted in 1909 and for the first time, laid out the expectations clearly:

> It is expected of every Scout that he belong to one form of religious denomination or another.

> Where a troop is composed of members of one particular form of religion, it is open to the Scoutmaster to arrange such denominational religious observance and

---

7   MJM, Oral History Recordings, J217.

8   Robert Baden-Powell, *Scouting for Boys, The Original 1908 Edition* (Mineola, NY: Dover Publications, 2007), p. 260.

9   Ibid., p. 261.

10   Robert Baden-Powell, *Boy Scouts Scheme* (London: The Scout Association, 1908), p. 24.

instruction as he, in consultation with his chaplain, or other religious authority, may consider best.

> Where a troop consists of Scouts of various religions they should be encouraged to attend the service of their own denomination and in camp, any form of daily prayer and of the weekly divine service should be of the simplest character – attendance being voluntary.[11]

It is clear that although Scouting as a whole was not attached to any specific denomination, it was expected that all Scouts were active in their own religion, and that their involvement in the movement should aid them to become more involved in worship. The policy was approved by a number of religious figureheads, including the Chief Rabbi, demonstrating the organizations' sensitivity to religious diversity.

The policy for the Guide Association was very similar and was clearly repeated from one body to another. In a pamphlet detailing the organization of the Guide movement, Baden-Powell stated that 'The religious training would be very similar to that of the Boy Scouts, that is, in the hands of the Captain as regards the form, or where members of different religions are in the same company it will be entirely unsectarian.'[12] By 1914 the organization as a whole had come under scrutiny regarding its religious policy, and it was felt necessary to clarify the expectations. It was stated that 'there is a definite religious basis to the movement, for every Girl Guide is expected to be a member of some religious organization. Every facility is given for the formation of companies in connection with the various denominations with almost every religious body in the country.'[13] As with the Scout Association, the openness of the religious policy allowed for Jewish troops and Companies to be formed under the national organization in a way that the Boys' Brigade, with their Christian basis, did not.

11   TSA Vol. i/51 *The Scout Movement and Religious Policy*, 1909. This version is after Baden-Powell's handwritten amendments.

12   Robert Baden-Powell, *A Suggestion of Character Training for Girls* (London: The Scout Association, 1909), p. 11.

13   *Girl Guide Gazette*, No. 7, July 1914.

While religious diversity was encouraged on official lines, Michael Rosenthal has argued that Baden-Powell himself, as well as the movement as a whole, were 'concerned about the behaviour and values of the Jew, whom they viewed largely through the prism of a traditional anti-Semitic stereotype'.[14] Rosenthal bases this assumption on the fact that Baden-Powell exhibited a number of anti-Semitic tendencies, including a positive reaction to *The Protocols of the Elders of Zion*, which he read in the 1930s, and a public declaration that Jews were responsible for the communist revolution in Russia. Rosenthal claims that Baden-Powell was so much the figurehead of the organization, that any of his beliefs and public statements were taken to be the official stand of the movement. Nevertheless, the ways in which Jewish religious observance was incorporated into national and international events casts a doubt on such an assertion: it is crude and misleading to suggest that the Scout Association was simply anti-Semitic. Instead, the steps taken by individuals and troops to accommodate religious requirements were far from hostile, and on occasion, especially when confronted by members of Hitler Youth as occurred during international camps in the 1930s, the movement can be seen as pro-Jewish, defending the presence of Jews within the organization.[15] Whilst Baden-Powell revealed *political*, conspiratorial, anti-Semitic prejudice, the movement as a whole did not and welcomed its Jewish members, and it would be misleading to assume that Baden-Powell's personal views were the views of the movement as a whole.

In light of the clearly defined policy, there was little criticism regarding the quantity of religious programming in the Scouts. Even so, the *Jewish Chronicle* did feature a letter from a gentleman in Philadelphia, USA, who was concerned that Scouting was incompatible with the Jewish religion. His concerns focused on three areas. First, trips were arranged for Saturday and Sundays and that these took children away from the synagogue and Sunday schools. Second, fire and tower building contests were always arranged on a Saturday and thirdly, 'camp life makes it essential that the Jewish Scouts all eat forbidden food or go hungry'.[16] The writer of the youth column

14   Rosenthal, *The Character Factory*, p. 268.
15   *Adelaide (Australia) Advertiser*, 16 November 1933.
16   *JC*, 6 October 1916.

('The Children of the Ghetto' – by one of them) was concerned about the implications of these statements, although he did not believe that the wholly Jewish groups would have arranged for events to take place on Saturdays. The following month, the columnist published a further article having received correspondence from a number of Scouters who stated that not only was the Scout programme adaptable, but that each troop was independent from others and they 'should have no difficulty of maintaining the desired Jewish atmosphere without any way detracting from the utility of the movement'.[17] The concern about the incompatibility between Scouts and Jewishness was more relevant to individual Jewish Scouts in mixed or predominantly Christian troops. For specifically Jewish troops, as each group ran its own activities, there was no real danger of groups breaking the Sabbath or not providing *kosher* food. In Liverpool, the 11th Toxteth (Jewish) Baden-Powell Boy Scouts certainly were able to adapt their programme to meet religious requirements by arranging trips on Sundays (rather than having their members attending the centrally run trips on Saturdays) and by not participating in events on Friday evenings, stating that 'owing to the nature of the group we cannot take part officially in *any* Friday night activity'.[18] As this was the only criticism of the movement's religious practices or lack thereof published in the mainstream Jewish press, it is fair to suggest that the Boy Scouts were not seen to have been neglecting the religious aspect of their work, or creating barriers to members of any religious denomination. Indeed, the frequency of positive reports in the Jewish press indicates that the community viewed these groups as acceptably Jewish.

Religious Activities

In many youth groups the fostering of a religious 'spirit' in club activities was important. For the JLB, as has been shown, the importance of a religious spirit was downplayed. Scouting followed the example of non-uniform

17   *JC*, 17 November 1916.
18   TSA 263.

groups more closely than that of the JLB. Like other clubs, many of the individual troops included a religious element in its objectives. In 1916, it was reported that a Jewish group in Dublin existed and that 'special care is taken to see that Scouts (particularly when camping away from home) carry out their religious obligations'.[19] Whilst there are no specific details given here, it is safe to assume that like in all other boys' clubs, these religious obligations included, at a minimum, observing the Sabbath and ensuring that the boys had access to *kosher* food. The 7th Stepney Troop B. P. Scouts in 1921 also ensured that their members carried out their religious obligations and were encouraged to practice 'simple Judaism without any tendency towards either extreme Orthodoxy and Reform'.[20] The 11th Toxteth Troop, in a publicity poster from 1937, stated that their 'aim was to foster Jewish Tradition, Cultural Activity and to help the boy to acquire Self-reliance, Resource and Character through Camping, Wood Craft [skills relating to living in the woods] and Nature Study'.[21] Whilst the religious aspect is not the only element mentioned in the group's activities, it is the first thing listed, indicating that the group may have believed this to be the most important– or at least their most marketable aim. For these troops, throughout the early twentieth century, religion was seen to be an important part of their activities; fostering Jewish tradition amongst their members was a duty that these clubs took seriously. Even so, not all Jewish Troops included religion in such a way. The 36th Stepney Troop, attached to the Oxford and St George's Street Club, did not have such a religious element, which is particularly noteworthy as the troop belonged to the same club in which Basil Henriques insisted a Jewish spirit be included. Wellesley Aron, the Scoutmaster of the 36th Stepney and later the founder of the *Habonim* movement, was criticized by Henriques 'who often charged him with being un-Jewish for omitting all Jewish overtones from his Scouting activities'.[22] Yet this lack of religious sentiment in a Troop was the exception. Moreover, it is wrong to assume that there was no religious element

---

19   *JC*, 3 November 1916.

20   *JC*, 22 June 1921.

21   TSA 263.

22   Helen Selman-Cheong, *Wellesley Aron: Rebel with a Cause, A Memoir* (London: Vallentine Mitchell, 1992), p. 27.

simply because Henriques thought that this was the case, as he had much greater expectations with regard to the quantity and content of religious programming than many of the other youth group leaders of the time.

Many of the Jewish Scout Troops had their own chaplain. Often the Troop itself was attached to a particular synagogue, enabling close links with local clergymen. Unlike in many of the other youth groups, Rabbis often became deeply involved in Scouting, attending camps and helping at weekly meetings. In the 19th Finchley Troop, at an investiture in 1938 (an occasion when Scouts and Scouters made their Scout promise and were formally inducted into The Scout Association.) 'Rabbi Dr I. Pouisch, minister of the [Finchley District] Synagogue, was the first to be invested, receiving his Scout badge. He was inducted into the synagogue as chaplain of the group.'[23] This level of involvement by religious authorities is significant, as it was with the JLB. Not only does it imply that the Scouts were concerned with the religious elements of its work, but it also shows that the synagogues supported the Scouts in a way that they did not support other youth groups, potentially due to the Scouts' inherent Britishness and their association with a decorated war hero. This connection with a religious figure helped to promote gendered expectations that boys engage more formally than girls with religion.

Guide Companies were not connected with religious figures in the same way as Scout Troops or the JLB were. As an organization for girls, it barred Rabbis and other male religious personnel from official membership of the organization, as it was felt that too great a male influence on girls' lives would result in girls losing their femininity.[24] There were, however, a small number of religious figures who did become involved with specific companies or areas in a less formal way. In Dublin, Rev. Mr Gudansky was associated with the 1st Jewish Troop of Girl Guides and often attended meetings, leading them in prayers.[25] Rabbi Salis Daiches was associated with the company of Guides attached to the Glasgow Jewish Girls' Club, and led a service each year, as well as attending occasional meetings to deliver

23   *JC*, 27 May 1938.
24   Proctor, *On My Honour*, pp. 24–5.
25   *JG*, 25 June 1926.

addresses on various subjects.[26] In London, during the 1920s Rabbi Gollop and Rev. Vivian Simmons gave sermons each year at *Chanucah*, and the former was involved with the Association for Jewish Girl Guides.[27] Whilst the involvement of religious figures in Guiding was not as extensive as was seen in Scouting, due in part to the prohibition of men joining the Guide movement, the presence of a small number of religious figures would have helped to promote Judaism within Jewish companies, at the same time as ensuring that girls were not encouraged to take on a masculine role of leading formal worship.

One of the unique ways in which the Scout and Guide Associations were able to include a religious element within their programme was with the consecration of Troop and Company Colours. Unlike the majority of youth groups, Scouts and Guides were, from the beginning of the movement, encouraged to have their own Union Flag and their own Troop flag for use at parades and official events. Ceremonies were conducted for either a Scout Troop's or for a Guide Company's colours; however, on most occasions, both Scouts and Guides were present in the congregation. The presence of Guide companies at these formal events in the synagogue indicates an important departure from gender norms, and instead places greater importance on religious participation and displays of nationalism generally rather than on maintaining strict gender divisions in common with other, singularly Jewish clubs. Girls' attendance at public worship has been noted from a variety of different organizations in the UK. In Sheffield Chanty schools from the 1780s, for example, it was expected that teachers take the girls to church on Sundays, demonstrating a long history of allowing girls to take part in public worship.[28] Within the Guide organization, Christian girls were encouraged to attend church parades, such as local parades attended by the 6th Slough troop in the 1930s and the city wide parades in Bournemouth companies recorded as early as

26   *JW*, 26 November 1925.

27   See, *JC*, 22 November 1929, *JG*, 22 October 1926, and *JW*, 26 November 1925, 24 November 1927, among others.

28   John Roach, 'The Sheffield Boys' and Girls' Chanty Schools 1706–1962', *Journal of Educational Administration and History*, 31 (1999), pp. 114–29 (p. 116).

1914.[29] In other Jewish girls' clubs synagogue attendance, in contrast, was not encouraged as part of a group activity and the maintenance of strict private spheres of worship, which required a level of devotion on a domestic and personal rather than public level, was encouraged instead. The Guide Association, however, encouraged girls to attend public worship as part of a group and thus fell outside of the strict norms seen in other Jewish girls' clubs. Instead, they followed traditional practices from within the UK more generally.

For Scout troops, consecrating their flags provided an opportunity for the group to attend synagogue and experience a sermon, often from a Rabbi attached to the Scout troop. In 1914, the West Ham Boy Scouts held their consecration at the West Ham Associate Synagogue. The service was conducted by the Reverend A. Katz and an address was given to the boys which encouraged the Scouts to think positively about the UK and the fact that in this country 'the throne was builded on righteousness'.[30] Here, the sermon was used in much the same way as they were in the Jewish Lads' Brigade; that is to say they encouraged young people to appreciate the country in which they lived and to foster a feeling of British nationality amongst the boys. The consecration of 6th Cricklewood Guide Company's flag in 1927 had a similar theme. The address given by Dayan Lazurus stated 'that as peace loving and law-abiding citizens they had met together … to represent their duty towards their sovereign and their country'.[31] At the consecration of the colours of the 235th Glasgow Girl Guides in 1932, the sermon placed an emphasis on the Union Flag, which was placed in the centre of the synagogue and was repeatedly referred to in the service, which implored the young people to see it as a symbol of

29   Mary Claire Martin, 'Roman Catholic Girl Guiding in Sussex 1912–1919: Origins, Ideology, Practice', in *Youth Policy*, 111 (2013), <http://www.youthandpolicy.org/wp-content/uploads/2013/10/martin-roman-catholic-girl-guiiding.pdf> [accessed 8 March 2014], p. 10; and Joyce Cranshaw, 'Reminiscences from 60 years of Guiding', <http://www.leics.gov.uk/index/leisure_tourism/local_history/recordoffice/recordoffice_exhibitions/recordoffice_currentexhibs/girlguiding.htm> [accessed 8 March 2015].

30   *JW*, 22 July 1914.

31   *JC*, 13 May 1927.

dawn, purity and heaven. These virtues were related to the ideals of the Guide movement and to Judaism and helped to underscore the young people's identities as both British and Jewish.[32] This provides an example of the way in which Jewish Guides could adjust practices to suit their own, in this case religious, needs.

In Scotland, the 155th Boy Scout Troop (1st Glasgow Jewish) used the consecration of their colours in 1930 to demonstrate combined loyalties towards their Jewish, British and Scottish identities.[33] Through the use of the Union Flag within the service and Jewish imagery pictured on the troop flag, the group was demonstrating both national and religious loyalty. In addition, the members of the troop wore kilts as part of their uniform, further highlighting national loyalties by demonstrating the inherent Scottishness of the members. By wearing a very visible symbol of Scottish identity, the troop was able to demonstrate to the wider public within Glasgow the loyalty of Jewish Scouts to the nation. The use of kilts in particular provided a very visible link between Jewish Scouts and Scottish notions of freedom, independence and heroism – qualities that Scouts were also expected to possess.[34] It is also worth noting that the youth branch of the National Party of Scotland in 1932 deemed the kilt to be the 'healthiest form of dress yet devised for youth groups' as it allowed unrestricted movement at the same time as demonstrating national allegiances.[35] These Scottish Scouts were thus demonstrating local loyalty through the adoption of a relevant uniform. Through the combination of British, Scottish *and* Jewish images, this troop was able to use synagogue attendance to display the members' religious and patriotic allegiances.

32   *Jewish Echo* (hereafter *JE*), 3 June 1932 and Scottish Jewish Archives Centre (hereafter SJAC) 'Coming of Age of the Girl Guide Association and the Dedication of Colours for the 235th Glasgow Girl Guides', 29 May 1932, SOC SCO 0001–0002.

33   SJAC PHO.S.0005, c.1930.

34   Beatriz Oria Gomez, 'Rob Roy an Anti-English Hero', in Christopher Hart (ed.), *Heroines and Heroes: Symbolism, Embodiment, Narrative and Identity* (Kingswinford: Midrash Publishers, 2008), pp. 196–206 (p. 198).

35   Hayden Lorrimer, 'Happy Hostelling in the Highlands: Nationhood, Citizenship and the Inter-War youth Movement', *Scottish Geographical Magazine*, 113 (1997), pp. 42–50 (p. 47).

The services held at the consecration of colours were, throughout the history of both the Guide and Scout movement, used within Jewish groups as a way to emphasize the importance of remaining British, including within a 'local' national context. In this way, religion was not used to promote gender divisions but instead to promote national loyalty with no reference to accepted male/female identities.

Within the Scout Association, in addition to encouraging loyalty to their country, the consecrations also served as a way in which to promote the public school ideals of character and self-reliance (also the Scout ideals). In Nottingham in 1925, the boys were encouraged by the Rev. A. Levene to embrace Scouting principles as he stated that 'the Scout idea laid stress on character, the development of which was the chief aim of all true education. He begged the boys always to hold up the name of Jew in honour and affection, and to make themselves worthy of the Scout movement.'[36] This sentiment was echoed two years later at the joint consecration of the 35th Stepney and 27th Willesden Troops at Cricklewood Synagogue. In this instance the Chief Rabbi delivered the sermon which

> stressed the fundamentals of good Scouting, honour, radiating happiness, self-abnegation, illustrating each point from Jewish history. In stirring sentences he called on the boys to stand firmly and loyally to their Judaism and their Scouting principles.[37]

Unlike other sermons, here there was a clear mention of the relevance of Judaism to the (essentially masculine) principles of Scouting providing examples relevant to the boys. Whilst these sermons, on the whole, were a further opportunity for leaders and religious figures to encourage children to become good British men and women, these events also allowed for an additional exposure to a religious event – one which other Jewish clubs did not possess.

Troop-run events in the synagogue were not confined to the early days of each Troop. A number of Jewish troops attended services at their local synagogue on a regular basis. The 1st (Hull) Jewish Troop of Boy Scouts,

36   *JW*, 13 August 1925.
37   *JG*, 18 March 1927.

which had approximately seventy members, was in the 1920s involved in the weekly services at their local synagogue where 'every Sabbath morning a synagogue parade is held'.[38] The 187th Scout Troop in Glasgow also held frequent synagogue services that were advertised in the local Jewish press.[39] This level of engagement with a synagogue was quite unusual amongst youth clubs – particularly amongst those for boys. There is no evidence that other troops held weekly parades; but, troops often took part in services during the year. As the services held for consecrating colours, the speakers often implored the Scouts to develop their character in line with Scouting ideals and Jewish traditions. In Leeds, a service attended by Scouts in 1925 encapsulated these themes perfectly. At this event the service was held at the Great Synagogue and led by the Rev. J. Abelson:

> The preacher said that character would always play a predominant part in the life of a Jewish Boy Scout. This character displayed itself principally in service to others. He trusted that the lads who belonged to the Scout movement would gain spiritual as well as physical health, and be enabled to stand in the vanguard of Jewish progress and prosperity all over the world.[40]

This sermon was typical of those given at events for Scouts. In speaking of character and giving service to others, the boys were being encouraged to engage themselves in their community and their country and at the same time remain Jewish. These services therefore provided a vital way for the Troop leaders to engage their Scouts in Jewish religious life, at the same time they promoted manly British values, which were such a vital part of the Scout programme.

Links between Jewishness and Britishness were also present in special services held for Guide companies. During the twenty-first anniversary of the Guide Movement, a number of special services were held by Jewish Companies across the UK. The service held in London reiterated to the girls the good qualities of the Guide Association, stating that 'the movement had striven from its inception to inculcate into young womanhood a

38   *JW*, 15 March 1926.
39   See *JE* from 1910 onward.
40   *JW*, 9 April 1925.

sense of loyalty to God and man, to king and country, a sense of reverence for truth and honesty, physical health and moral strength'.[41] These themes were often mentioned in the sermons of youth groups, and helped to create a sense of Britishness amongst the young members. In Liverpool, the service led by Rev. S. Frampton used the principles of the Guide Association to encourage devotion to Judaism. He said that 'loyalty to their movement would teach them loyalty to their obligations, especially to their religion, and help them to become not only good and useful women but faithful Jewesses'.[42] Once again, Guide companies attending the synagogue is significant as it underscored the differences between ideal Jewish femininity as seen in non-uniformed Jewish clubs and that encouraged within the Guide Association, although as noted earlier this was not necessarily a distinction found within non-Jewish girls' organizations. Both Guide and Scout sermons, whilst one of the most overt forms of religious activity in their programme, can also be seen as a platform for creating a feeling of Britishness by drawing members' attention to their loyalty to their country and monarch, whilst also maintaining a distinctly Jewish atmosphere. Unlike in other clubs, however, the services were not used to promote gendered qualities to the same extent.

In addition to weekly services and parades, Jewish Scout and Guide groups attended synagogues for religious holidays. From 1912 there are reports of Jewish Scout Troops attending the JLB and Children's *Chanucah* services, both in London and in the provinces. These services provided Jewish Scouts with a way to engage with their religion as well as their peers from outside of the Scout movement. In Liverpool, the *Chanucah* service in 1937, where a sermon was given on Scouting principles, served an additional purpose as non-Jewish Scouts were invited to join in. Both the *Liverpool Echo* and the *Liverpool Evening Express* reported on the event, stating that the 'a large party of Scouts of the non-Jewish faith representative of the full organization participated in a delightful gathering at the synagogue where the minister (Mr Phillips) welcomed them in

41   *JW*, 16 June 1932.
42   *JC*, 3 June 1932.

good scouty-straight-from-the-shoulder sentiment'.[43] In this instance, in addition to ensuring that Scouts attend the synagogue at *Chanucah*, the service helped other young people to experience Judaism and to show the local community that their organization was just as British as the other non-Jewish Troops.

For Guides in London and the Home Counties, *Chanucah* was an important festival, as a yearly parade of all Jewish Guides was held in London. The service was organized by the Association for Jewish Girl Guides and the sermon given by Rabbi Gollop, with approval by the chief Rabbi. The event featured a number of hymns and Psalms, with Psalm 121 and the Old Hundredth both featuring in a number of the *Chanucah* sermons.[44] Interestingly, none of the hymns or readings mentioned relate to a feeling of national loyalty or to self-improvement, instead focusing on God and belief in God. The lack of national feeling in readings is in contrast to other sermons Guide and Scout groups attended and to sermons given by a number of non-Scouting boys' clubs. It is significant that not only were girls once again formally encouraged to attend the synagogue, but that they were encouraged to do so during *Chanucah*, a festival associated with militarism and courage, traditionally masculine qualities. Whilst this does not necessarily contradict non-Jewish clubs' and schools' experience of public worship for girls, it does counter the ideal promoted by other Jewish clubs in relation to formal and structured public worship.

Whilst *Chanucah* was the most universally commemorated religious festival amongst the Scouts and the Guides as well as in other youth clubs, there is evidence that a number of Scout troops commemorated *Purim*. The *Jewish World* reported in 1933 that Jewish Boy Scouts from across the country attended a special 'Rally' (a daytime gathering of a large number of Scouts from different Troops) at the East London Synagogue for *Purim*. This service, organized on a grand scale, enabled Troops from all over London to engage with a synagogue. Individual Troops also ran their own *Purim* events. The Toxteth group reported two *Purim* celebrations

---

43 *Liverpool Echo*, 4 December 1937.

44 *JG*, 22 October 1926, and *Girl Guide Gazette*, Vol. 14, No. 168 (December 1927), p. 368.

in their log book in 1937 and 1938. For the first service, the boys 'went to the synagogue (informally) and at 5.30, after the reading of the *Megillah*, Ping-Pong and *marbles* and Quarterstaff were indulged in.'[45] In attending the synagogue informally, not only were the Troop leaders encouraging the boys to attend the service, but they also encouraged them to attend without the ostentation of participating in a Parade. In 1938, the *Purim* celebration was very different. Rather than attend the synagogue, the boys ran a short 'Scouts-Own' ceremony at the end of the meeting where the Troop leader officiated and 'Freiser [an assistant leader] said a few words about the significance of *Purim*.'[46] The 'Scouts-Own' (and Guide-Own) ceremony was encouraged throughout the Scouting movement, requiring the members themselves to plan and produce a simple service, rather than rely on the presence of a Chaplain or other formal religious figure. There are records of these services taking place in groups attached to a number of faiths. The 10th Belfast Troop records weekly Scouts-Own services from the 1920s, which included passages from the Bible, hymns and prayers as well as discussions on various papers, read on local and Scouting interest.[47] The Christian 14th Salisbury Troop included a short open-air Scouts-Own service involving a number of hymns and reflections in each of its camps.[48] Instructions on how to hold these ceremonies were printed in a number of official publications, including the *Girl Guide Gazette*, which included lists of prayers, dedications and blessings that each troop could include in their services.[49] The list, including the Lord's Prayer and multiple references to Jesus, was clearly written with Christian troops in mind. There was, however, an expectation for groups of different faiths to adjust the content accordingly. In this way, the Scouts-Own services provides evidence that, like young members personalizing their uniforms, Scout

45   TSA 263 (original emphasis).

46   Ibid.

47   Andrew Totten, *Straight and Ready: A History of the 10th Belfast Scout Group 1908–1988* (Belfast: Nelson and Know, 1989), p. 52.

48   Salisbury, Private Collection, *The Log of the 14 Salisbury Scout Troop*. See for example, 2 August 1936, 1 August 1937 and 8 August 1938.

49   *Girl Guide Gazette*, see for example, May 1914, p. 8.

troops and leaders were able to adapt Scouting for their own purposes in this case, their own religious purposes. This informal style of worship was something often seen in girls' clubs, but rarely in boys' clubs and indicates that the group felt confident in working outside gender norms in order to provide religious activities. The celebration in 1938 was much less formal than that of the previous year, probably due to the fact that there was no official service during the weekly meeting as *Purim* fell on a different day of the week from the Scout evening. It could, however, signify that Troop leaders felt more confident in letting the boys themselves take a role in worship.

Other religious holidays were observed by Jewish Scout groups, although less uniformly. *Succoth* was one of the more commonly observed festivals, alongside *Chanucah* and *Purim*. The typical format of these celebrations involved Scouts attending a service in the synagogue, followed by a reception in the *Succah*. This model of service was taken as the form for the 27th Willesden Troop's event in 1926. For the sermon, Dayan Lazurus 'delivered an address on the significance of the *Succah* and the value of the Scout movement.'[50] Once again, it is evident that the service was used to extol the virtues of Scouting. In 1938, London Scouts celebrated *Tu B'Shevat*, an occasion not often observed by Jewish youth groups. More than 100 Scouts gathered at Gilwell Park, Scout Headquarters, in order to plant a number of trees and 'the Rev. E. Lipson, M.A., who conducted the religious service, said that they had planted trees in the land of their birth. As a symbol they were also planting a tree in the King George V. jubilee forest in the land of their fathers.'[51] This was a significant symbol for the boys who came from immigrant families; by showing that Britain was their land, the club leaders were able to emphasize the Britishness of the young people. By mentioning that Palestine was the land of their fathers, the leaders were underscoring their religious and ethnic loyalties. By including both elements of the members' identities, they were able to demonstrate that their religious background did not counteract their national loyalties.

50   *JW*, 7 October 1925.
51   *Scouter*, February 1938, Vol. 32, No. 2, p. 46.

Summer Camps

As with other boys' youth clubs, the Scouts saw camping as a vital part of
their work, and as such, camps formed a large part in the Troop calendar. As
each Troop was able to plan its own event, and often had three or four camps
each year, it is impossible to determine exactly how each group included
religion at each different event. However, as with the JLB and other clubs,
religious observances at camps were included through daily prayers and
Sabbath services. Depending on the troop and the camp's location, there
were three main ways in which the different troops incorporated religion.
The first was for a troop to attend a local synagogue on a Saturday morning. Making links with Jewish Scouts where the troop was camping often
facilitated this. The 155th (1st Jewish) Glasgow Scout Troop camped near
Newcastle in 1938 and attended services at the synagogue with Newcastle
Scouts.[52] When camping abroad, this was also a popular option for troops.
Groups would form links with the local synagogue and attend on multiple occasions during their visit. Other troops favoured holding their own
services at the campsite, similar to the drumhead services run by the JLB.
These would be small scale and the Troop leader would act as *Chazan*.
The Scouts-Own is the third way in which Troops included religion, and
no parallel can be found in other clubs. The Scouts-Own gave ownership
of the service to the Scouts themselves and directly engaged them in the
religious element and encouraged informality and engagement with the
surroundings, rather than the boys acting as passive spectators. This was
an important deviation from masculine norms found in the JLB and other
clubs, particularly as boys could join Scouts from the age of eleven. Many of
the boys within Scouting, therefore, were under *Bar-Mitzvah* age and would
therefore have had limited experience in planning structured worship that
older boys would have been familiar with, unless as part of their upbringing, they attended services. For boys' clubs there was less emphasis on
encouraging members to explore their own religion and a greater emphasis

52   *JC*, 15 July 1938.

on observing the ritual. The Scouts-Own ceremony reflects the opposite, allowing boys to explore their own religion in a way that was more commonly found within girls' clubs. Scouts-Own services were run during the joint camp of the 16th Stepney and 28th Southwark Troops where 'Divine services were held every morning and were conducted, after the first two days, by the lads themselves, with great success.'[53] This allowed the Scout leaders to promote ideals of self-sufficiency and independence. Whilst for Scout Troops, religion at camps did not have the same grandeur as that included in JLB camps, the services were certainly more intimate, mirroring the experience of religion in girls' clubs more closely than that of boys' clubs. Additionally, through the Scouts-Own services, Troops were able to engage children practically in religion and ensure that they were developing their own sense of Jewishness.

For girls' clubs as a whole, camping and holidays were less common than in boys' clubs, and it is only in the late 1920s that camps began to be a regular feature in club life. The Guides, however, began camping earlier than their non-guiding counterparts. In 1924, in addition to local camps, a 'World Camp' was held in the New Forest, where selected girls from all over the world attended. At this event, the religious element was included daily in the form of communal prayers for the whole camp, as well as on the Sabbath for Jewish campers. The arrangements were made by a Jewish Guider, Miss Landau, who ensured that the needs of Jewish campers from the UK, Palestine, America and South Africa were met. The *Jewish Guardian* reported that 'a special hut has been provided for the Friday night and Sabbath meal, during which Sabbath table hymns are sung'.[54] Unlike the efforts made for boys during camp, the religious provisions for Guides focused on the more domestic elements of observance, such as the Sabbath meal. This account, like others from girls' clubs, places emphasis on the Sabbath meal and thus on the kitchen table as the heart of the Sabbath experience, contributing to the relationship between

53　*JC*, 12 August 1932.
54　*JG*, 25 July 1924.

femininity and domesticity.[55] This would have been seen as a way for the leaders to promote acceptable gender roles to the girls, as well as to ensure that the members were being sufficiently prepared for their future roles in passing on their faith to their children.

During the 1930s, small company camps became more popular for Guides. At these camps, religion was observed in a way that was similar to that in boys' club camps. Jewish troops from Glasgow and Edinburgh came together to camp in Fifeshire where 'a special feature of the camp were the services held daily and on the Sabbath'.[56] In Birmingham, the Jewish Guides attended a camp in 1934 where 'prayers were said every day, and Kasher food was provided direct from Birmingham'.[57] In the same year, Guides from Glasgow and Edinburgh attended camp in Aberdour. Here, *Adon Olam* and *Yigdal* were sung and the *Shema* was recited each morning. Services were held on the Sabbath and, as in the larger camps, emphasis was placed on the Sabbath meal. The *Jewish Echo* reported:

> Surely a familiar odour must have reached the nostrils of the Jewish visitors to Aberdour during the cooking of the fish and chips in readiness for the first Sabbath meal, and welcome glances were thrown at the appearance of a white table cloth, Challahs complete with cover, two candle-sticks with their accompanying candles and even a small bottle of wine. Each guide joined joyfully in the *Kiddush* and *Moitzee*.[58]

In Manchester during camps in the 1930s, the Jewish Guide Group did not hold a formal Sabbath service, however, they did pay attention to the Sabbath meal where they had fried fish and salad, games and ensured the meal was 'a little bit different' from others at camp.[59] The absence of the sermon and concentration on the meal demonstrates adherence to gender norms in a way that most other Guide companies did not. Whilst

---

55   See Kate Barclay, 'Place and Power in Irish Farms at the End of the Nineteenth Century', *Women's History Review*, 21 (2012), 571–88, for a discussion on the role of the kitchen table in constructing women's identities.

56   *JC*, 21 September 1934.

57   *JC*, 31 August 1934.

58   *JE*, 24 August 1934.

59   MJM Oral History Recordings J217 and J17.

it is clear that religion *was* observed on Guide camps, it does not seem to have differed greatly from that of Scout camps, or indeed from the camps of other Jewish boys' clubs with the exception of the emphasis on the Sabbath meal. The content of the sermons and prayers in Guide camps are not expanded upon, but it seems reasonable to assume that this mirrored the sermons given at other points of the year, focusing on the domestic and more feminine pursuits, rather than military and masculine ideals. In terms of the amount and format of the religion included, the Guide units appear closer to the religious observance of boys' clubs than non-Guiding girls' clubs – something that certainly could not have helped with the image of Guides as tomboys. This might have added to early fears that the Guide Association was encouraging young girls to become less feminine, however, as the association began to include more feminine activities as part of their programme, this would have been less of an issue. Within Orthodox Jewish clubs gender norms were the key way to assert British identities whilst retaining an element of Judaism within their activities. Guides were, in contrast, able to assert Britishness through areas other than religion.

The Council of Jewish Scouters and the Association for Jewish Girl Guides

The religious activities of the Jewish Scouts and Guides can be seen through the work of the Council of Jewish Scouters and the Association for Jewish Girl Guides. The existence of these organizations signified a sizeable number of Jewish Scouts and Guides who needed particular religious considerations. Indeed, both the Council of Jewish Scouters and the Association for Jewish Guides catered specifically for the religious needs of members in their respective organizations. As a result, the activities of these two groups reflect the religious activities of both Jewish Scouts and Jewish Guides as a whole. As a consequence of the popularity of Scouting in the Jewish community, a Council of Jewish Scouters was officially formed in May 1929, although

it had existed informally before then.[60] The council met on a regular basis
and had links to the main Scout Association Headquarters. Rather than
dictate what should be done on a Troop level, the Council was concerned
with large-scale events such as Rallies and Jamborees (large camps at which
Scouts from all over the world are present). For larger camps, the Council
would co-ordinate suitable catering and arrange Sabbath services; they
organized an annual service for all Jewish Scouts held in London and
encouraged Troops to be set up in conjunction with every synagogue in the
UK. The Council ensured that the religious needs of Jewish troops were
met on a national level, through their engagement with Headquarters.[61]

The potential of Scout-run sermons as a tool in which to engage the
boys in their religion was recognized early on. In 1912, it was suggested
that the Scouts run a special service in order to encourage existing members to attend the synagogue, but also to encourage new members to join
Scouting.[62] Whilst it is unclear whether any such service was arranged at
this time, by 1925 Jewish Scouters were holding annual services for London
Scouts, similar to those held by the JLB at *Chanucah*. This service, held in
March of each year, gave an opportunity for approximately 500 Scouts and
Cubs to get together at the Great Synagogue in London.[63] Herbert Martin,
the non-Jewish International Commissioner for the Scout Association,
was invited to attend this service and published a report of the event in
the *Scouter* magazine:

> Fully 500 Jewish Scouts turned up and in the course of the service I had the pleasure
> of leading them in the recital of the Scout laws and the renewal of their promises. The
> service, most of which was unaccompanied singing, was beautifully rendered, and
> I was impressed by the reverent and hearty way in which these hundreds of Jewish
> Scouts joined in the prayers and Psalms; they did not just leave it to the choir, but
> every boy joined in with heart and soul. In that they set an example to some of us
> Christians. The Rabbi gave us an admirable address in which he expressed the special
> interest of all Jewish Scouts in the international aspect of Scouting and its world

60   *JC*, 22 November 1929.
61   See for example *JG*, 3 May 1929 and 14 June 1929.
62   *JC*, 13 December 1912.
63   See *JW*, 9 April 1925, and *JC*, 24 March 1933.

brotherhood. He further laid stress on their devotion to the chief Scout and Imperial Headquarters. We have no more loyal boys than our Jewish Scouts.[64]

The detail that was given in this account is remarkable. This is likely due to the fact that it was provided by someone who was not familiar with Judaism to an audience that was predominantly non-Jewish. The service produced for the boys, whilst containing a sermon of relevance and interest to the young members, was a traditional one. As in sermons throughout the year, this encouraged loyalty, including within the imperial realm, amongst the boys, especially important as the loyalty of the Jewish population on the whole was consistently under question. Indeed, the surprise and admiration that Martin exhibits regarding the participation of the Scouts in the service indicates that this level of engagement was not as common amongst Christian Scouts.

In 1920, the first Scout Jamboree was held in Kensington, and since then, Jamborees have been held approximately every four years in various countries around the world. At the first Jamboree, troops of Jewish Scouts were present and *kosher* food and trips to synagogues for Sabbath services had been arranged in advance.[65] The visits to the synagogues allowed the Scouts to present an image to the public of well-disciplined and ordered Jews. This would have contributed to the positive image of Jews that club leaders were attempting to promote. In 1929, the next Jamboree to be held in the UK, the newly formed Council of Jewish Scouters took an active part in making arrangements for Jewish Scouts attending the event. Prior to the camp, the Council placed adverts in the Jewish press asking for numbers of Jews attending and promising that arrangements would be made for them. At the Council's annual conference held after the camp, their report stated that 'every facility and much help had been given by camp authorities in connection with religious observance and the supply of *Kasher* food'.[66] The Council was able to secure a chaplain to attend the camp and arrange services for the Scouts as well as arranging that meat was

64   *Scouter*, Vol. 27, No. 4, April 1933.
65   *Headquarters Gazette*, Vol. 14, No. 8, August 1920, p. 153.
66   *JC*, 22 November 1929.

'provided already porged and *koshered* so that with separate utensils there will be no difficulty as regards food'.[67] Similar arrangements were put in place at the 1933 Jamboree in Hungary and at the 1937 event in Holland. By 1937, the Scout movement had grown considerably and featured a large number of Jewish troops and members from all over the world. It is therefore not surprizing that provisions for Jewish Scouts to observe their religion became even more prominent. The Jamboree's newspaper simply stated that 'the Jewish Scouts held their own service'.[68] The *Jewish Chronicle*, offered more information:

> The religious services ... were held in the open air, and these must have created a lasting impression not only upon the participants, but upon the large numbers of members of other denominations who were reverent onlookers. The Chief Rabbi of Holland, Rabbi Frank, addressed a large gathering at *Mincha* on Sunday ... and the chief Scout of America, Mr James West addressed the Jewish Scouts at the Sabbath evening service. Jewish Scouts could be observed at prayer each morning with *Talit* and *Tefilin*.[69]

The attendance of the Dutch Chief Rabbi at the camp shows that a certain amount of priority was given to the Jewish Scouts fulfilling their religious obligations and emphasizes the formality of the event. Additionally, the level of cooperation given by the Scout movement to the needs of the Jewish campers, particularly during a time of increased anti-Semitism demonstrates that the Scout movement was one that accepted and embraced diversity.

Jewish Guiders also recognized the importance of having a central organization to deal with Jewish matters. As Guides did not attend Jamborees, Jewish Guiders were not concerned with the same issues as Scouts, such as ensuring Jewish worship at a predominantly Christian event. Despite this, Jewish Guiders still recognized areas where a national organization would be beneficial. In 1914, an early group was set up with Captains of all of the Jewish companies in England in order 'to discuss any purely

---

67 *JW*, 1 August 1929.
68 *Jamboree Post Kampdag Blod Wereld Jamboree*, 2 August 1937.
69 *JC*, 13 August 1937.

Jewish Questions'.[70] This group remained informal until the 1920s, when the number of Jewish Companies had increased. In 1927, the Association for Jewish Girl Guides was well-established, and consisted of a number of Jewish Guiders as well as a committee of interested people who were not members of the organization, including Rabbi Gollop and the Rev. Vivian Simmons. The aims of the organization were to encourage 'our children to be good Jews as well as good Guides', which was achieved by organizing two large services each year.[71] First, the annual *Chanucah* service, which, as shown previously, was organized by Rabbi Gollop with the approval of the Chief Rabbi, and second, was the Annual Service of the Association, which began in 1924. Both of these services included Guides from a number of companies across London and the Home Counties. They were led by respected figures in local synagogues, which would have helped to familiarize young members with the synagogue and with religious figures. Both events emphasized formal synagogue worship – something not frequently seen to this extent in non-uniformed girls' clubs, in particular the observance of *Chanucah*. Whilst women were not excluded from *Chanucah*, or similar, celebrations, the level of observance and the public nature of the event more closely resembles the observances of Jewish boys' clubs, rather than that of the girls'. This again indicates that for the Girl Guides religion was more important than preserving the strict gender ideals, which were seen in Orthodox girls' clubs.

Conclusion: Jewish Scouts, Guides and Religion

Both the Scout Association and the Guide Association can be seen to have made a significant effort to accommodate diverse religious needs. Individual Troops and Companies had the expectation that they ensured their members attended a religious service, although it was not dictated which this should

70   *Girl Guide Gazette*, Vol. 2, No. 28, April 1916, p. 59.
71   *JW*, 26 November 1929.

be. Such openness helped to avoid the issues that many other Jewish youth groups had of which variation of Judaism to follow. Troops were allowed to arrange their own programme, which meant that leaders were able to take into account their own members and arrange services that suited the young people themselves. Amongst Jewish Scout Troops, services in the synagogue seem to have been more popular than in other boys' clubs; however, the sermons given at these events served a similar purpose: to ensure that Jewish boys were encouraged to be good and respectable British citizens, this time through the ideals of the Scout movement. In contrast, the Guides observed more formalized religion – such as more frequent synagogue services than their non-Guiding counterparts. Rather than placing the emphasis on spirituality, the Guides instead emphasized attending events. This focus is not surprising, considering that the Guide Association laid a much greater emphasis on adventurous activities than other girls' clubs and was closer to mirroring boys' clubs in terms of activities provided than other girls' clubs of the period. The content of the religious programming was also influenced by that experienced in boys' clubs, but did draw in a few elements that were expected from girls, such as the emphasis on the domestic element of Judaism. What remained the same in the Guide Association were the themes of character training and loyalty that were frequently brought into sermons, ensuring that the members of the Guides, like members of all other Jewish youth clubs, became good Jewesses and good British women.

Uniformed Religion?

For the Jewish Lads' Brigade (JLB), strict gender roles were promoted through religion, with an emphasis initially on manliness through militarism and then later through courage and independence, although it appears that overall, religion had a limited role. Within the Brigade religion was observed with ceremony and was often public, or open to the public eye. For the Scouts, religion also encouraged masculine qualities. Even so, boys were also encouraged to explore their religious side further on a less grand scale than the Brigade and, on occasion, the boys were encouraged to take an active role in planning worship. This marked a departure from the traditional masculine qualities encouraged within the Jewish Lads' Brigade and in non-uniformed groups. For Guide groups, religion was less marked by gender expectations than in other Jewish girls' clubs. Whilst Guides did include a domestic element of observance not found within the Scouts or the JLB, this was minimal in comparison with the differences between the non-uniformed boys' and girls' clubs. The attendance of Guide companies at synagogue parades and the importance of *Chanucah* within the Guide calendar also marked a difference from non-uniformed girls' clubs. Indeed, for Guides religion was less marked by expectations of femininity than their non-uniformed counterparts. This is hardly surprising as the association maintained close links with the Scouts and was seen as encouraging tomboyism through their activities. Though most organizations sought to highlight femininity, the more masculine religious observance of Jewish Guide groups certainly would not have helped to counter this tendency and thus the membership of Guide groups was likely limited to those who were more comfortable with less traditional observance for girls. The JLB, Scouts and Guides all operated within national organizations that allowed the groups to make alterations to their programme according to locality (such as the promotion of kilts in Scottish Scout groups) and to financial circumstance through the introduction of cheaper uniforms and savings schemes. The adaptations, however, served to identify each group as different from the national model in the same way that Scouts and Guides could symbolize their belonging or their difference through the purchase of certain uniform items. The uniforming of youth groups within the Scouts and the Guides can therefore be seen not only to have applied to clothing, but within the Guides and the Scouts, to some extent at least, to gender divisions within religion. For the JLB, however, religion served to heighten gender divisions in line with wider expectations.

CHAPTER 5

The West Central Jewish Girls' Club, 1893–1939

The clubs looked at in previous chapters, and indeed all but a small minority of the Jewish youth groups in the early twentieth century, were formed in line with Orthodox Judaism. However, within London two of the largest clubs – the West Central Jewish Girls' Club (WCGC) and the Oxford and St George's Jewish Boys' Club – existed not within Orthodox Judaism, but within Liberal Judaism. The following two chapters will look at these clubs in turn to show the ways in which the Liberal clubs were able to include religion, which reflected the ideals of the Liberal Jewish movement.

There are limited surviving records for the West Central club as most of these were destroyed in the Second World War when the club building was hit in an air raid. The documents that do remain are printed sources, including a number of books written by Lilian Montagu (the founder of the West Central Girls' Clubs), newspapers from the Jewish community, records of sermons and a limited number of oral history testimonies of former club members conducted during the 1990s. Montagu wrote a number of books focusing on her religious and social work that provide a detailed (though somewhat idealized) explanation of the motives of her club work and her beliefs of the religious nature of the club. Whilst the documents used do not include a large amount of evidence from the members themselves, these sources do provide a sense of the club's character. This chapter will examine the ways in which the West Central Girls' Club incorporated prayer and celebrated Sabbath services and religious festivals as well as the presentation of a number of religiously significant gifts from the young women to the club leaders. This section will add nuance to the work of Spence and demonstrate that in contrast to Livshin's work on Jewish youth in Manchester, religious elements played a key role in the life of the West Central Girls' Club and adhered firmly to gender norms. This religion was, however, of a firmly Liberal Jewish character. Prior to examining the work of the club, it is vital to understand Liberal Judaism as a movement. Whilst this section by no means provides a detailed account of the origins, it offers an overview of Liberal Judaism and the criticisms levied upon it by the Jewish community.

Liberal Jewish thinking emerged in the late nineteenth century and by the 1920s Liberal Judaism had taken on distinct beliefs and structures. Before the Second World War, Liberal Judaism was confined to London and was influenced by key individuals, namely Claude Montefiore, Lily Montagu and Israel Mattuck. It grew in popularity in the first decades of the twentieth century: in 1912, it consisted of approximately 150 members, in 1915 this had grown to nearly 450 and by the mid-1920s membership had expanded to around 1,500.[1] Despite the growth of the movement, Kessler notes that there is a paucity of scholarly work on Liberal Judaism's origins in England; indeed, many (though not all) of the accounts of Liberal Judaism have focused not on the movement itself, but on individuals associated with it.[2]

Prior to the emergence of Liberal Judaism, Anglo-Jewry was largely Orthodox with a small Reform Jewish community who believed in 'elevating the Bible while derogating the Talmud'.[3] Unlike its German counterpart, Reform Judaism in Britain failed to attract a large number of adherents and only spread to three cities outside of London.[4] Orthodox Judaism was centrally organized under the auspices of the Chief Rabbi and was largely concerned with maintaining an acceptable English form of Judaism. The United Synagogue, the umbrella organization for Orthodox synagogues, was 'concerned with the preservation of Judaism in an English milieu, through a framework of a large modern English organization and

---

1   Daniel R. Langton, *Claude Montefiore: His Life and Thoughts* (London: Vallentine Mitchell, 2002), p. 89.

2   See for example, Edward Kessler (ed.), *A Reader of Early Liberal Judaism: The Writings of Israel Abrahams, Claude Montefiore, Lily Montagu and Israel Mattuck* (London: Vallentine Mitchell, 2004), p. 1; and Langton, *Claude Montefiore*.

3   Michael Meyer, *Responses to Modernity: A History of the Reform Movement in Judaism* (Detroit, MI: Wayne State University Press, 1988), p. 172.

4   For more information on Reform Judaism in Europe see Meyer, *Responses to Modernity*.

by synagogues of the Western model'.[5] The Reform community, which had adopted limited reforms to practices, emerged in the 1840s and by the end of the nineteenth century had stagnated. Orthodoxy remained the dominant form of Judaism within England.

From the background of inconsistent religious observances of many Orthodox Jews, advances in the scientific understanding of the Bible brought about by Darwin and growing criticism of Biblical accuracy, Liberal Judaism developed as a 'protest movement' against Orthodoxy, particularly for some middle-class Jews.[6] A number of speeches and writings from Montefiore helped to develop early Liberal Jewish thinking and in 1899 Montagu's article 'The Spiritual Possibilities of Judaism Today' published in the *Jewish Quarterly Review*, laid the foundations for the creation of the Jewish Religious Union (JRU), the forerunner to Liberal Judaism, in 1902.[7] Early Liberal Judaism and the Liberal Jewish clubs were particularly concerned with creating a 'living Judaism' to 'help Anglo-Jewry redress by revitalizing the religious life of the community' and this clearly captures its opposition to Orthodoxy. By 1910, when the organization opened its first synagogue, Liberal Judaism had firmly established itself as a completely separate organization, setting itself apart from both Orthodoxy and Reform traditions.[8]

The nature of Liberal Judaism evolved and over the first three decades its self-definition became more concrete. In 1891, Montefiore formulated a straightforward definition establishing what would become the basic beliefs of Liberal Judaism. In a response to Biblical criticisms he stated that the two foundations of Judaism – the belief in a theistic God and the moral law – would remain the same. He claimed that it was the 'practices and rituals peculiar to Judaism', which set Jewish beliefs apart from those of other religious traditions.[9] In 1920, Montefiore established a code of beliefs for Liberal Judaism, similar to that provided by Maimonides' thirteen

<hr>

5   Kessler, *Reader*, p. 3.
6   Langton, *Claude Montefiore*, p. 17.
7   Kessler, *Reader*, p. 6.
8   Langton, *Claude Montefiore*, p. 77.
9   Ibid., pp. 72–3.

principles of faith but taking into account Biblical criticism. He stated that Liberal Judaism was concerned with

> Accepting results of Biblical criticism
> Abandoning doctrines of verbal inspiration
> Accepting a human element in the Hebrew Bible
> Accepting moral imperfection and growth within the Hebrew Bible
> Accepting the concept of progressive revelation
> Regarding the past as authoritative but not binding
> Separating the 'universal' from the particular
> Emphasizing the mission of Israel to the world.[10]

This code of belief not only sets out Liberal Jewish in opposition to Orthodoxy, but this opposition establishes the essential tenets of Liberal Judaism.[11] Montefiore and other figures within Liberal Judaism stressed that the two denominations were not opposed to each other. In Montefiore's monograph on Liberal Judaism, he stressed that 'Liberal Judaism was still a legal religion', underscoring the similarities with Orthodoxy and high-lighting its essential Jewishness.[12]

The differences between Orthodoxy and Liberal Judaism can be seen in the discussions of what Liberal Judaism was. Liberal Jewish practices served to emphasize further the differences between Liberal Judaism and Orthodoxy. The first circular promoted by the JRU in 1902 advertised adapted services, which were held on Saturday afternoons, were approximately one hour long, conducted in English with music and instrumental accompaniment and had no division of men and women.[13] This

---

10   Langton, *Claude Montefiore* p. 81. Montefiore rejected a number of Maimonides' principles, mostly those that were at odds with Biblical criticism. Liberal Judaism did not believe in article 6, which stated that the words of the prophets were true, article 7, that the prophecy of Moses was absolutely true, article 8, that the entire Torah was given to Moses, and number 9, that the Torah may never be changed. Liberal Judaism also objected to article 12, which asserts faith in the coming of the Messiah, instead stressing the coming of a Messianic age.

11   Ibid.

12   Claude G. Montefiore, *Outlines of Liberal Judaism for the Use of Parents and Teachers* (London: MacMillan, 1923), p. 220.

13   Langton, *Claude Montefiore*, p. 81.

demonstrated a departure from Orthodox services, which were conducted in Hebrew, took place on Saturday mornings and featured no instrumental accompaniment with men and women seated separately. In addition to demonstrating its rejection of a number of Orthodox traditions, these Liberal services stressed the modern elements of worship which allowed for Sabbath employment and took into account an element of gender equality as well as calling for a return to the 'spirituality' of religion, rather than basing itself solely on tradition. Langton has highlighted the important differences between Liberal and Orthodox Judaism. Liberal Judaism was anti-Zionist, held a different stance on the authority of Rabbinic Literature and took a sympathetic view towards Christianity.[14] Much as the theoretical basis for Liberal Judaism defined itself against Orthodoxy, so did the practices, which stressed the differences between what Liberal Jews saw as out-dated Orthodox Judaism and a modern Liberal tradition.

As Liberal Judaism defined itself in opposition to Orthodox Judaism, it understandably faced a large amount of criticism from members of the Jewish community. Public figures attacked Liberal Judaism and the JRU from its earliest days and the Liberal Jewish Clubs were not exempt. The Chief Rabbi called the JRU a 'menace to Judaism' and both the *Jewish Chronicle* and the *Jewish World* newspapers frequently attacked Montefiore and the movement.[15] In particular, the way in which the services were run was a source of complaint for many, with the early JRU services seen as un-Jewish because of the scarceness of Hebrew prayers, lack of Scripture readings and the use of hymns taken from 'unacceptable' (Christian) sources.[16] The Sunday afternoon services held in the first Liberal synagogue were seen as 'a menace to Judaism calculated to sap the most sacred institution of our race' and Montefiore himself was denounced as 'an anti-Jewish missionary'.[17] In abandoning many of the traditions in Orthodoxy and adopting a more Anglicized and at times Christianized religion, Liberal Judaism opened itself to attacks from traditional Orthodox Jewry: 'opposition to the traditional

---

14   Langton, *Claude Montefiore*, p. 74.
15   Kessler, *Reader*, p. 7, and Langton, *Claude Montefiore*, pp. 138–9.
16   Langton, *Claude Montefiore*, p. 79.
17   Ibid., pp. 82 and 139.

Jewish institutions combined with the failure to provide something people could recognize as a replacement, goes a long way to explaining why the Jewishness of Montefiore's movement was so often called into question.'[18] Despite the criticism that the movement faced, Liberal Judaism continued to develop and attract members. The role of the West Central Jewish Girls' Club and the Oxford and St George's Jewish Youth Club were pivotal in promoting Liberal Judaism in London.

What is significant about both of these clubs is their growth. Both clubs started small, but by 1939 had become settlements (a neighbourhood social welfare organization designed to improve living standards within a certain area). Both settlements incorporated boys' and girls' clubs, welfare centres, employment bureaus and health visitors among other services. Only two of the Orthodox clubs grew in this way (the Brady Club and the Stepney Club) and both of these did so much later in their history. The settlement movement began in London with the creation of Toynbee Hall in 1884. It began with the idea that all individuals should take part in their community. This concept was applied to impoverished areas and encouraged university-educated men to live and interact with the lower classes in order to promote social change whilst avoiding what settlement activists saw as the patronizing elements of existing poor relief.[19] After the opening of Toynbee Hall, settlements followed across London and by 1900 existed in cities including Glasgow, Bristol, Manchester and Edinburgh as well as outside the UK. The Jewish settlement movement, which began later than its Christian counterparts, likewise shared the aim for upper and middle classes to live with the people they sought to help. The Oxford and St George's Settlement (later the Bernhard Baron Oxford and St George's Settlement) grew from the boys' club after the realization of Rose Henriques (née Loewe) that the community needed an infant

---

18   Ibid., p. 140.

19   S. A. Barnett, 'University Settlements', in W. Reason (ed.), *University and Social Settlements* (London: Methuen, 1898), pp. 11–27; and Katherine Bradley, 'Poverty and Philanthropy in Central London 1918–1959: The University Settlements' (unpublished doctoral thesis, University of London, Institute of Historical Research, 2006), pp. 12–14.

welfare provision.[20] This opened in the boys' club premises, which was below the lodgings of the club leaders. Similarly, the Stepney settlement grew from the work of Alice Model and her Day Nursery, which became incorporated into the boys' club.[21] The outbreak of war in 1914 encouraged the rapid growth of the Jewish settlements as they were expanded to help individuals and contribute to the national cause. The Jewish settlements, whilst beginning later and evolving more organically through identifying community needs, followed the pattern of social welfare found within the settlement movement more generally.

The development of the Liberal Jewish clubs into settlements marks a significant difference between the scope of Liberal groups and their Orthodox counterparts. Part of this can be attributed to the support given by Montefiore. Montefiore was dedicated to philanthropy, supporting a number of causes including the Hartley Institute (later the University of Southampton) and the advancement of Liberal Judaism, but 'a favoured cause was the advancement of women and children. He was associated with the work of Lily Montagu in the West Central Club for Jewish Girls and with Basil Henriques in the St George's and Bernhard Baron Settlement in the East End.'[22] This support, both financial and otherwise, helped both clubs to grow in their early years. Whilst many clubs lacked funds in the first few years of their existence, this was not such a concern for the Liberal groups. Additionally, as Liberal Judaism was an evolving movement, this allowed both Henriques and Montagu to develop their own personal beliefs in line with their club work, allowing their commitment to charitable causes to advance their religious views. Whilst the development of the settlements is not the focus of this chapter, it is important to consider that the settlement grew out of the leaders' Jewishness, as well as the success of the clubs.

It is remarkable that both clubs were able to attract members from the largely immigrant, Orthodox population. The Liberal Judaism promoted in both groups was clearly at odds with the Orthodox practices; however, the increase in membership demonstrates that the groups were able to

---

20　Rose L. Heniques, *50 Years in Stepney*, Pamphlet, 1966, pp. 8–9.

21　Ibid., pp. 9–10.

22　Langton, *Claude Montefiore*, p. 11.

attract members in spite of this, though some defenders suggested that
Henriques did not try to influence children away from their parents' religious traditions This is likely due to the personalities and commitment of
the club leaders. In both instances, it is evident that the leaders' personalities helped to make the clubs a success and place the groups as part of the
London Jewish landscape. Indeed, both clubs were very much attached to
the legacy of their leaders. It is possible to speak not of the West Central
Club, but of Montagu's club and the same can be said for Henriques. The
personalities and beliefs of both individuals were therefore pivotal in the
creation of the groups and within their success.

Background and Ethos

Lilian Montagu was born in 1873 to observant Orthodox parents. During
her lifetime, she campaigned for industrial reform, encouraged girls to join
trade unions, and was known for her pioneering social work amongst Jewish
working girls in London. In 1937, as a result of her work within the community, she was appointed OBE. As a teenager, she began to question the
traditions of Orthodoxy and she became a leading figure in the creation of
Liberal Judaism, despite opposition from her father, which likely increased
her enthusiasm for the cause.[23] Montagu was involved with Liberal Judaism
throughout her life and the West Central Jewish Girls' Club was frequently
tied to her personal beliefs. The Liberal nature of religion included within
the club attracted criticism from figures within the Orthodox community;
the Chief Rabbi in particular was concerned that Montagu was having a
damaging effect on the Jewish community.

23   For a thorough understanding of Montagu's life see Jean Spence, 'Working for Jewish
      Girls: Lily Montagu, Girls' Clubs and Industrial Reform 1890–1914', *Women's History
      Review*, 13 (2004), 491–509 and Geoffrey Alderman, 'Montagu, Lilian Helen (1873–
      1963)', *Oxford Dictionary of National Biography*, Oxford University Press, 2004
      <http://www.oxforddnb.com/view/article/40837> [accessed 13 September 2013].
      Langton, *Claude Montefiore* p. 78.

Like other clubs that emerged at the end of the nineteenth century (both Jewish and non-Jewish), the West Central Girls' Club existed to provide 'wholesome' recreation for young Jewish women who were largely impoverished, foreign-born or of foreign parentage and were from Orthodox backgrounds. Providing 'wholesome' entertainment was a method of policing girls' leisure time. Cox, in her work on girlhood, welfare and justice, noted that girls' clubs from all communities in Britain shared the same aims, specifically 'to divert the girls from dangerous pleasures ... to encourage their girls to keep to their particular faith; and to provide, in some cases, basic skills training to allow girls to support themselves economically and to learn the lessons of regular work'.[24] The entertainment provided by the West Central Girls' Club included both lectures and educational classes designed to attract members away from undesirable pastimes, such as visiting music halls or socializing on the streets. Girls were able to attend the club each evening (except for the Sabbath) at a small cost. The club opened in Dean Street, London in 1893 where a small group of girls attended who were housed in one room. Montagu, along with her Sister Marian, assisted with the formation of the club inspired by the former's volunteer work with a Bible Class.

Montagu and club leaders were keen from the outset to establish that the work of the club was firmly rooted in religious principles. Both the motto, 'If I strive not after my own salvation, who shall strive for me, and if not now, when?' (taken from Hillel's Maxim), and the object, 'to bring brightness and refinement into the lives of Jewish working girls' show the club leaders' aim that a religious ethos underpin the both the aims and daily activities of the club.[25] The religious element within the motto is clear; within the object, 'brightness' referred to both a spiritual and social 'brightness', which combined to situate religion at the centre of club life. Montagu believed the club owed some of its success to the religious element of their work and in 1911 she stated that the accomplishments of the club were due to 'the fact that our club work is inspired by a living faith in

24   Pamela Cox, *Bad Girls in Britain: Gender, Justice and Welfare, 1900–1950* (Basingstoke: Palgrave Macmillan, 2013), p. 69.
25   Levy, *The West Central Story* p. 2.

God, and we seek to express our religion, our Judaism, in the daily life of our club, believing that we serve our God when we serve one another'.[26] The idea of a 'living faith' underscored the Jewish nature of the WCGC, and this remained constant throughout the life of the club. Through the emphasis on spirituality in the club's aims, the club conformed to gender norms which expected that generally, women should be more spiritual than men (though the examples of Claude Montefiore and Basil Henriques within Progressive Judaism are significant counter-examples). By focussing club work on this appropriately gendered version of religion through both the motto and founding statement, the club showed that its religious work was twofold; it sought to provide for the religious needs of the members at the same time as presenting a commitment to providing religion which enabled the development of the girls' identities within wider English gender norms.

The other club leaders promoted religious spirit through activities as well as through their own personal faith; in particular, Montagu played a pivotal role in the development of the club's Jewish character. Montagu's role with the development of Liberal Judaism, and her own personal beliefs, understandably influenced the way the WCGC included religious practices into its work. This was acknowledged by Montagu:

> I have been influenced by Liberal Jewish teachings and believed that if we would serve our God who is father of all men, we must translate His word in the changing circumstances of life. It was important that we should ask all those under our influence to discover God's word, and try to live in accordance with it in our everyday lives. If they lived truly by His word, they could worship him all day long, whatever they were doing, and not only at Sabbath services.[27]

The West Central Girls' Club also took the religious beliefs of other adult volunteers seriously, as Montagu felt that club leaders had an important role to play in producing the religious spirit of the club that members would

---

26   London Metropolitan Archives (hereafter LMA), ACC Lily Montagu, *Address Given by the Hon. Lily Montagu at the New Theatre on the Occasion of the Annual Display of Work*, 1911, 3529/3/16.

27   Lily H. Montagu, *My Club and I: The Story of the West Central Jewish Club* (London: Herbert Joseph, 1941), p. 41.

appreciate. In Montagu's review of the work of the WCGC, she commented on the religiosity of the leaders, claiming that it was through the example of the leaders that a religious element was included within club life.[28] Through personal beliefs of the leaders, the club was able to emphasize its Jewish identity and promote a 'Jewish spirit', which promoted acceptably English identities amongst the girls. Certainly, the Liberal Jewish element was similar to English traditions in a way that Orthodoxy, with its adherence to ancient traditions and customs, was not. By promoting Liberal religion, club members were encouraged to become familiar with and adapt to more typically English behaviours than Orthodox traditions allowed for.

Religious Activities

Like other Jewish girls' clubs, the WCGC held prayers at the end of each evening, which included hymns and prayers in Hebrew and English, as well as the *Shema* in order for 'the real meaning of [club] work be brought home to each of [the] members.'[29] In contrast to Orthodox Judaism, which used formulaic prayer, prayers with the club were extempore and thus had more similarities to prayer in Protestant England, providing the members further exposure to English traditions. Montagu felt that the girls valued the inclusion of these prayers within the club routine stating that the members 'responded most readily to this effort and constantly told me that these "made up" prayers meant a great deal to them'.[30] Attendance at the services was compulsory for all members who had been to the club that evening. The compulsory nature of the services is something that was only found within girls' clubs and highlights the importance of prayer in acceptably feminine religion.

28　Ibid., p. 48.
29　*JC*, 22 February 1901.
30　Lily H. Montagu, *The Faith of a Jewish Woman* (London: George Allen and Unwin, 1943), p. 21.

Montagu viewed the services as a crucial way of instilling religious spirit amongst the members and engaging the young people with their Jewish identities. She claimed that the members were 'glad to add their supporting faith to the proclamation of the *Shema*, by which we conclude our brief evening service'.[31] Unfortunately, there is little direct evidence from the members to support Montagu's belief. One example, however, is provided from 1910, when a younger member at the children's service was overheard praying for a club leader. The child said 'Please God, I am going for my holiday to Ealing. When you go for your holiday, please do not forget the lady who is ill.'[32] Whilst this incident certainly does not provide evidence to Montagu's claim that the prayer services made the members aware of their Jewishness, it indicates that for some of the members at least, the prayer service had an impact on their religiosity. As Orthodox prayer followed strict patterns, the child who made up this prayer could only have been influenced by her experiences of prayer within Liberal Judaism, which allowed for this type of extempore prayer. The use of prayer in this way corresponds to Montagu's notions of a child's relationship to prayer: 'all observances should be connected with prayer in the child's mind – prayer in which he must take part, which he must understand thoroughly'.[33] The creation of the prayer for the ill leader demonstrates that the child understood the nature of prayer itself and was able to take part in the process of prayer as supported by Montagu. The prayer was thus Liberal in its character and in moving away from the Orthodox patterns and expectations of prayer, fitted more closely with English religious traditions found within Protestantism, therefore helping to Anglicize the young members.

In addition to the prayer services at the end of the club evenings, Montagu promoted prayer to club members with the production of a booklet *Prayers for Working Girls* in 1895. The book, which encouraged the members to pray in their everyday life, featured prayers for apprentices, domestic workers, those whose work prevented them from keeping

31   Ibid., p. 48.
32   LMA, ACC, Lily Montagu, *Address Given by the Hon Lily Montagu at the Queens Theatre on the Occasion of the Annual Display of Work 1910*, 3529/3/15.
33   Lily H. Montagu, *Thoughts on Judaism* (London: Adelphi, 1904), p. 69.

the Sabbath and those who had recently become engaged or married.[34] Girls' who fell into these categories were the target demographic for the group and it is likely that Montagu saw these groups as 'at-risk' of losing their religious faith. The prayer book would have helped to counter the threat of growing irreligion, which both increased employment on the Sabbath and marriage outside of the Jewish community were seen to have contributed to. These prayers featured in the pamphlet allowed for the girls to maintain their Jewishness at the same time as encouraging them to continue assimilating into English society through acceptable employment for girls such as domestic service and through the pursuit of the ideal of marriage. The emphasis on prayers and the content of the service remained consistent throughout the period, although there were changes in some of the subjects discussed, mirroring changes seen within wider society. The continued importance placed on prayer fell within Liberal Jewish ideals of the centrality and relevance of prayer, demonstrating one of the ways in which Montagu's own beliefs influences club work.

In addition to promoting the Jewish character of the club through prayers, the club leaders encouraged Sabbath observance amongst its members as a way further to promote Jewish identities. The club, from its beginnings, remained closed on Friday nights as Montagu stated that 'it desired to strengthen not supplant the love of home'.[35] The club therefore encouraged the members to undertake the pivotal role of women in creating the Sabbath meal and in welcoming the Sabbath, a role that fell within idealized English gender roles for Christian women as well as Jewish ones. As it did through the circulation of the prayer book, the club sought to provide practical means of strengthening the girls' involvement within the Sabbath by producing a Friday evening service. Badges, depicting the Shield of David, were also distributed amongst members and it was hoped these would encourage home worship by using the specifically Jewish imagery to provide a visual reminder of their faith and religious obligations.[36]

---

34   Levy, West Central Story, p. 3 and Montagu, Faith, pp. 23–4.
35   *JC*, 22 February 1901.
36   Montagu, *My Club and I*, p. 44.

In addition to encouraging involvement at home, the club adopted additional measures in order to increase formal Sabbath observance, despite the gendered expectations that girls should distance themselves from formal religious worship. For girls who worked on Saturday mornings (the usual time for Sabbath services), the club introduced its own service held on Saturday afternoons. Young people had been condemned by Jewish religious society for missing Sabbath services due to work or social engagements. The club, by providing afternoon services, allowed the members to maintain employment and their faith at the same time. Unlike Orthodox services, which were conducted in Hebrew, the club services were mainly given in English, helping to promote national pride and pride in the English language – an important consideration for the club leaders when working with immigrant girls. The services also differed from Orthodox ones as only prayers with a specific meaning for those in attendance were included rather than including traditional ceremonial prayers and instrumental music was included, reflecting services given by the JRU. These services were thus Liberal in their character and therefore in opposition to the Orthodoxy of many of the members, large numbers of whom would have come from Orthodox Eastern European backgrounds. This does not appear to have been a barrier to the members; one girl, herself Orthodox, recalled attending these services as she liked the way Montagu conducted them and stated that many of the Orthodox girls similarly attended the services despite their Liberal stance.'[37] The services were, as a result of the Liberal characteristics, more accessible to the young members and thus increased the exposure of young members to religion. This helps to explain the success of the club in attracting girls from primarily Orthodox backgrounds. Whilst the inclusion of a service itself is more attuned to expectations of worship for boys, the informal nature of the worship was more in line with feminine expectations, although also reflecting the informality found within Liberal Judaism. The influence of these services grew within the early years of the club. Initially the services were small, informal gatherings but by the end of the 1930s, these were increasingly formal – though not as formal as those

---

37   JML, *Interview with Esther Goldstein (Neé Levine) Interviewer Iris Dove January 14 1990*, Tape 215.

within Orthodoxy. This reflects the growing confidence of Montagu as a religious leader who, in line with the increased acceptance of women as preachers within Liberal Judaism, took on a more structured role. Sabbath observance, as a result, became more formal within the West Central Club, although still not as formal as services held by Orthodox boys' clubs.

The content of sermons encouraged club members to remain loyal to their religion and to ensure that they were working to be 'good Jews', as well as working to promote gendered expectations. In 1914, Montagu delivered a sermon based on a play presented by members of the dramatics class. In this play, a deeply religious grandmother sees her son, a *Yom Kippur* Jew (one who only attends synagogue on the high holidays) move to America. Montagu used this to advocate the importance for young people to remain religious and ensure that they pass on their faith to their future families.[38] This reflected gendered concerns that women were responsible for ensuring the continued religious observances of their family. At a service in 1937, Montagu again emphasized the work needed to remain Jewish, asking the girls to 'carry always this thought that *faith* and *effort* are needed today if we would feel at one with God'.[39] These sermons were a key way for Montagu to promote the notion that religion was something that needed to be worked at, particularly for girls who had a familial responsibility to promote religiosity. These services show continuity in the club's religious aims, as they both, despite being twenty-three years apart, promoted similar themes, emphasizing the centrality of religion to the individual and to the family through stressing the importance of the woman's role in ensuring the Jewish upbringing of her family.

The WCGC held services on religious holidays, ensuring that the girls could find a place to worship at religiously significant times of the year. The club, during its early years, included services on the High Holy Days such as at *Yom Kippur*, the holiest day in the Jewish calendar, where visiting ministers were invited to speak.[40] The visitors were often connected with

---

38　LMA, ACC Lily Montagu, *Address Given at the West Central Jewish Working Girls' Club on Saturday February 28 1914*, 3529/3/19.

39　LMA, ACC Lily Montagu, *Children's Sermon*, [1937], 3529/3/6/B (original emphasis).

40　Montagu, *My Club and I*, p. 26

the Liberal Jewish movement and included Claude Montefiore, the leader of Liberal Judaism in England. Despite the Liberal associations, there is, as with the Sabbath services, no evidence that this dissuaded Orthodox girls from attending. Like Orthodox girls' clubs looked at in chapter one, the club provided opportunities for the members to be involved in the planning of celebrations. A selection of young members formed a committee, overseen by a club leader, to plan *Chanucah* parties and make gifts for the younger siblings of those involved with the group – a tradition that continued throughout the club's history.[41] The skills that the members gained from creating entertainment for children based on a religious festival reflected a gendered expectation that girls – as future wives and mothers – were expected to be skilled at childcare and providing domestic entertainment.

Summer Holidays

The club, in addition to the activities run on evenings and weekends, held a summer holiday each year, providing seaside recreation for its members, often at a subsidized rate. Originally, the club provided one holiday a year, but by the First World War, as the club grew, so did the number of holiday opportunities. In all instances, religion was a significant part of the experience. As in daily club life, prayer formed a vital part of daily worship. As in the club services, the prayer on holidays was extempore and made relevant to the girls, allowing the members to explore their own emotions, reflecting Liberal Judaism and therefore a more Protestant experience than that provided within Orthodox prayer. Discussions on religious topics were also a key feature of the holiday through nightly 'talks under the tree', which encouraged girls to examine their religious beliefs by asking questions such as 'can a good Jew be a bad man?'[42] This sort of questioning was a further indication of the Liberal Jewish character of the club and was thus directly

41 Levy, *The West Central Story*, p. 12 and p. 25.
42 Montagu, *Faith*, p. 21.

opposed to the Orthodox traditions of the young people which encouraged its adherents to unquestioningly follow the laws laid down in the Bible.

In addition to prayer and religious discussions, religion was promoted on holidays through the Sabbath. The Friday evening events included the traditional family meal, during which the lighting of the Sabbath candles (a woman's religious obligation) was emphasized:

> We had our little service before supper. Everybody wore her freshest clothes and there prevailed a lovely feeling of friendliness and peace. In lighting the Sabbath lights we burned up any ugly remains of little misunderstandings and dissensions. The emblem of purity suggested self-control for the individual and the realization of family purity. We had pleasant readings after the service and talks on fundamentals and extempore prayer, which revealed our strivings and hopes, and brought unity between us and all the homes we had left in London. We felt the spirit of our beautiful Sabbath bride.[43]

The recollections of the Sabbath meal and the worship mirror those found within recollections of Sabbath observances within the Orthodox Jewish Girls' Club. In both clubs the details of the candles, the emotional feel to the service and the details of the clothing worn, were mentioned specifically. These accounts demonstrate a very domestic expression of religion, one that enhanced the dual identities of the members as Jews and as English women.

In addition to the domestic observance of the Sabbath meal held during the year, Sabbath services played a role in the club's holidays. When the group stayed in hotels they ensured that a room was acquired in which they would not be disturbed and during a trip to Belgium in 1939, it was reported that 'the club will lose a day of its holiday so as to avoid travelling on the Sabbath'.[44] Although the service was a feature of the club holiday, no accounts featured recollections of the services indicating that greater emphasis was placed on the domestic element of the Sabbath meal, rather than the more formal element of worship. This reflects the gendered experience within Judaism (and within wider English society). In Jewish boys' clubs, the emphasis was placed on ceremonial aspects such as elaborate rituals, services and parades, neglecting the domestic contrasting with the emphasis

43   Ibid., p. 26.
44   Levy, *The West Central Story*, p. 7 and *JC*, 26 June 1939.

given in girls' clubs. In this way, the West Central Girls' Club followed the traditions of other Jewish girls' clubs in rejecting the emphasis placed on the ceremonial, preferring instead to emphasize the more feminine elements.

There are limited existing records of holiday Sabbath sermons which are published versions of the services given by Montagu and indicate that the services emphasized the feminine expectations of marriage and family life. At the 1916 holiday, Montagu led two Sabbath services, which focused on love specifically the importance of parental love, love between a husband and wife, a brother and sister and on friendship. During the sermon the girls were told that true love was part of their duty to God emphasizing the importance of marriage in fulfilling religious duty: '... marriage may be holy; since love is a form of worship given to us by God'.[45] This emphasizes the importance of the feminine responsibilities of being a wife and mother. Along with the attention placed on the family meal, this clearly indicates that the club was concerned with promoting both Jewish and English family values, expecting the members to adhere to these norms.

With the limited remaining records, it is difficult to ascertain how the members themselves viewed the religious work of the club. The evidence of gifts given to the club leaders on two occasions provide (somewhat limited) evidence that the girls were, at the very least, aware of the work undertaken in this respect. In 1923 at the end of the Sabbath service, the young people presented a *Sepher Torah* (a scroll of the *Torah*) to the Montagu sisters and Miss Lewis, the three most prominent leaders at the time. The members stated that:

> We ... ask you to accept this scroll as a gift from us to be used for club services, realising that all your work has been done in obedience to the Laws of God, and that through personal influence ... many of us have been awakened to the full significance of the laws and teachings of Judaism ... We trust that with the Law of God placed permanently (by its members' desire) in our club, it may grow from strength to strength and become a worthy testimony to the work of our dear and beloved leaders.[46]

In presenting an item of religious significance, rather than a secular one, the members showed that they were aware the leaders wanted a *Sepher*

---

45   LL, M379, Lily Montagu, *Addresses given on the Club Holiday at Littlehampton 1916*.
46   *JC*, 18 January 1923.

Torah in the club, rather than continuing to borrow one from local congregations. The speech also shows the girls were, to some extent, aware of the club leaders' efforts in getting the girls to engage with Judaism. That several members were 'awakened' to Judaism as a result of their involvement within the club, demonstrates that the leaders had some success in influencing the members to live a more religiously-minded life.

A similar presentation occurred in 1929, when both the Montagu sisters were presented with religiously significant gifts. The gifts were purchased through donations from over 1,600 former club members and were presented with an address from one of the active club members:

> To Miss Marian, the faithful friend … they presented an Ark and to Miss Lily also a reading desk, both silent messengers of God's word to be used for the glorification of the Jewish faith. No gifts could be more appropriate to both who have laboured so unceasingly to spread the Jewish faith. These gifts cannot adequately express how grateful we are for your life and work. You have made our life the better and richer for having known you and you have given the best in friendship and service, all the while proving by your lives that by your faith you live.[47]

This shows that both members and former members continued to be mindful of the managers' efforts to introduce a religious element into the life of the club. It is possible that the members were simply saying what they knew the leaders wanted to hear; however, the repetition of these sentiments on two occasions combined with the limited testimonies from former members looked at earlier indicates that this was not the case. Instead, a number of girls demonstrated a heightened religious faith as a result of their club life.

West Central Girls' Club and Religion

Despite assertions from previous studies that have recognized Montagu's religiosity but questioned that of the club, it is clear from the examples of how the West Central Club included religion in their work, that religion

47   *JC*, 12 July 1929.

was *not* neglected. Religious work was vital in the development of the identities of young people within the West Central Club and these activities contained more nuance than has previously been assumed. As a result of the wide reach of the club, the religious activities not only influenced the identities of young people but were also significant in creating identities within the Anglo-Jewish community as a whole. Club leaders, led by Montagu, were able to provide for the religious needs of the girls through prayer and weekly services. These activities helped to fill a gap between the what the leaders perceived as the ideal religious experience and the religious experience members had within their homes. The recollection of club members and records of the speeches and gifts given by club members to the leaders demonstrate that the girls were aware of the religious element of club work and, to some extent, to the efforts to which club leaders went to include religion within club life. Criticism of the club alleging that the it was run on Liberal Jewish lines, was well-founded; although, this did not appear to limit the engagement of the young people within the religious life of the group. The Liberal traditions helped to present a more 'Anglicized' image of religion, reflecting modern Enlightenment thinking within wider English society. The creation of acceptable English Jewish women, in line with recognized notions of femininity, was central to the religious character of the club throughout the period.

CHAPTER 6

The Oxford and St George's Jewish Youth Club, 1913–1939

Born in 1890, the youngest of five children, Basil Henriques, like Lily Montagu from the West Central Girls' Club, grew up in a background which emphasized religion and charity work. In contrast to Montagu's Orthodox upbringing, Henriques was brought up in a Reform tradition where he 'was taught to kneel in prayer, and understood Judaism to be based on faith and love of God rather than upon a body of ceremonies, all of which echoed contemporary Evangelical Protestant practices and left him almost entirely unfamiliar with those of Jewish Orthodoxy'.[1] His early beliefs clearly resemble those of Liberal Judaism, and certainly enabled Henriques to develop the religious element in the Oxford and St George's Club.

Henriques began the Oxford and St George's Jewish Lads' Club in 1913 with a total of twenty-five boys aged between 14 and 18. By 1939, the club had expanded to include a girls section and membership was at 3,000. After finishing his studies at Oxford, Henriques moved to St-George's-in-the-East in London's East End in order to create a club for boys, modelled on the time he spent volunteering at the Christian Oxford and Bermondsey Mission. The aspect that Henriques particularly admired was the way in which religion was used in everyday life at the mission, reflecting his own upbringing. He sought to create Jewish clubs that incorporated religion in the same way. At the time, the population of St-George's-in-the-East was heavily immigrant, filled with boys from Yiddish-speaking families who observed strict Orthodox customs and lived almost entirely within their

---

1   Daniel R. Langton, *Claude Montefiore: His Life and Thoughts* (London: Vallentine Mitchell, 2002), p. 66.

own Jewish enclave. In contrast, due to his Reform upbringing, Henriques was unfamiliar with many of the Orthodox practices and was unable to speak Yiddish. Even so, he was able to start and run a successful club in the area. For Henriques, who disliked the way Orthodox teaching allowed the boys to memorize certain religious obligations without understanding their meaning or feeling the spirit of religion, he desired to teach the boys the ways in which Judaism could be relevant to their everyday life, and thus absorbed Liberal Jewish teachings into his club.[2]

Very little has been written on the history of the Oxford and St George's Club, beyond a number of short accounts from relatives of the club leaders, passing reference to the club in the few biographies of Basil Henriques and mentions in a few volumes on the Jewish East End. As a result, the impact of the religious programming of the group on the character of Anglo-Jewry has not been discussed. Like the West Central Club, the group involved large numbers of London Jewry and, as such, deserves to be studied in order to fully understand the development of the religious character of Anglo-Jewry prior to and beyond the Second World War.

In this section I will examine the activities and the ethos of the Oxford and St George's Club. I will look at the ways in which religion was seen by Henriques to work within the club, as well as statements given at the founding of the group and at significant events within club history. This chapter will also look at the ways in which religious elements were included within the programme, specifically through prayers, classes and the Sabbath both during the year and at camp. Through this, I will show that religion in the Oxford and St George's Club transgressed gender boundaries and emphasized spiritual elements of belief. As a result, the club faced criticism from the Jewish community due to a lack of focus on formal and therefore more masculine elements – a reflection of the Liberal Jewish nature of the club – which ultimately led to the club being seen as not providing for the religious needs of boys.

2   L. L. Loewe, *Basil Henriques: A Portrait* (London: Routledge and Kegan Paul, 1976), p. 15.

Background and Ethos

From the outset, Henriques was keen to include religion as a vital part of the Oxford and St George's Jewish Club activities. The religious element was clear from his early writings and discussions on the club and emphasized the need for an explicitly religious basis in the group. Henriques frequently drew this religious element out, comparing his proposed activities to the lack of religion found in other Jewish boys' clubs: 'since we are determined to have a definite *religious* influence in the new club, I believe that it would be *impossible* for us to introduce into one of the existing clubs what would to a very large degree be an entirely novel influence. We must start with that influence at the very beginning.'[3] Henriques' intent can therefore be seen to clearly include a religious element, one that he viewed as lacking in other clubs. Lily Montagu of the West Central Girls' Club noted the novelty of including such a blatant religious element into a boys' club. Montagu showed her support to Henriques in a letter written six months before the opening of the club where she stated 'I want again to tell you how glad I was to be alive yesterday. For *years* I have wanted a boys' club on religious lines and it's just splendid to know it's coming.'[4] This demonstrates that within Liberal Jewish circles, the informal religious education of both boys and girls was seen to be in great need. This presents a contrast between those in charge of Orthodox groups who valued informal religious education for boys significantly less than they did for girls, partially as a result of the more thorough education boys received in religion through synagogues and schools.

The Reform Jewish Synagogue at Upper Berkeley Street supported Henriques' plans. Henriques wrote to the synagogue asking for support for the club. 'My desire is not so much for financial support as for *moral* support. I am trying to organize a Jewish boys' club in St George's in the

---

3   SUA, MS132 AJ220 3/6/7 *Oxford and St George's Jewish Lads' Club: A proposal* (original emphasis).

4   SUA MS132 AJ 220 3/2/2 Letter from Lily Montagu to Basil Henriques, 3 November 1913.

East ... There would of course be the ordinary activities of a boys' club, but it is my hope also that a dominating factor will be a positive religious influence. I should therefore like the club to be associated with the synagogue.'[5] It is significant here that the club was not asking for simply financial support. Where many Orthodox boys' clubs were concerned primarily with financial matters, this was not the case for the Oxford and St George's Club. Instead, the plea for moral support demonstrated Henriques' desire to promote religion, placing religious concerns as a priority where most boys' clubs did not. Henriques' own comments on the basis of the club also support the idea that religion was key in the activities and purpose of the club. Prior to the foundation of the group Henriques commented that 'I simply long to achieve my object which is to make religion an attractive reality among the Jews up here. At present it is far from being a reality or in the smallest part attractive.'[6] Prior to the club's founding, religion was therefore placed firmly at the centre of the club's activities and outlook. The desire for *moral* support in particular demonstrates this clearly. From the outset therefore, religion was a key motivation in the formation of the Oxford and St George's Club.

With religious elements so evident in the club's origins, it was logical that the club would emphasize the religious element throughout its history. At a meeting with potential supporters in 1914 Henriques again emphasized the specifically religious features of the club: 'Now, this club is to be called the Oxford and St George's *Jewish* Boys' Club. How can we justify ourselves in calling the club a *Jewish* boys' club unless we have a *Jewish* influence in the club? And by that I mean, and from my own point of view could only mean, a Jewish *religious* influence.'[7] This description of the club is a clear attack on the majority of Orthodox clubs which excluded a religious element despite calling themselves Jewish. By emphasizing this side of the proposed club, Henriques was underscoring the difference between the Oxford and St George's Club and other existing boys' clubs. This religious position was

---

5   SUA MS132 AJ220 3/1 Letter from Basil Henriques to Mr Belisha, Upper Berkley St Synagogue, 23 October 1913.

6   Loewe, *Basil Henriques*, p. 15.

7   SUA MS132 AJ220 3/6/7 (original emphasis).

not just evident in the early life of the club. At the annual concert in 1924, Henriques stated that 'the main objects of the settlement were to teach the boys and girls in the locality the better sense of life, and to encourage them to become good Englishmen and women and to be as proud of their Judaism as they were of their English citizenship'.[8] This provides an element of continuity in the clubs' religious work, indicating that religion was still a concern a decade after it opened. Two years after this concert the club again demonstrated its commitment to religion, but it offered a slightly different justification. According to its Annual Report in 1926, the purpose of the club was to 'stop the growing tide of irreligion and to rouse fresh religious fervour [is] perhaps the most far reaching and important branch of settlement work'.[9] The emphasis here, unlike in previous statements was placed on the growing irreligion of the area. Taken alone, this statement certainly supports the notion that religious activities in the club were strengthened during the interwar years; however, when viewed within the context of the club's previous aims, it is clear that this is not as straightforward as it appears. Rather than adjusting the religious activities, the club instead adopted a new justification, which made club work relevant to the contemporary situation.

Throughout the 1930s, the Oxford and St George's Club and Henriques maintained the religious position of the group. Henriques in particular, and by extension the club, continued to promote religion as the central part of club life. 'Religion must be the controlling factor in the club ... It is perfectly useless talking of "prayers at the end of the club evening" and saying "we have a religious club" ... Religion MUST be the basis on which the club is built.'[10] The centrality of religion can be seen from the way the club included closing prayers at the end of every evening. Similarities can be seen in this statement and the one made before the club opening, in particular, the notion that religion should be central to club work. Once again, Henriques in his statement was drawing a contrast between the

8   *JG*, 8 February 1924.
9   *JG*, 22 January 1926.
10   SUA, MS132, AJ220 3/4/4 An address on 'The club and the Religious Problem' Given by BLQH at the Anniversary Conference of the Association for Jewish Youth, 4 April 1930.

Oxford and St George's Club and Orthodox groups, commenting that the role of prayers within Orthodox groups was often seen as proof that the club was religious. Throughout the history of the group, the club (and Henriques) was keen to maintain its religious position and place religion firmly at the heart of club life. Former club member Mark Fineman, whose parents and grandparents emigrated from Russia and Poland, noted this. He was brought up in line with his grandparents' Orthodoxy, observing the Sabbath and Jewish festivals in the home and attended *Cheder* as a boy. When interviewed in 1986, he recalled the motivation for club work:

> CS: [The strong religious element was] probably necessary to reassure the parents that, er, the children weren't going to, er … I mean would encourage
> MF: Yes
> CS: the parents to send their children
> MF: No, I think in that respect … Henriques and his wife, who was a very talented woman, they were very sincere. They did want this religious element. They thought it played a very important part in the development of people.[11]

Fineman's recollections on the motivations behind religion support the statements made by Henriques. Religion, in the eyes of Henriques and noted by (at least one of the) former members was a key part in club life. It is also clear that religion was included not just to satisfy members of the Jewish community but because of belief. This belief was evident to members, who were aware of the motivations behind Henriques' desire to include religion.

Religious Activities

The evidence of a clear religious basis as mentioned by Henriques can be found most obviously in evening prayers. Writing in 1930, Henriques spoke of the importance of prayer in club life:

11   JML, Tape 50, Interview with Mark Fineman, 27 January 1986.

The spirit of the club must be created through the club prayers. If you cannot deliver a sermon, at any rate pray with the boys. Lose your Singer Prayer Book and every other kind of prayer book. Say the simplest prayer you like, but at any rate recognize the great unseen manager of the club, recognize the Commander-in-Chief of your Brigade. Do something before you go home to show that you acknowledge God. Do it with the boys and the girls. I do not think that club prayers ought to last more than 8–10 minutes in all – the talk, an English or Hebrew Hymn, or the *Shema*, the prayer and the valedictory verse.[12]

Given this position, it is natural that the Oxford and St George's Club therefore included prayers as a central part of the club routine. From the outset, the club ran prayers at the end of every evening. This small service was called 'time' and was optional for boys who had attended club activities during the evening. A letter from Henriques regarding the first two nights of the club illustrate his commitment to holding 'time':

First Night 3rd March 1914 I started straight off with prayers on closing. They very seriously said the *Shema* together, and then I started an extemporary prayer. This made them roar with laughter! Most disconcerting and I finished as quickly as I could. ... Second Night 4th March 1914 Last night we said the *Shema* and I read a prayer from Singer's Prayer Book, which I thought they would know and the behaviour was perfect.[13]

The reception of the boys to these prayers indicate that some elements of Liberal Judaism – in particular the extemporary prayers rather than formalized prayers – were not initially well received by the members. The change in prayer style between the first and second night shows the willingness of Henriques to adapt his own religious practice in order to promote his religious ideals. There is, however, evidence that the reception of more liberal traditions improved. The following year, the boys demonstrated that they had adapted to the extemporary style of prayer promoted by Henriques and there was 'a large attendance at prayers. When SEF [a club member] announced that he had joined the navy the boys were deeply moved and

12   SUA MS132 AJ220, 3/4/4 The Club and the religious Problem.
13   Basil L. Q. Henriques, *The Bernhard Baron St George's Jewish Settlement: Fiftieth Anniversary Review, 1914–1964* (London: Private Publisher, 1964), p. 7.

cheered and sang for "he is a jolly good fellow".[14] This demonstrates that, even within the first year of the club, Henriques had had some success in promoting Liberal Judaism amongst club members despite initial assertions that the club would not introduce Liberal Judaism into Orthodox families, although familiarity with Liberal Jewish style prayers may not have meant that the boys were ideologically committed to Liberal Judaism. The involvement of the boys within the prayer service, even though the boys were not necessarily involved in direct prayer, demonstrates that the young people felt comfortable involving themselves within the religious life of the club. This certainly marked a change from the first evening in the club, where the young men were not receptive to any unstructured religious element within 'time'.

The tradition of prayers at the end of the club evening continued, even when Henriques was called away to serve on the front. Other club managers and visitors to the club took the service. Solomons, an instructor within the group, took prayers in November 1915 despite previously being uninvolved with the service: 'I took prayers and hope I got home – I felt rather awkward as I did not know quite how you did it – still I did my best and I am quite happy to know that I am doing something at this critical hour.'[15] The continuation of the prayer service, despite the absence of Henriques, shows that prayers had become an established part of club life that was not solely dependent on Henriques himself. Through 'time', religion had therefore become an established part of club life.

The boys showed themselves to be receptive to these prayers. Visitors to the club frequently noted that the behaviour of the young people during the service was good; Lily Montagu commented that the boys were 'splendidly responsive' to the prayers during a visit in 1915. In 1915, Samuel, of the Stepney Club, noted that the boys 'seem to behave much better than ours, not only in the prayers, but in the club'.[16] The behaviour of the boys

14   SUA MS132 AJ220 1/3/2 Diary of Basil Henriques, Entry Saturday 30 January 1915.

15   SUA MS132 AJ220, 3/3/1 Letter from HE Solomons to Basil Henriques, 2 November 1915.

16   SUA MS132 AJ220 3/2/2 Letter from Lily Montagu to Basil Henriques, undated, 1915 and SUA MS132 AJ220 3/6/2 Letter from Samuel to Basil Henriques, 3 June 1915.

during 'time' indicates that the members were aware of the special significance of prayer and therefore were able to behave appropriately. This marks a significant departure from the behaviour of boys during prayers in Orthodox groups,. Records show that boys in Orthodox clubs frequently displayed behaviour and attention less desirable than that shown by members of the Oxford and St George's Club such as in the accounts of the Stepney Club from the 1930s (mentioned earlier) where members were reported to use prayers as a 'subterfuge for a late night game of ping-pong'.[17] The tradition of holding 'time' continued throughout club history and, at special events, the prayers took on a greater significance. At the opening of the new settlement building in 1930, the clubs held a special 'time' service, which acknowledged the importance of the day. Henriques reported that on each groups' first evening in the club he 'gathered them all into the games room for two minutes silent prayer'.[18] Through this, Henriques was able to show that prayers were important on a daily basis and that they could also be used to note the significance of important events.

The subjects discussed during these prayers sessions have some similarities with the religious content found within sermons of other boys' clubs, although with some key differences. Henriques' early diaries detailing his club work frequently mention the prayers and the subject discussed. In 1915, prayer topics included those which dealt with 'manliness' and sportsmanship such as the sermons on cricket, military life and patriotism and topics dealing with more religious matters such as the services on Friday evenings, 'the love of God for His children' and spiritual welfare.[19] The focus of the subjects discussed present an interesting contrast to the subjects discussed in other boys' clubs. There was less emphasis placed on the subjects typically considered 'manly'. Although these topics were still present, they constituted less than half of the subjects discussed and thus placed less emphasis on the concerns of promoting an acceptably English masculinity. In contrast, more emphasis was placed on the more 'spiritual' and directly religious topics than can be seen in other boys' clubs services.

---

17   SUA MS172 AJ250 *Stepnian*, October 1934.
18   Henriques, *Fiftieth Anniversary Review*, p. 26.
19   SUA MS132 AJ220 1/3 – 1/10 Basil Henriques' Diaries.

Whilst the focus on 'spiritual' matters was not a concern solely for women in Anglo-Jewry during this period, the *emphasis* the club placed on spiritual matters certainly falls outside of the experiences within other boys' clubs. This deviation is particularly important as it demonstrates that the club was less concerned with promoting subjects perceived as especially masculine in the way that other boys' clubs did. Instead, the club promoted religiosity and spirituality, something traditionally emphasized as feminine and frequently seen within girls' clubs.

Given the general emphasis on prayer as a whole, it is therefore natural that many former members would later recall the prayer services and the impact that they had on their lives. During the Second World War, many former members wrote to the club with recollections of their time in the group as well as commenting on their current activities. One of the original members of the club wrote stating that: 'Twenty two years ago I sat and listened to your first "Time" … something you said then has stuck in my mind ever since "Once you belong to the Oxford and St George's Club, and are really imbued with its spirit, you belong to it forever".'[20] Whilst this member was not recalling any specifically religious part of 'time', it is clear that the member remembers the service and that it stayed with him thereafter. The same can be seen from a later member, who wrote 'I still remember my handshake after prayers and the feeling of comfort of mind, and security … when I first said goodnight on my first night of membership almost 10 years ago.'[21] Whilst, again, this memory contains no recollection of a specifically religious element, the prayer service in general clearly had an impact on this member. The significance of the prayers in creating a religious atmosphere was also noted by former members. In 1986, a member recalled 'we always ended the evening with a prayer … so there was a very strong religious element in the club.'[22] These three accounts of the prayer services demonstrate that the prayers were not just tolerated by the boys, but were significant and remembered. Despite the lack of specific

---

20   Basil L. Q. Henriques, *Fratres: Club Boys in Uniform* (London: Secker and Warburg, 1951), pp. 109–10.

21   Loewe, *Basil Henriques*, p. 64.

22   JML, Audio Tape 50, Interview with Mark Fineman, 27 January 1986.

religious emphasis in the first two memories, it is clear that the boys were aware of the significance of prayers within the club, and believed that it constituted a large part of the group's identity. One of the most significant factors of the prayer service is not that the boys remembered the events, but the way in which the subjects and the service itself transgressed gender roles. By including a spiritual element of prayers into the evening, the club was confirming that religion was more important than maintaining such clearly defined gender roles as promoted in Orthodox groups. Indeed, the recollections of the boys certainly support this notion – that religious elements, regardless of their adherence to gender stereotypes, were observed and appreciated within the group.

In addition to ceremonial expressions of religion through prayer, the Oxford and St George's Club provided an opportunity for members to get involved in formal learning of religious history and endeavoured to imbue all of its activities with a 'Jewish spirit'. A Jewish history class was run during the early years of the club. In addition to providing formal learning opportunities, the club was also encouraged to discuss issues relating to the Jews both 'religiously and racially'.[23] In these discussions, the members were encouraged to think about both the history and the future of Jews and to apply their learning to the contemporary situation. In the 1930s, Henriques was still promoting classes such as these within the clubs, with the aim that the club should 'teach Israel with classes in Jewish history, biblical and post biblical, on prophets'.[24] Although there is no direct evidence supporting the existence of these classes in the 1930s, it seems reasonable to assume that the club continued to hold some sort of Jewish history class. Whilst the notion of post-Biblical history and secular Jewish history may not seem to include any specific religious training, a contemporary view held that *all* Jewish history, whether explicitly religious or not contributed to the religious education of young Jews: 'instruction in Jewish history [throughout the ages] is then ... above all, instruction in the history of Judaism and of

23   SUA, MS132 AJ220 1/3/2 Monday 3 January 1915.
24   SUA, MS132 AJ220 3/4/4.

Jewish religious life'.[25] Whether this view was mainstream, or shared by the leaders of the classes within the Oxford and St George's club, is difficult to say; however, to some these classes were considered to have provided an element of religious education though the inclusion of history.

As the club expanded in the late 1920s and 1930s, the number of activities expanded likewise. These activities were categorized by Henriques to describe whether they cared for the physical, mental or spiritual fitness of club members. Those that catered for the 'spiritual needs' of the club members were the synagogue, family-style prayers nightly, club Friday evening services, religion school, Jewish history and camp.[26] Many of these activities were provided by the settlement rather that the club itself, particularly the synagogue, and will therefore not be explored here. However, this list demonstrates that the club was concerned with finding religious activities for the boys whether these were provided by the club itself or by the settlement. It is also interesting to note that the term 'spiritual' is used, rather than religious. This certainly marks a departure from the religious activities in many boys' clubs who sought to distance themselves from the notion of spirituality as this was seen as too feminine for their members. Whilst such gender concerns had declined by the 1930s when this list was produced, it was still a consideration and such a blurring of these gender lines was the exception, even in 1934, rather than the norm.

Praise for the religious provisions found in general club activities came from an unlikely source. The 'Young Judean', Orthodox correspondent to the *Jewish World* paper, who was usually highly critical of the Oxford and St George's Club, wrote in 1933 'I would like to take this opportunity of congratulating the St George's Settlement upon its presentation of "The Dybbuk" which was not alone a splendid performance, but brought valuable contact and spiritual association with Jewish history and Jewish customs.'[27] This praise is highly significant coming from a normally fierce critic of

25   Joseph Morris, 'Jewish Religious Education', *Jewish Quarterly Review*, 9 (1897), 631–68
      (p. 653).
26   THLA, 360.1 Bernhard Baron St George's Jewish Settlement Fifteenth Annual
      Report, 1933–1934.
27   *JW*, 28 March 1933.

Liberal Judaism and the club. It indicates that the religious element found within the play satisfied not only Liberal, but also Orthodox Jewish requirements. The religious and Jewish history classes, as well as additional activities within the club (and in the settlement), therefore allowed religion to be included within club life. This religion, on occasion, transgressed gender boundaries and certainly, at times, was seen as acceptable to Orthodoxy, highlighting once again the importance placed on religion over maintaining gender roles and Liberal Judaism.

Henriques recognized the importance of ensuring that prayers were not the only religious activity in the club and encouraged Sabbath observance amongst the boys. In the early years of the club, the services were held with other boys' clubs. In 1915, the club boys attended services for all Jewish boys' clubs, held at the Stepney Club. These services grew in success: 'the members who attend have increased from 6 to about 20. There seems to be a real interest taken in these services.'[28] The club, through these services, made a clear provision for a formal element of observance, and one which was tied more to Orthodox traditions, rather than Liberal ones. The growing interest in these services indicate that religion was increasingly a part of club life and that success had been made in promoting the formal (and therefore more masculine) elements of observance, rather than solely through prayers and spiritual elements of religion. Despite the 'real interest' taken in these services, there was, however, an element of poor behaviour. In August 1915, 'the behaviour of Morris and Alohen [club members] was not very satisfactory as they walked in, after the service has commenced with a good deal of swank and a girl of notoriously bad reputation.'[29] Through this behaviour, the boys were able to demonstrate their 'manliness' to their peers. This shows that whilst the services provided an element of more masculine religion, the services were viewed by some as an area for promoting themselves as more masculine within a specifically Jewish context. This was perhaps a conscious intention from the club in order to attract attendees.

28   SUA MS132 AJ220 1/3/2 Saturday 20 March 1915.
29   Ibid., Saturday 6 August 1915.

Sabbath services within the club itself began in late 1915, 'the synagogue can be said to have begun in 1915 when [Rose Henriques] used to hold "informal" services in the boys' club in Cannon Street Road, to which Basil used to come and preach when he could get leave from his regiment. ... It seems that the boys held aloof for some months until shamed by the girls into joining. Thus for Saturday 28th August we read "15 to synagogue – 11 boys – huge triumph".'[30] It is interesting to note the gender reversal here. The service was both run by and attended (at least initially) by girls and women. The more informal setting of holding events at the club certainly indicates a more feminine version of religion in comparison to a service at a synagogue in another boys' club and can, perhaps, go some way to explain the lack of attendance of boys. The services continued within the settlement synagogue after the end of the First World War. One member, whilst serving in the Second World War recalled the services held at the Settlement: 'some of your old sermons came to life again. I could almost hear the rise and fall of your voice, the dramatic pauses, the occasional gestures: speaking in a whisper that gradually gained momentum, you reached a terrific crescendo and descended to normal again ... there was one sermon in particular, the text of which was "Do you well to be angry".'[31] This memory provides clear evidence that the services played a role in the lives of club members. That a boy could recall services years later demonstrates clearly the impact these events had on his life. Yet, there were problems with the services. In 1933 the club was aware of the indifference of club members to the synagogue and held a special committee meeting in order to 'thoroughly debate the reasons why so few members attend either our own or any other synagogue and to think out some provision for a finer religious fellowship among the members'.[32] The lack of attendance at the synagogue coincides with a general decline in religious observance nationwide. The continued focus of the club on these services, however, attests to the *continued* desire to promote formal religion within the club setting.

30   Loewe, *Basil Henriques*, p. 66.
31   Henriques, *Fratres*, p. 109.
32   SUA MS132 AJ220/1/8/2 March 1933, Agenda for Committee Meeting.

In addition to providing formal services on the Sabbath, the club also opened on Friday evenings. This was a controversial element with boys' clubs generally, but Henriques maintained the usefulness of these events throughout the club history. The club evenings were clearly different from those during the rest of the week. Rather than open for games and structured activities, the boys 'came in for a quiet evening. After reading some fiction, two sermons were read and the evening closed with a short service.'[33] The emphasis on the Friday evening programming was placed on 'quiet' activities, in contrast to those provided during the rest of the week. The notion of quiet activities was something that Henriques continued to emphasize and in 1930, he stressed the importance of maintaining a quiet atmosphere on the Sabbath. He stated that clubs should refrain from billiards, ping pong, boxing and other 'normal' club activities and instead provide activities which highlighted the importance of the day as one of rest not idleness as 'idleness leads to more vice' outside of the club.[34] In keeping the club open on Friday evenings, Henriques and by extension the Oxford and St George's Club were therefore demonstrating awareness of contemporary issues and placed the club in a position to combat the dangers alternative leisure placed on religious observance. In providing Friday evening events, the club was once again stressing the importance of religion in life and was able to show that observing the Sabbath, whilst not in the strictly Orthodox manner, could be incorporated into the weekly routine. Through both formal Sabbath services and Friday evening services, the club was able to demonstrate the importance of religion and showed its commitment to Jewish (albeit Liberal) observance.

As well as provisions for observing the Sabbath in the club, the group also organized observance for religious festivals and Holy Days. These services, like Sabbath services, began on a small scale with events held at the club. For *Purim* in 1915, the group held a short service and address on Friday followed by a *Megillah* service at 7.30 a.m. and 'a *Purim* treat was given to about 120 brothers and sisters between the ages of 6 and 10 from 3.30–9 p.m. Games, skipping, recitation, singing and boxing by the smallest

33　SUA MS132 AJ220 1/3/2 Friday 19 February 1915.
34　Basil L. Q. Henriques, *Club Leadership* (London: Humphrey Milford, 1934), p. 172.

boys followed by a very large tea made the treat a great success.'[35] This event was not unlike those held in other clubs for *Purim*. But, in contrast the focus of the event was not solely on the 'treat'. Instead, the club was clearly providing for the religious element of the festival, not just the fun side. In this way, the club distanced itself from the boys' clubs, which solely concentrated on the celebration to the detriment of the religious elements. The club also focused its attention on the more religiously significant days. Early in the club's history these services, like the Sabbath services, were small and informal: 'during the war years, the Missus [Rose Henriques] held informal services for club members in the Boys' Club on the High Holy Days.'[36] The inclusion of these services within the boys' club goes some way to both promote and counter gender norms. First, the informality of the services was much more typical of what was found within girls' clubs and thus represents a way in which the inclusion of religion transgressed gender norms. Second, the holding of such structured services, like those for the Holy Days, presented a more masculine side and was a typical expression of 'manly' religion. These small and more informal services therefore both conformed to and contradicted gender norms.

With the expansion of the settlement, and the creation of the Settlement Synagogue, the services took on a more formal role. 'A *Chanukah* service was held in Whitechapel Art Gallery for the Play Centre, Brownies, Wolf-cubs, Scouts, Guides and a sprinkling of older club members.'[37] This was very typical of a club service, whether Orthodox or Liberal. The focus on *Chanucah* is reflective of its status as a more 'fun' and 'child-friendly' holiday, and was therefore, like *Purim*, celebrated in the majority of Jewish youth clubs. Unlike *Purim* and *Chanucah*, the High Holy Days were neither seen as 'fun' nor particularly 'child-friendly', however, the Oxford and St George's Club provided services on these days with large attendances. A record of the services in 1922 recorded 650 attendees on *Rosh Hashanah* and over 1,000 attendees on *Yom Kippur* as well as large numbers of attendees at

35   SUA, MS132 AJ220, 1/3/2 27 to 28 February 1915.
36   Henriques, *Fiftieth Anniversary Review*, p. 12.
37   Ibid., p. 23.

other festivals in the period.[38] Whilst a large number of these attendees were drawn from the settlement community, rather than the clubs themselves, the services were promoted in the clubs and a number of members attended. From the 1920s, the Settlement took over the Holy Day celebrations and these were no longer held in the club. As a result, it is increasingly difficult to determine how successful these services were amongst club members. The presence of a fully functioning synagogue within the settlement community also allowed for more formal worship from club members, as seen in the services in 1922. The observance of Holy Days and religious festivals in the clubs initially fell within the same scope as found within Orthodox groups. Only with the growth of the synagogue did the religious activities become more formal. This should be seen less a reflection on the gendered roles of boys as girls' club members also attended, but rather as a result of a general expansion of the community.

Summer Camps

Prayers, services and regularly scheduled activities were the largest part of club work. One of the most memorable parts, and the one which appeared to be the most enjoyable part, was the annual summer camp. Like most clubs prior to 1939, the Oxford and St George's Club held a week long camp at a location in the countryside or close to the sea. Not only was this significant from the boys' point of view, but, Henriques noted it was also significant from a religious point of view:

> the time when we have the greatest opportunities for dealing with boys religiously is on camp. It is there that we can really take advantage of the fundamental way of teaching the knowledge of God for we can make nature and beauty and goodness and joy and happiness another word for God.[39]

38   Ibid., p. 16.
39   SUA, MS132 AJ220 3/4/4.

For Henriques, camp therefore provided a way for the leaders to increase their religious influence over the boys and impact upon the religious lives of club members. Religion was included in two main ways during the camps, first through prayers which, as they did in club evenings, held a particularly prominent place within the routine and second, the Sabbath, which was further emphasized as a day of rest and used to promote religion.

The structure of camp prayers was largely similar to those held during the year. The emphasis was placed on sincerity and experience, rather than following Orthodox traditions: 'on a fine night when "Time" was to be taken [Henriques] would lead his flock up to the top of the hill on which the camp stood and talk to them under the stars in the belief that the beauty of the scene would make their consciousness more sensitive to the direct religious impact of his words'.[40] The creation of an outdoor religious space allowed Henriques to create links between religion and the environment which emphasized the symbolic power of the natural world rather than rely on the finite space of a building and the traditional symbols of Judaism.[41] In emphasizing the creation of an outdoor religious space Henriques was thus able to remove an element of formality and structure from the club experiences of religion in camp. This is an interesting contrast to prayers seen in other boys' clubs camps, which preferred to emphasize the formality of the prayers, such as in the Jewish Lads' Brigade, where boys were paraded in full uniform, passages were read from scriptures, and were led by the camp chaplain. An account of 'time' from the 1915 camp further emphasizes the differences between the formality of prayers in other boys' clubs and the informality in the Oxford and St George's Club:

> The conversion of the chapel into a synagogue and the wonderfully sincere prayers were the highest moments of each day. A religious spirit pervaded the services, the hills and the trees asked for it, and the boys responded. A fairly large number, which unfortunately diminished during the week went to lay *Tephillin* at early morning prayers. The whole club assembled before breakfast for prayers which were generally

40　Loewe, *Basil Henriques*, p. 65.

41　David Harvey, 'From Space to Place and Back Again'. In David Harvey (ed.), *Justice, Nature and the Geography of Difference* (Cambridge: Blackwell, 1996), pp. 291–326 (p. 305).

brief, an address being given only twice. In the evening the synagogue, lit up by candles arranged on a suspended hoop of a beer barrel presented a glorious spectacle. Addresses were given each time, a Hebrew Hymn sung and English and Hebrew prayers recited. Finally, when the boys were all tucked up in bed, two minutes silence was called to enable those who wanted to confess and offer secret thoughts to the Father who rewarded himself.[42]

From these accounts, it is clear that Henriques was concerned with promoting the spiritual rather than the ritual elements of prayer. This contrasts firmly with other boys' clubs, which emphasized masculine notions of religion through formality, ritual and grandeur. Indeed, these prayer services in their simplicity and spirituality resemble services found within Jewish girls' clubs, particularly in the recollection of the decoration of the synagogue. There were, however, structured elements to these services. The club showed its willingness to accommodate the laying of *tephillin*, a formal and Orthodox ritual, demonstrating that the group was able to include an element of masculine religion and one that did not fit with the Liberal beliefs of Henriques.

The club had a 'camp prayer', which was written by Leonard Stern, a prominent youth worker and member of established Anglo-Jewry before his death in 1915:

> Our God, who art in heaven, be with us the members of this club, when we pray to thee. Grant that our prayers may come not from our lips, but from our hearts. Thou art with us at all times and in all places. Do then open our eyes so that we may see and never forget this. Remove from us the temptation and evil thoughts which make life ugly; let us seek only what is good. Keep us from bad companions until we feel that we have the strength to lead our friends towards thee instead of yielding ourselves to what is base. [Here in the fields which thou hast made,] let us not have the shame of knowing that we brought evil, where there was only good before we came; but let the thought of thee colour all we say and do with light. Grant us health of body and of mind so that we may bear our troubles manfully and use our brains to overcome them. Through us, bless our homes and make us a source of happiness to our parents and our sisters and brothers. Bless the troop which thy goodness has

42 SUA MS 132 AJ 220/1/3 Basil Henriques' Diary, Entry under August 'Camp'.

inspired and help us to hold its honour sacred; so may we forget ourselves and do only our duty to Thee and to those about us. Amen.[43]

This prayer, whilst providing an element of structure was much less formal than its Orthodox counterparts. In addition, the prayer has many similarities with the Christian 'Lord's Prayer'. The opening works of the prayer, 'Our God who are in heaven' can be compared to the opening lines of the 'Lord's Prayer' which begins 'Our Father, who art in heaven'. A later section of the club prayer asks 'remove us from the temptations and evil thoughts which make us ugly'. This phrase closely resembles the section in the Lord's Prayer, which asks 'lead us not into temptation, but deliver us from evil'.[44] The similarities between these two prayers certainly did not emphasize the Jewish elements of the club. Rather than adopt many traditional elements of Jewish observance, the club prayer highlighted the more Christian elements of Liberal worship such as those encouraged by Montefiore, who viewed the Bible as a form of progressive revelation in which moral and ethical teachings were developed. Significantly, this 'progressive revelation' also included the New Testament, which Montefiore viewed as a Jewish book. Indeed, many Liberal Jewish services included references to the New Testament, or allusions to Christian teachings.[45] This would have been a significant declaration for the club and this prayer, rather than showing its allegiance to Judaism, instead indicated that specifically Jewish elements of worship were less significant that the act of worship itself. Indeed, not much of the camp prayer can be seen as specifically Jewish, rather than generally religious. However, when recited in context, along with the *Shema* and Hebrew prayers and hymns, rather than on its own, the prayer can be seen in a more Jewish light, complementing more explicitly Jewish elements.

Henriques showed himself, despite the lack of Judaism in the camp prayer, to be sensitive to more typically Jewish, in particular Orthodox, practices. In 1930, he addressed the concerns of a number of his critics that the club sought to limit the Orthodoxy of club members:

43   SUA, MS132 AJ220, 3/1, 'Camp Prayer' by Leonard Stern.
44   Ibid. and Matthew 6.9–11.
45   Ibid., p. 83.

> I think we ought to have as a camp rule that 'those boys who lay *Tephillin* should bring their *Tephillin* with them. We cannot allow them not to do things or to do things that they would not be allowed to or would be forced to do at home ... After these early morning prayers there should be club prayers, similar in respect of their informality, to the kind I have suggested for the prayers at the end of an ordinary club evening. Don't let the boys put hankerchiefs on their heads – it makes a farce of it, instead get them to put their hands on their heads, or leave it uncovered. Don't let them race – insist on decorum.[46]

In this, Henriques showed that, whilst he did not promote formality he was at least aware of the need to allow boys to observe the more formal elements of observance. Unlike in other boys' clubs, the formality, and therefore the masculinity, whilst acknowledged, was not emphasized within this realm. Instead, the concern was, once again, placed on the more individual spiritual and therefore traditionally feminine types of religion.

Henriques illustrated the overall attitude of the club to prayers in camp in his 1930 handbook of club leadership:

> Perhaps the most marvellous experience of all, are the prayers at the end of the day. The whole life in camp is living in the presence of God. His Goodness, His Love and His Glory are apparent at all times. To worship him at the close of a happy day is but a natural climax to all that has happened. There can be no formality or empty ceremonialism about camp prayers ... there is scarcely a boy who will not think, even if he does not say, some inarticulate prayer before he goes to sleep, perhaps a prayer of gratitude for his happiness ... whatever it is will be sincere and real.[47]

The emphasis of prayer in both this statement and the accounts seen previously, is a spiritual one, which is not evident in Orthodox boys' clubs who chose to emphasize formality in their prayers. Within Judaism, there was an expectation for men to lead prayers and thus the inclusion of a prayer service does not necessarily appear to fall outside of these gendered roles. However, the extempore nature of these prayers (rather than the formality of following structured prayer) advocated by Henriques had more in common with feminine notions of religion which rejected the rigidity required by

---

46 SUA MS132 AJ220 3/4/4.
47 Henriques, *Club Leadership*, p. 156.

men. As a result, the Oxford and St George's Club prayer services can be seen to have promoted a more feminine version of religion through these club prayers, which had more in common with religion found in Orthodox girls' clubs, rather than in those for boys.

Like prayers, the camp Sabbath also emphasized the spiritual and traditionally feminine forms of worship. The emphasis was placed on the attractiveness of the Sabbath to the boys, rather than the fulfilment of religious laws, which was common within Orthodox boys' clubs, something which can be attributed in part to the Liberal Jewish nature of the club. This was especially true of the Friday night meal, which was not emphasized in any other boys' group:

> The planning of the Sabbath in camp must be above all on the basis of delectability. The family feast on a Friday evening in the dim light of the Sabbath candles on the white table; the quality and quantity of the food provided, the glow that comes through saying the sanctification … the peace, the love, the sense of brotherliness … the Friday evening fails completely and utterly in camp unless those who attend it have had deeply imprinted on their hearts that it is something good in itself, something to be emulated and repeated in their daily lives at home.[48]

This level of focus on a meal was unusual for a Boys' Club, as most wished to distance themselves from this domestic and therefore feminine activity. Certainly, men were responsible for conducting the Friday evening service and as such, were not excluded from this element of observance. It is, however, the club's focus on the more domestic elements of the meal that is noteworthy as this demonstrates willingness for the group to focus on that, which was seen as too feminine for other clubs. It is especially interesting that the boys were encouraged to emulate the meal in their homes. This was something that was repeatedly stressed in girls' clubs as the managers sought to make good wives and mothers out of the young people. This element significantly was not found within any other boys' club and demonstrates that for Henriques and the Oxford and St George's Club the focus was less on maintaining strict gender boundaries but more on maintaining a religious atmosphere.

---

48 Loewe, *Basil Henriques*, p. 65.

In addition to the meal, Henriques did, like other boys' clubs, hold services on Fridays and Saturdays. These services were included from the first camp in 1915 where the ceremonies were described as 'impressive'.[49] Whilst the inclusion of a service indicates a more formal element of ritual, Henriques' recollections dispute the formality of these events. Instead, the emphasis was placed on the 'inner meaning' of religion, which again corresponds to more feminine versions of religion as well as to Liberal Judaism. Elements of formality were observed in camps in the 1920s, where Henriques recalls that he 'preached on "come before the lord rejoicing" [Psalm] 100, extemporary but it seemed to go down well' and that he 'preached from Isaiah 35 which ... was most appropriate'.[50] The inclusion of biblical passages in the description of the service is traditional amongst boys' clubs, however, the passages chosen are unlike sections read at services in Orthodox boys' club services. Both Psalm 100 and Isaiah 35 focus on the joys of worship and the glory of God, rather than focusing on militarism and manly qualities favoured by God. Again, this marks a way in which the religious observances in the Oxford and St George's Club more closely resembled that found in girls' clubs than in boys.

At times, the choice of scripture was even further from Orthodox traditions than merely departing from gender norms. 'As regards formal worship, what Henriques offered was liable to be idiosyncratic, sometimes – within a Jewish context – to the point of absurdity. He was fond, for example, of using for a Sabbath "scriptural" at camp St Paul's lyrical homily on love (i. Cor. 13) amidst a company of youngsters the majority of whose parents or grandparents fled Czarist Russia'.[51] This explicit use of Christian teachings and Christian scripture was an interesting move for a Jewish club, and could not have helped to dispel concerns that the club was not authentically Jewish. The use of such a blatantly Christian text, and the

---

49   SUA MS132 AJ220 1/3/2, August 1915.
50   SUA MS132 AJ220 1/4/3, Saturday 10 and Friday 11 August 1923.
51   R. Loewe, 'The Bernhard Baron Settlement and the Oxford and St George's Club', in *The Jewish East End*, ed. by the Jewish Historical Society of England on behalf of the Conference Organising Committee (London: The Jewish Historical Society of England, 1981), pp. 143–6 (p. 144).

camp prayer resembling the Lord's Prayer, is problematic and symbolizes a closer relationship with 'ethical monotheism' and Liberal Judaism rather than anything specifically, or Orthodox-ly, Jewish. Nevertheless, recollections of the service from former members demonstrate the impact that the service had and they show no real memory of a specifically Jewish element. During the Second World War, a former member recalled 'the aims and ideals which we are fighting for in this great struggle we learnt from those glorious and memorable services on Highdown [the campsite] when we had peace and happiness and hatred for no-one'.[52] Whilst this certainly shows that the religious programming had a lasting impact, there is certainly no evidence of an enduring *religious* impact. Indeed, the qualities that were mentioned – peace, happiness and hatred for no-one – could as easily have come from a non-denominational service as a Jewish one.

A Jewish Club?

The lack of a specifically Orthodox element and the inclusion of New Testament scripture caused controversy in the Jewish community. Observers, who believed that the Liberal character of the club was eroding Orthodoxy and Jewish religious adherence, frequently criticized the Liberal nature of the club. Henriques was adamant that the club was neither Orthodox nor Reform, stating that he wanted to teach a religion that was 'Judaism pure and simple'.[53] Prior to the opening of the club, he firmly refuted claims that he would teach Reform Judaism and set out his aims:

> It has been suggested and the suggestion seems very plausible, that because we are being financed by the Reform Synagogue of Upper Berkeley St and Hiss Street that we are going to try to introduce Reform Judaism into the East End by a kind of side door. Ladies and Gentlemen, I *cannot* too emphatically tell you that it is not our

52   Henriques, *Fratres*, p. 116.
53   Loewe, *Basil Henriques*, p. 29.

motive: that nothing is further from the minds of those who are promoting this club: that we should not do anything so MEAN. We shall not seek to destroy any portion of the boys' faith: we shall not seek to interfere with any religious practice or rite; our work will be constructive. We want to deepen and fortify, not to upset or undermine. Construction must be our motto or all times and in everything we shall teach the boys they must above all honour their father and their mother.[54]

This demonstrates a clear desire at the beginning of the club's history to promote Judaism without an adherence to a particular type. For most other Jewish clubs, the groups firmly allied themselves with Orthodoxy, here the Oxford and St George's Club was setting out with a different aim. In the early years, the club enjoyed the support not only of the Reform synagogues, but also of the Chief Rabbi, who consecrated the club premises, attended the club, led 'time' and gave messages of support stating that he would 'do everything in [his] power to assist [the] movement … The object of us all at this time must be to unite Judaism and not to separate it.'[55] The support of the Chief Rabbi was crucial in allaying the fears of the Jewish community that the club was *too* Reform. That the Chief Rabbi involved himself in the club's activities rather than just giving distant support shows that the club was making efforts to ensure Orthodoxy was promoted among members. After the war, coinciding with the growth of the Settlement and the creation of the Liberal Settlement Synagogue, the club's relationship with Orthodoxy became more strained. In 1919, the Chief Rabbi severed ties with the club as he believed that the most pressing need for the East End was not to Anglicize the immigrants, but to create a greater Jewish element. He believed that the club was 'tampering' with Judaism and therefore not fulfilling the goal to emphasize the correct form of Judaism in the community.[56] The alienation of the Chief Rabbi and the withdrawal of official support signalled a formal split from Orthodoxy. From this point, the club began to face strengthened criticism from the Jewish community. As Henriques developed his own beliefs, the criticism of the club increased. In 1930, Henriques stated that in the club the ideal that ceremony equals

---

54   SUA MS132 AJ220, 3/6/7.
55   Ibid. Henriques, *Fiftieth Anniversary Review*, p. 8; Loewe, *Basil Henriques*, p. 34.
56   Loewe, *Basil Henriques*, p. 34.

religion must be ignored and instead that 'the spirit of God be made to mean something',[57] and that the club should 'make sportsmanship, happiness, cleanliness identical with religion – that a good game of ping-pong is a kind of prayer and that a foul game of football is a kind of sin'.[58] In both of these instances, he was showing that he was concerned with religion. Even so, in neither instance does he define anything that can be seen as a specifically Jewish element. Indeed, Henriques himself noted this, stating that 'we can teach what you may call "ethical monotheism" If we have done that we have done something gigantic ... How are we going to make ethical monotheism into Jewish ethical monotheism? 1. Emphasise Israel, 2. Emphasise Jewish Holidays, 3. Emphasise Sabbath.'[59] Critics noted the promotion of 'ethical monotheism' with one member of the community writing to the *Jewish Chronicle* criticizing Henriques' position:

> From end to end [his] purpose seems to me to disrupt and breakdown traditional Judaism and to substitute for it, so far as the settlement has any influence, a sort of ethical monotheism to use the term employed by [Henriques], with a Jewish tinge ... In his unmeasured zeal Mr Henriques appears as a rampaging iconoclast prepared to uproot all true Jewish sentiment and to set at nought much that is valuable in Jewish belief and practice.[60]

Although strongly worded, the correspondent's views were justified when looking solely at Henriques' speeches and writings. These works were designed for both Jewish and Christian audiences, therefore removing explicitly Jewish elements from the texts was logical as it allowed for Christian clubs to use the basic structure of the services for their own, Christian audiences. In the speeches, Henriques managed to promote an ethical monotheism that limited a specifically Jewish element. A glance at the club's religion, especially religion at camp, supports the view of the correspondent that the club practiced an ethical monotheism. This certainly lacked the ritual and ceremonial elements traditionally associated

---

57   Henriques, *Club Leadership*, pp. 161–2.
58   SUA MS132 AJ220 3/4/4.
59   Ibid.
60   *JC*, 18 July 1930.

within Jewish boys' clubs. However, through the religious history classes, the promotion of the Settlement Synagogue and the opening of the club on Friday evenings as well as the emphasis on the Sabbath at camp, the club can be seen to have included elements designed to add a *Jewish* element to ethical monotheism.

There can be no doubt that, especially post-1919 and the loss of the Chief Rabbi's support, religion in the Oxford and St George's Club was of a Liberal, rather than Orthodox, character. The particular emphasis on spirituality certainly emphasized the Liberal character, especially in a boys' club where this was seen in Orthodoxy as a feminine element of religion and therefore less important than observing rituals and ceremony. The early claims of the club to teach a Judaism free from Orthodoxy or Liberalism were, ultimately, unsuccessful as the religion in the club took on strong Liberal characteristics. Although members were allowed to (and encouraged) to preserve their own beliefs, this was certainly (after 1919) not promoted officially by the club, whose identity as a part of a Liberal Jewish Settlement was firmly established.

In contrast to many of the Jewish clubs looked at in previous chapters, this religious influence was a continual feature of club life. The religious activities introduced at the start of the club's history, such as prayer services, continued to be a part of club life up until the Second World War. In this way, the club, like the West Central Girls' Club showed that it was committed from the outset to including a religious element, not only when society demanded it.

This was a controversial element of the club's religious policies and led some to criticize the club's Jewishness. Its Jewish history class, an emphasis on the Sabbath and the promotion of synagogue services throughout the year as well as on Jewish Holy Days certainly indicates a specifically Jewish element. Nevertheless, the emphasis on the spiritual meant that this religion was considered to be less formal and therefore less appropriate for boys than the traditional observances noted in other boys' clubs. This emphasis on spirituality and the idea that boys took religious practices into their homes was something that was noted in girls' clubs, both Orthodox and Liberal. Boys would have been expected to bring certain elements of Judaism into the home – particularly leading services. However, this was not a focus for boys' clubs, which rejected the emphasis placed on the domestic space. In contrast, girls' clubs emphasized the religious responsibilities of women in the domestic setting, a traditionally feminine space. Indeed, the religious policies of the Oxford and St George's Club mirror the policies of Orthodox girls' clubs closely. Whilst this attention to the domestic was acceptable in girls' clubs, this was not so within a boys' club. As a result of the emphasis on spirituality and the omission of ceremonial rites, the religious element in the club was doubted. Additionally, the 'Liberal' element of the club drew criticism from the community and helped to underscore fears that the club was not a religious one.

The examination of the religious activities of the club shows that the group *was* concerned with religion and, indeed, religion occupied a prominent place within club life. Henriques, and consequently the Oxford and St George's Club, proved that he was committed to the promotion of Judaism over the promotion of gender ideals. Ultimately, this is why the club faced such criticism from the Jewish community. Whilst the type and amount of religious observance in the club was considered inadequate for a boys' club, it would have been seen as acceptable – and perhaps even commendable – within an Orthodox girls' club. In rejecting gender norms, the club therefore rejected any potential acknowledgement that the group included an acceptable religious element.

Conclusion: The Oxford and St George's Club and Religion

Despite contemporary criticism, activities in the group did take on a distinct *religious* character. First, through observing Holy Days and festivals such as *Chanucah* parties and *Rosh Hashanah* services; second, through retaining certain distinctly Jewish customs including the reciting of the *Shema* and maintaining dietary laws; and, third, through observing the Sabbath as, perhaps not a day of rest, but as a day apart from the rest of the week. Despite criticism in the press, the club *was* religious and featured elements of 'ethical monotheism' as well as distinctly Jewish practices.

The most striking difference between the Liberal and non-Liberal clubs was the criticism that was laid on each group. In the West Central Club there was little disapproval of the amount of religion included in the group, instead negative attention was placed on the Liberal nature of religion. In the Oxford and St George's Club, however, not only was the club attacked for its 'Liberal' style of worship, but it was also concerned with the general lack of Jewish religion within the group. This is an interesting contrast, as the religious activities in the Oxford Club did not differ largely from those included in the West Central Club. The contrast between the criticisms levelled at both clubs is telling. Both clubs adopted a progressive attitude towards religion. Indeed, they included religion more frequently than Orthodox clubs by including prayers. This was seen as religious in the West Central Club as these concepts conformed to prevalent gender norms, with criticism focusing on the Liberal nature of religion rather than on a perceived lack of religion. Thus, religion, whilst disagreeable in form was seen to be present. In the Oxford and St George's Club, however, religion did not conform to gender roles and, as a result, the club was seen to be ignoring religion.

Finally, by adopting a more feminine form of worship, the Oxford and St George's Club was seen as problematic with regard to religion. In contrast, the West Central Club adopted gender appropriate worship and therefore religion was more acceptable (if still open to criticism). The opposition to the Oxford and St George's Club cannot be seen purely in terms of objections to its association with Liberal Judaism, as the West Central Club did not face such disapproval. Whilst the Girl Guides included elements of ungendered religion, they did not come in for such attacks. This was due to two reasons. First, Guiding was an essentially British organization that did not appeal solely to Jewish immigrants and their families and, second, Guides largely adhered to certain gender norms, for example, the promotion of domesticity. The Oxford St George's Club, however, deviated from both of these points. Rather than having a national appeal, it was an organization operating in an impoverished and essentially immigrant Jewish community and although the club did maintain elements of masculinity in its religious teachings, these shared equal time and importantly equal emphasis with more feminine traits of domesticity and love. For the Oxford and St George's Club, it is possible to argue that it was the opposition to gender norms and the closer adherence to traditions of girls' clubs rather than boys' clubs (in combination with the Liberal nature of the group) that resulted in the criticisms laid on the group. This demonstrates not only the importance of Orthodoxy within the Jewish community but also the importance of gender-based religion. For religion to be seen as legitimate it *must* be gendered.

Religion in the Clubs

Jewish youth clubs played an important role within late nineteenth and early twentieth century British Jewish society. The groups served to provide links between British Jews who financed and ran the organizations and immigrants and their children who were the club members. This connection was not neutral but was of a patriarchal kind, where Anglo-Jewry were able to exert social control over young, impoverished Jews by guiding them to live in what wealthier classes considered to be a respectable way, that is to say, in a manner that corresponded to upper- and middle- class British expectations. The clubs were also important in instilling a sense of patriotism and national pride amongst the young, which established British Jewry deemed to be in need amongst the immigrants. Additionally, the clubs sought to cultivate and present a positive image of Jewish youth, which fell in line with idealized versions of British behaviour. Overall, the clubs aimed to exert social control over young people, including the religious observance of its members. Indeed, club managers sought to promote a highly Anglicized form of religion which corresponded closely to gender norms for both boys and girls, respectively.

Despite the numerous clubs in existence prior to 1939 and the varieties of geographical locations and religious affiliations (whether Liberal or Orthodox), religious programming was remarkably similar, which indicates that a particular affiliation did not impact on religion to a great extent. The Jewish Lads' Brigade in Glasgow was similar to the Jewish Girls' Club in Bristol. Indeed the different clubs sought to achieve their aims through comparable methods; the inclusion of Holy Day services, prayer and the use of appropriately gendered language. Because of this homogeneity, subtle deviations from the norm become an important indication of what was, and what was not, considered acceptable. Good point.

For the majority of boys' clubs, religion was characterized by formality and structure. Synagogue parades and services formed a frequent part of religious observances, which highlighted the link between masculinity and the public sphere, as well as military influenced discipline.[1] The public nature of worship adopted in boys' clubs helped to underscore the importance of separate spheres for boys within British gendered traditions. In promoting this goal within clubs, the leaders were helping to promote religion at the same time as Anglicization. Clubs promoted religion in line with the public school 'sports ethic' defined by Mangan as 'the belief that important expressive and instrumental qualities can be promoted through team games'.[2] This allowed the clubs to further their Anglicizing aims in line with religious expectations laid out by the British Jewish community. With the boys' clubs, the focus of religious programming changed between 1880 and 1939. Prior to the First World War, religious activities highlighted militarism and espoused patriotic virtues that were seen as integral to the formation of masculine identities. This was strengthened during the war as clubs adopted war prayers, such as that in the Stepney Club, and celebrated the activities of members and leaders who were serving in the armed forces.[3] After 1918 however, the nature of religious programming changed in line with popular opinion, which turned against militarism; throughout the 1920s and 1930s, courage, self-reliance and bravery were emphasized. These changes can be seen clearly in the celebration of *Chanucah*, where the focus of pre-war services was on the aggressive militaristic element of the story and after the Armistice was on courage and bravery.[4]

In contrast to the changeable nature of religious programming within boys' clubs, religion within girls' clubs remained largely constant between 1880 and 1939. This was due to two elements. First, militarism, which was seen as a vital component of masculine identities, was seen as a negative influence within the female sphere. As a result, there was no need to adjust

---

1   See John Tosh, *A Man's Place: Masculinity and the Middle-Class Home in Victorian England* (Bath: Bath Press, 1999), p. 189.

2   J. A. Mangan, 'Grammar School and the Games Ethic in the Victorian and Edwardian Era', *Albion*, 15 (1983), pp. 313–55 (p. 314).

3   For the Stepney Club War Prayer see The London Library, M397, *Prayers: Stepney Jewish Lads' Club* (London: Eyre and Spottiswoode, 1915).

4   See *JC*, 10 December 1915, and *Jewish Guardian*, 6 January 1922 for examples.

the religious content in girls' clubs, as was the case within boys' clubs. Second, femininity was considered to be unchangeable and immutable; thus, the continuity found within feminine religion reflected a woman's position as a continuous force.[5] Throughout the period, religion in girls' clubs emphasized prayer and placed spirituality and the notion of a 'living religion' at the centre of their religious activities. The Jewish Girls' Club, for example, described the moral and religious element of their work as 'the most vital' part of their programming.[6] By placing an emphasis on prayer, the groups were equipping girls with skills that they were expected to have learned before they had their own families. Indeed, the centrality of family was an important characteristic of female-focused Judaism, as many of the activities were designed to develop skills or knowledge that the members could later bring to the home.

The majority of Jewish clubs, by including highly gendered programming reflecting wider societal concerns within their religious activities, were promoting national identities within a specifically ethno-religious context. They emphasized the public and private divide of gender roles within young people, something that was not always visible within Eastern European Jewish identities – particularly in regard to the acceptance of women going out of the home to work. This helped to reinforce acceptable notions of Britishness within first and second generation immigrant children. To counter specifically Jewish concerns brought about by stereotypes of male Jewish effeminacy and female Jewish promiscuity, the clubs gave additional attention to the ideas of sports and gentlemanly behaviour for boys and purity and the importance of the family for girls. In the majority of clubs, therefore, gendered constructions of religion provided a way to reinforce the importance of the ideals of Anglicization and the need to maintain distance from negative images of Jews prevalent in British culture, society and politics.

5   See George L. Mosse, *Nationalism and Sexuality: Respectability and Abnormal Sexuality in Modern Europe* (New York: Howard Fertig, 1985), p. 23.
6   THLA, 360.1, Leman Street Girls' Club, *52nd Annual Report, 1937–1938*.

There were also a number of important deviations from these common tendencies. Within girls' clubs, synagogue attendance was encouraged at certain times, such as the Beatrice Club Sabbath services within the New West End Synagogue, although these were small-scale and used 'feminine' traits (such as an emphasis on beauty) to promote Judaism.[7] Within boys' clubs, domestic ideals were promoted through religiously significant events such as holding a *Seder*, including the one held at the Brady Club in 1933.[8] These instances, however, were not significant enough to have an impact on the overall message provided by the Orthodox clubs, including the JLB. Within the Guides and the Scouts, there were more gender deviations. This is particularly evident within the Guides, who were often encouraged to attend the synagogue and to take part in parades through consecrations of colours. The involvement of Guides within public worship was considered to be acceptable as the organization as a whole had explicit links to Britishness through the founder Baden-Powell. The annual *Chanucah* service of Jewish Girl Guides fits more closely with the experiences found within boys' clubs, emphasizing the formal and structured element of observance. For Scouts, members were often encouraged to develop the spiritual side of religion through the use of the Scouts-Own ceremony and the inclusion of evening prayers to a greater extent than was found in other boys' clubs. Despite these deviations, there were few instances of criticism against the Scouts and Guides. These factors allowed social commentators to overlook transgressions from acceptably gendered religion, as the two groups were seen as fulfilling their duty sufficiently to overlook them. In all of these cases, these deviations from traditional gender norms demonstrate the complexities of religion: at specific moments, religious needs were more significant than the need to promote appropriate gender roles.

In contrast to the acceptance of gender deviations within Scouts and Guides, the case of the Liberal Jewish clubs provides another important insight into the importance of gender in religious programming. The West

---

7   The National Archives, ED 41/262, *19th Annual Report of the Beatrice Girls' Club, Year Ending Dec 1919*.

8   THLA, 360.1, *Brady Associated Clubs Annual Report 1933*.

Central Girls' Club provided a religious programme, which was firmly within religious expectations of Liberal Judaism, and *did* fall within gender norms. Whilst the club faced criticism because of its Liberal Jewish element, it was not accused of abandoning Judaism entirely. This was not the case with the Oxford and St George's Lads' Club. This club focused on the creation of a religious spirit and placed prayer firmly within its programming. The language of religion within this group, whilst mentioning sports, patriotism and courage, traditionally associated with masculinity, placed an *equal* emphasis on traditionally feminine qualities of love, beauty, friendship and the home. The criticisms against this club focused more on the absence of Judaism rather than 'ethical monotheism' and the damage caused by such a religious policy which left boys ill-equipped to participate in traditional elements of Judaism. It is not sufficient to argue that this criticism is based on the Liberal Jewish affiliation of the group, as the West Central Club did not face such concerns. Instead, the criticisms, arguably, should be seen as a result of the ungendered quality of religion – as the group was not promoting a suitably 'masculine' religion, it was seen to be failing in its duty to promote acceptably British Jewish identities. The promotion of differentiated gender identities was thus central to whether a club was deemed successful in its Jewish obligations.

The religious element of club work prior to 1939 reflected Anglo-Jewry's vision of acceptable religion and was promoted in order to further the Anglicizing aims of club work. This is significant as it demonstrates the ways in which the Jewish community was able to adapt religious practices in order to conform to contemporary concerns. Moreover, this book has shown that gendered religion within the clubs was a vital element in the construction of Jewish identities prior to the Second World War. Although at times religious needs were seen as more pressing than promoting acceptably feminine or masculine identities, largely the clubs followed similar patterns to each other, emphasizing appropriate gender norms. The importance of gender in the construction of religious identities in clubs can be seen through the Oxford and St George's Jewish Lads' Club, which chose to emphasize spirituality rather than 'masculine' religion. In doing so, the club was seen as not specifically Jewish. Through the example of this club, this study has thus shown that not only was the relationship between religion and gender important, it was indeed considered to be *vital*. Without a suitably gendered religion, clubs were seen as 'un-Jewish'. It thus has illustrated the centrality of gender differentiation within youthful religiosities.

Bibliography

Section 1. Primary Sources

1a. Archive Collections

Guide Association Archives (GAA)
    Girl Guide Gazette
    Misc. Photographs and Unit Records
Jewish Museum London (JML)
    1991.30 – Papers of the West Central Jewish Girls' Club
    T293 – Papers of the Jewish Girls' Club
    1993.78 – Papers of the Stepney Jewish Girls' Club
    19913.72.2 1993.79 – Papers of the Butler Street Club
    1992.9.7 – Papers of Habonim
    1990. 2.3 – Magazines of the Hutchison House Club
    Museum of Jewish Life Oral History recordings
    Miscellaneous records
London Metropolitan Archives (LMA)
    ACC/3529 – Lily Montagu Papers
    ACC/2999 – Victoria Boys' Club Papers
    ACC/2712 – United Synagogue Papers
Liverpool Records Office (LRO)
    296 JGC, M364 CHC/98 – Papers of the Liverpool Jewish Girls' Club
    296 JLB – Papers of the Liverpool Jewish Lads' Brigade
    296 LJS, 296 LJE – Papers of Liverpool Jewish Scouts
Manchester County Records Office
    MS 130, 2340–2346. Records of the Jewish Lads' Brigade
Manchester Jewish Museum (MJM)
    J17, 142, 157, 217, 237 and 268 – Oral History Project

The Montagu Centre, Liberal Jewish Archives
    8B – West Central Girls' Club Papers
    Audio tape collection
The National Archives (TNA)
    ED 41/253 – West Central Girls' Club Papers
    ED 41/262 – Beatrice Club for Jewish Working Girls' Papers
Scottish Jewish Archives Centre, Glasgow (SJAC)
    SOC SCO 0001–0004 – Records for Guide Companies
    PER G 0001 – Oral History Collection
    PHO G 0011 – Photographs of Brownies and Guides
    Cabinet of Jewish Lads' Brigade Records
Scout Association Archives
    Vol i/51–3 – Collections of letters and records
    263 – Log book of the 11th Toxteth Jewish Scout Group
    Scouter Magazine
    Headquarters Gazette
Tower Hamlets Local History Archives (THLA)
    360.1 – Papers of the Stepney Juvenile Organization, Oxford and St George's
    Settlement, Association of Jewish Youth, Leman Street Girls' Club, Stepney
    Lads' Club and Brady Boys' Club.
University College, London Archives (UCL)
    GASTER/1/A/NOT/1 – Nottingham Jewish Girls' Club Papers
University of Southampton Archives (SUA)
    MS116 – Small Papers
    MS127 – Norwood Archives
    MS132 – Henriques Papers, 1854, 1894–1970s
    MS152 – Papers of the West Central Jewish Lads' Club 1887–1929
    MS172 – Papers of the Stepney Jewish Lads' Club 1924–63
    MS223 – Papers of Stanley Rowe
    MS231 – Papers of Sharman Kadish
    MS244 – Papers of the Jewish Lads and Girls' Brigade 1897–1991

1b. Published Primary Sources

1921 census of England and Wales, General Report with Appendices, Table 35; 'Number
    of Males and Females in Various Age Groups in 1000 Persons at all Ages in Several
    Countries', in *A Vision of Britain Though Time*, <http://www.visionofbritain.

org.uk/census/table_page.jsp?tab_id=EW1921GEN_M35&show=> [accessed 5 January 2014]

Baden-Powell, Robert, *Boy Scouts Scheme* (London: The Scout Association, 1908)

——, *Scouting For Boys: The Original 1908 Edition* (Mineola, New York: Dover, 2007)

——, *A Suggestion of Character Training for Girls* (London: The Scout Association, 1909)

Barnett, S. A., 'University Settlements', in W. Reason (ed.), *University and Social Settlements* (London: Methuen, 1898), pp. 11–27

Evans-Gordon, William Eden, *The Alien Immigrant 1903*, reproduced by (London: Elibron Classics, 2006)

Frank, Ray, 'Women in the Synagogue', in *Papers of the Jewish Women's Congress Held at Chicago, September 4, 5, 6 and 7th 1893* (Philadelphia: Jewish Publication Society of America, 1894), pp. 52–65 (p. 64), in *Internet Archive* <http://archive.org/stream/papersofjewishwooojewiuoft/papersofjewishwooojewiuoft_djvu.txt> [accessed 12 July 2013]

Henriques, Basil L. Q., *The Bernhard Baron St George's Jewish Settlement: Fiftieth Anniversary Review, 1914–1964* (London: Private Publisher, 1964)

——, *Club Leadership* (London: Humphrey Milford, 1934)

——, *Fratres: Club Boys in Uniform* (London: Secker and Warburg, 1951)

Henriques, Rose L., *50 Years in Stepney*, Pamphlet, 1966

Hourwich, Isaac A., 'The Jewish Laborer in London', *Journal of Political Economy*, 13 (1904), pp. 89–98

Jewish Year Book 1924, The (London: The Jewish Chronicle, 1924)

Joseph, Morris, 'Jewish Religious Education', *Jewish Quarterly Review*, 9 (1897), pp. 631–68

Levy, Nellie, *The West Central Story and its Founders, the Hon Lily H. Montagu, CBE JP DD and the Hon Marian Montagu 1893–1963* (London: Leeway Business Services, 1969)

Mattuck, Israel, I., *Jewish Ethics* (London: Hutchinson University Library, 1953)

Montagu, Lillian H., *The Faith of a Jewish Woman* (London: George Allen and Unwin, 1943)

——, 'The Girl in the Background', in *Studies of Boy Life in Our Cities*, ed. by E. J. Urwick (London: Dent, 1904), pp. 233–54

——, *My Club and I: The Story of the West Central Jewish Club* (London: Herbert Joseph, 1954)

——, 'The Role of Women in Religious Life' reprinted in *A Reader of Early Liberal Judaism: The Writings of Israel Abrahams, Claude Montefiore, Lily Montagu and Israel Mattuck*, ed. by Edward Kessler (London: Vallentine Mitchell, 2004), pp. 127–12

——, *Thoughts on Judaism* (London: Adelphi, 1904)

Montefiore, Claude G., *Outlines of Liberal Judaism for the Use of Parents and Teachers* (London: MacMillan, 1923)

Pethick, Emmeline, 'Working Girls' Clubs', in *University and Social Settlements*, ed. by W. Reason (London: Methuen, 1898), pp. 101–14

Royal Commission on Alien Immigration (London: H. M. Stationary Office, 1903), Q17877

Stanley, Maude, *The Way to Start and Manage a Girls' Club* (London: MacMillan, 1890)

1c. Printed and Electronic Ephemera

British Library (BL)
    1976.dd.20.(06–10) – Jewish Lads' Brigade Records of Service
    ORB30/4931 – Stepney Jewish Lads' Club Papers
    ORB40/77 (8) – Bethnal Green Jewish Girls' Club Papers
    P.P.1149.bb. – West Central Jewish Lads' Club Papers
    Oral History Collections – Family Life and Work Experience Before 1918, Millennium Memory Bank, Living Memory of the Jewish Community collections
Harvard University Library
    560307 – Habonim Handbook
The London Library (LL)
    M329, M332, M341, M407, M413, M431, M512, M536, M558 – West Central Girls' Club Papers
    M351, M375, M376, M405 – Oxford and St George's Club Papers
    M395, M397 – Stepney Jewish Lads' Club Papers
The Log of the 14th Salisbury [Scout Troop] (Private Collection)
Reminiscences from 60 years of Guiding by Joyce Cranshaw, <http://www.leics.gov.uk/index/leisure_tourism/local_history/recordoffice/recordoffice_exhibitions/recordoffice_currentexhibs/girlguiding.htm> [accessed 8 March 2015]

1d. Newspapers

Adelaide Advertiser
Daily Telegraph
Girl Guide Gazette
Headquarters Gazette [Boy Scout Association]

Jewish Chronicle
Jewish Echo
Jewish Guardian
Jewish World
Liverpool Echo
Scouter

Section 2. Secondary Sources

Alderman, Geoffrey, 'British Jewry: Religious Community or Ethnic Minority', in *Jewish Identities in the New Europe*, ed. by Jonathan Webber (London: Litman Library of Jewish Civilization, 1994), pp. 189–92

——, 'Montagu, Lilian Helen (1873–1963)', *Oxford Dictionary of National Biography*, Oxford University Press, 2004 <http://www.oxforddnb.com/view/article/40837> [accessed 13 September 2013]

——, *Modern British Jewry* (Oxford: Oxford University Press, 1992)

Arnaut, Karel, 'Making Space for Performativity: Publics, Powers and Places in a Multi-Register Town Festival', in Bruno Boute and Thomas Småberg (eds), *Devising Order: Socio-Religious Models, Rituals and the Performativity of Practice* (Leiden: Brill Academic Publishing, 2012), pp. 81–102

Barclay, Kate, 'Place and Power in Irish Farms at the End of the Nineteenth Century', *Women's History Review*, 21 (2012), pp. 571–88

Becker, Annette, 'Faith, Ideologies and the "Cultures of War"', in *A Companion to World War One*, ed. by John Horne (Oxford: Wiley-Blackwell, 2010), pp. 234–47

Beavan, Brad, *Leisure, Citizenship and Working-Class Men in Britain 1850–1945* (Manchester: Manchester University Press, 2005)

Black, Eugene, *The Social Politics of Anglo-Jewry 1880–1929* (Oxford: Blackwell, 1988)

Black, Gerry, *JFS: The History of the Jews' Free School, London since 1732* (London: Tymsder, 1998)

Boyarin, Daniel, *Unheroic Conduct: The Rise of Homosexuality and the Invention of the Jewish Man* (London: University of California Press, 1997)

Bradley, Katherine, 'Juvenile Delinquency, the Juvenile Courts and the Settlement Movement 1908–1950: Basil Henriques and Toynbee Hall', *Twentieth Century British History*, 19 (2008), pp. 133–55

—— 'Poverty and Philanthropy in Central London 1918–1959: The University Settlements' (unpublished doctoral thesis, University of London, Institute of Historical Research, 2006)

Bruley, Sue, *Women in Britain Since 1900* (Basingstoke: MacMillan, 1999)

Burman, Rickie, 'Growing Up in Manchester Jewry: The Story of Clara Weingard', *Oral History*, 12 (1984), pp. 56–63

——, 'Jewish Women and the Household Economy in Manchester, c. 1890–1920', in *The Making of Modern Anglo-Jewry*, ed. by David Cesarani (Oxford: Blackwell, 1990), pp. 55–76

——, 'Middle-Class Anglo-Jewish Lady Philanthropists and Eastern European Jewish Women: The First National Conference of Jewish Women, 1902', in *Women, Migration and Empire*, ed. by Joan Grant (Stoke-on Trent: Trentham Books, 1996), pp. 123–48

Clarke, Michael, 'Jewish Identity in British Politics: The Case of the First Jewish MPs, 1858–87', *Jewish Social Studies*, 13 (2007), pp. 93–126

Collins, Kenneth, *Aspects of Scottish Jewry* (Glasgow: Glasgow Jewish Representative Council, 1987)

Connolly, Peter, *Approaches to the Study of Religion* (London: Continuum, 1999)

Cox, Pamela, *Bad Girls In Britain: Gender, Justice and Welfare, 1900–1950* (Basingstoke: Palgrave Macmillan, 2013)

Davidoff, Leonore, 'Class and Gender in Victorian England: The Diaries of Arthur J. Munby and Hannah Cullwick', *Feminist Studies*, 5 (1979), pp. 86–141

Davidoff, Leonore, and Catherine Hall, *Family Fortunes: Men and Women of the English Middle Class, 1780—1850* (London: Routledge, 1987)

Davin, Anna, *Growing Up Poor: Home, School and Street in London, 1870–1914* (London: Rivers Oram, 1996)

Dee, David, 'Nothing Specifically Jewish in Athletics? Sport, Physical Recreation and the Jewish Youth Movement in London, 1895–1914', *London Journal*, 34 (2009), pp. 81–101

——, *Sport and British Jewry: Integration, Ethnicity and Anti-Semitism, 1890–1970* (Manchester: Manchester University Press, 2013)

Delap, Lucy, 'Be Strong and Play the Man: Anglican Masculinities in the Twentieth Century', in *Men, Masculinities and Religious Change in Twentieth Century Britain*, ed. by Lucy Delap and Sue Morgan (Basingstoke: Palgrave Macmillan, 2013), pp. 119–45

——, and Sue Morgan, 'Introduction: Men, Masculinities and Religious Change in Post-Christian Britain', in *Men, Masculinities and Religious Change in Twentieth Century Britain*, ed. by Lucy Delap and Sue Morgan (Basingstoke: Palgrave Macmillan, 2013), pp. 1–29

Dove, Iris, 'Sisterhood or Surveillance?' The Development of Working Girls' Clubs in London 1880–1939' (unpublished doctoral thesis, University of Greenwich, 1996)

Dyhouse, Carol, *Girls Growing Up in Late Victorian and Edwardian England* (London: Routledge and Kegan Paul, 1981)

Elliott, Dorice Williams, *The Angel Out of the House: Philanthropy and Gender in Nineteenth Century England* (London: University Press of Virginia, 2002)

Endelman, Todd M., *The Jews of Britain, 1656–2000* (London: University of California Press, 2002)

——, *Radical Assimilation in English Jewish History 1656–1945* (Bloomington: Indiana University Press, 1990)

Feldman, David, *Englishmen and Jews: Social relations and Political Culture 1840–1914* (London: Yale University Press, 1994)

Ferris, Jillian L., 'What a Girl Needs: The Influence of Religion on the Girls' Friendly Society and West Central Jewish Girls' Club in the Late Victorian Era' (unpublished honor's thesis, Colgate University, 2008)

Fishman, William J., *East End 1888* (London: Gerald Duckworth, 1988)

Flanagan, Bud, *My Crazy Life* (London: Frederick Muller Ltd, 1961)

Galchinsky, Michael, 'Engendering Liberal Jews: Jewish Women in Victorian England', in *Jewish Women in Historical Perspective*, ed. by Judith R. Baskin (Detroit, MI: Wayne State University Press, 1998), pp. 208–26

Gartner, Lloyd P., *The Immigrant in England 1870–1914* (London: Vallentine Mitchell, 1960)

Giles, Judy, *Women, Identity and Private Life in Britain 1900–1950* (Basingstoke: MacMillan, 1995)

Gilman, Sander, *The Jew's Body* (London: Routledge, 1991)

Glasman, Judy, 'Assimilation by Design: London Synagogues in the Nineteenth Century', in *The Jewish Heritage in British History: Englishness and Jewishness*, ed. by Tony Kushner (London: Frank Cass, 1992), pp. 171–209

Gomersall, Meg, *Working Class Girls in Nineteenth Century England: Life, Work and Schooling* (Basingstoke: MacMillan, 1997)

Gomez, Beatriz Oria, 'Rob Roy an Anti-English Hero', in Christopher Hart (ed.), *Heroines and Heroes: Symbolism, Embodiement, Narrative and Identity* (Kingswinford: Midrash Publishers, 2008), pp. 196–206

Granot-Bein, Yael, 'An Urgent Social Problem? Jewish Juvenile Delinquents in Turn-of-Twentieth-Century London', *Journal of Modern Jewish Studies*, 9 (2010), pp. 369–96

Guy, Francis, *Women of Worth: Jewish Women in Britain* (Manchester: Manchester Jewish Museum, 1992)

Harvey, David, 'From Space to Place and Back Again', in David Harvey (ed.), *Justice, Nature and the Geography of Difference* (Cambridge: Blackwell, 1996), pp. 291–326

——, 'Space as Keyword', in N. Castree and D. Gregory (eds), *David Harvey: A Critical Reader* (Oxford: Basil Blackwell, 2006), pp. 270–93

Henriques, U. R. Q., 'The Jewish Emancipation Controversy in Nineteenth Century Britain', *Past and Present*, 40 (1968), pp. 126–46

Hirschfield, Claire, 'The Anglo-Boer War and the Issue of Jewish Culpability', *Journal of Contemporary History*, 15 (1980), pp. 619–31

Horn, Pamela, *Women in the 1920s* (Stroud: Alan Sutton, 1995)

Hyman, Paula E., *Gender and Assimilation in Modern Jewish History: The Roles and Representation of Women* (London: University of Washington Press, 1997)

Jackson, Carol, and Penny Tinkler, '"Ladettes" and "Modern Girls": "Troublesome" Young Femininities', *Sociological Review*, 55 (2007), pp. 251–72

Jeffs, Anthony J., *Young People and the Youth Service* (London: Routledge and Kegan Paul, 1979)

Jordan, Ellen, '"Making Good Wives and Mothers?": The Transformation of Middle-Class Girls' Education in Nineteenth Century Britain', *History of Education Quarterly*, 31 (1991), pp. 439–62

Kadish, Sharman, *A Good Jew and a Good Englishman: The Jewish Lads' and Girls' Brigade, 1895–1995* (London: Vallentine Mitchell, 1995)

——, 'Ironing Out the Ghetto Bend?: The Impact of the Jewish Lads' Brigade on the Jewish Immigrant in England 1895–1914', in *Patterns of Migration 1850–1914: Proceedings of the International Academic Conference of the Jewish Historical Society of England and the Institute of Jewish Studies, University College London*, ed. by A. Newman and S. W. Massill (London: The Jewish Historical Society of England, 1996), pp. 53–8

—— 'Katie Magnus', *Oxford Dictionary of National Biography* (Oxford: Oxford University Press, 2004), <http://www.oxforddnb.com/view/article/55630> [accessed 2 February 2015]

Kennedy, Rosie, *The Children's War, Britain 1914–1918* (Basingstoke: Palgrave MacMillan, 2014)

Kessler, Edward (ed.), *An English Jew: The Life and Writings of Claude Montefiore* (London: Vallentine Mitchell, 1989)

Kuzmack, Linda Gordon, *Woman's Cause: The Jewish Woman's Movement in England and the United States 1881–1933* (Columbus: Ohio State University Press, 1990)

Langton, Daniel, R., *Claude Montefiore: His Life and Thoughts* (London: Vallentine Mitchell, 2002)

Latham, Emma, 'The Liverpool Boys' Association and the Liverpool Union of Youth Club: Youth Organisations and Gender 1949–1970', *Journal of Contemporary History*, 35 (2000), pp. 423–37

Lerman, Tony, 'The '*Habonim*' Story – The formative years', *Jewish Quarterly*, 24 (1977), pp. 29–33

——, unpublished manuscript, personal collection, [n.d.]

Lipman, V. D., *A History of the Jews in Britain since 1858* (Leicester: Leicester University Press, 1990)

Livingston, Harvey M., *From Strength to Service, 100 Years of Service, 1903–2003: Celebrating the Centenary of the Glasgow Jewish Lads' Brigade* (Glasgow: Glasgow Jewish Lads' Brigade, 2004)

Livshin, Rosalyn, 'The Acculturation of the Children of Immigrant Jews in Manchester, 1890–1930', in *The Making of Modern Anglo-Jewry*, ed. by David Cesarani (Oxford: Blackwell, 1990), pp. 76–96

Loewe, L. L., *Basil Henriques: A Portrait* (London: Routledge and Kegan Paul, 1976)

Loewe, R, 'The Bernhard Baron Settlement and the Oxford and St George's Club', in *The Jewish East End*, ed. by the Jewish Historical Society of England on behalf of the Conference Organising Committee (London: The Jewish Historical Society of England, 1981), pp. 143–6

Lorrimer, Hayden, 'Happy Hostelling in the Highlands: Nationhood, Citizenship and the Inter-War youth Movement', *Scottish Geographical Magazine*, 113 (1997), pp. 42–50

Lowerson, John, *Sport and the English Middle Classes, 1870–1914* (Manchester: Manchester University Press, 1995)

MacDonald, Robert H., 'Reproducing the Middle-Class Boy: From Purity to Patriotism in the Boys' Magazines, 1892–1914', *Journal of Contemporary History*, 24 (1989), pp. 519–39

McCrone, Kathleen E., 'Play Up! Play Up! And Play the Game! Sport at the Late Victorian Girls' Public Schools', in *From Fair Sex to Feminism: Sport and the Socialisation of Women in the Industrial and Post-Industrial Eras*, ed. by J. A. Mangan and Roberta Park (London: Frank Cass, 1987), pp. 97–129

MacFarlane, Donald M., *First For Boys: The Story of the Boys Brigade, 1883–1993* (London: The Boys' Brigade, 1993), <http://www.boys-brigade.org.uk/ffb.pdf> [accessed 2 April 2013]

Mangan, J. A., 'Grammar Schools and the Games Ethic in the Victorian and Edwardian Era', *Albion*, 15 (1983), pp. 313–55

——, and Callum McKenzie, 'The Other Side of the Coin: Victorian Masculinity, field Sports and English Elite Education', in *A Sport Loving Society: Victorian and Edwardian Middle-Class England at Play*, ed. by J. A. Mangan (Oxford: Routledge, 2006), pp. 45–64

Marks, Lara, 'Carers and Servers of the Jewish Community: The Marginalized Heritage of Jewish Women in Britain', in *The Jewish Heritage in British*

History: Englishness and Jewishness, ed. by Tony Kushner (London: Frank Cass, 1992)

——, 'Jewish Women and Jewish Prostitution in the East End of London', *Jewish Quarterly*, 34 (1987), pp. 6–11

——, 'The Luckless Waifs and Strays of Humanity: Irish and Jewish Immigrant Unwed Mothers in London, 1870–1939', *Twentieth Century History*, 3 (1992), pp. 113–37

——, *Model Mothers: Jewish Mothers' Maternity Provision in East London 1870–1939* (Oxford: Clarendon Press, 1994)

——, 'Race, Class and Gender: The Experience of Jewish Prostitutes and other Jewish Women in the East End of London at the Turn of the Century', in *Women, Migration and Empire*, ed. by Joan Grant (Stoke-on Trent: Trentham Books, 1996), pp. 31–50

Martin, Mary Claire, 'Roman Catholic Girl Guiding in Sussex 1912–1919: Origins, Ideology, Practice', in *Youth Policy*, 111 (2013), <http://www.youthandpolicy. org/wp-content/uploads/2013/10/martin-roman-catholic-girl-guiiding.pdf> [accessed 8 March 2014]

Meyer, Michael, *Responses to Modernity: A History of the Reform Movement in Judaism* (Detroit, MI: Wayne State University Press, 1988)

Mills, Sarah, 'Duty to God/my Dharma/Allah/Waheguru: Diverse Youthful Religiosities and the Politics and Performance of Informal Worship', *Social and Cultural Geography*, 13 (2012), pp. 481–99

——, '"An Instruction in Good Citizenship": Scouting and the Historical Geographies of Citizenship Education', *Transactions of the Institute of British Geographers*, 38 (2012), pp. 412–23

——, 'Scouting for Girls? Gender and the Scout Movement in Britain', *Gender, Place and Culture*, 18 (2011), pp. 537–56

Mosse, George L., *The Image of Man: The Creation of Modern Masculinities* (Oxford: Oxford University Press, 1996)

——, *Nationalism and Sexuality: Respectability and Abnormal Sexuality in Modern Europe* (New York: Howard Fertig, 1985)

Nead, Lynda, *Myths of Sexuality: Representations of Women in Victorian Britain* (Oxford: Basil Blackwell, 1990)

Park, Roberta, 'Biological Thought, Athletics and the Formation of a 'Man of Character' 1830–1900', in *Manliness and Morality: Middle Class Masculinity in Britain and America, 1800–1940*, ed. by J. A. Mangan and James Walvin (Manchester: Manchester University Press, 1987), pp. 7–34

Pieren, Kathrin, 'Cultivating Jewish Britons in the Edwardian Period: Jewish Youth Work Between the Call to Empire and the Home Cinema', unpublished conference paper, *Cultivating Britons: Culture and Identity in Britain, 1901–1936*, Oxford University, 16 September 2008.

Pooley, Colin and Sian Pooley, 'Constructing a Suburban Identity: Youth, Femininity and Modernity in Late-Victorian Merseyside', *Journal of Historical Geography*, 36 (2010), pp. 402–10

Portelli, Alessandro, 'Oral History as Genre', in *Narrative and Genre*, ed. by Mary Chamberlain and Paul Thompson (London: Routledge, 1998), pp. 23–45

Presner, Todd Samuel, *Muscular Judaism: The Jewish Body and the Politics of Regeneration* (Oxford: Routledge, 2007)

Proctor, Tammy, M., *On My Honour: Guides and Scouts in Interwar Britain* (Philadelphia: Transactions of the American Philosophical Society, 2002)

——, '(Uni)Forming Youth: Girl Guides and Boy Scouts in Britain 1908–1939', *History Workshop Journal*, 45 (1998), pp. 103–34

Pryke, Sam, 'The Popularity of Nationalism in the Early British Boy Scout Movement', *Social History*, 23 (2008), pp. 309–24

Richmond, Vivienne, '"It is not a Society for Human Beings but for Virgins": The Girls' Friendly Society Membership Eligibility Dispute 1875–1936', *Journal of Historical Sociology*, 20 (2007), pp. 304–27

Roach, John, 'The Sheffield Boys' and Girls' Chanty Schools 1706–1962', *Journal of Educational Administration and History*, 31 (1999), pp. 114–29

Robinson, James, and Sarah Mills, 'Being Observant and Bing Observed: Embodied Citizenship Training in the Home Guard and the Boy Scout Movement, 1907–1945', *Journal of Historical Geography*, 38 (2012), pp. 412–23

Rose, Daniel, 'The World of the Jewish Youth Movement' (*The Encyclopaedia of Informal Education*, 2005) < http://www.infed.org/informaljewisheducation/ Jewish_youth_movements.htm> [accessed 21 August 2012]

Rosenthal, Michael, *The Character Factory: Baden-Powell and the Origins of the Scout Movement* (London: Collins, 1986)

Rubenstein, W. D., *A History of the Jews in the English Speaking World: Great Britain* (Basingstoke: MacMillan, 1996)

Selman-Cheong, Helen, *Wellesley Aron: Rebel with a Cause, a Memoir* (London: Vallentine Mitchell, 1992)

Smith, Mark, *Developing Youth Work: Informal Education, Mutual Aid and Popular Practice* (Milton Keynes: Open University Press, 1988)

Solomon, Norman, 'Judaism in the New Europe: Discovery or Invention', in *Jewish Identities in the New Europe*, ed. by Jonathan Webber (London: Litman Library of Jewish Civilisation, 1994), pp. 86–98

Spence, Jean, 'Working for Jewish Girls: Lily Montagu, Girls' Clubs and Industrial Reform 1890–1014', *Women's History Review*, 13 (2004), pp. 491–510

Springhall, John, 'Baden Powell and the Scout Movement before 1920: Citizenship Training or Soldiers of the Future', *English Historical Review*, 102 (1987), pp. 934–42

——, 'Building Character in the British Boy: The Attempt to Extend Christian Manliness to Working Class Adolescents, 1880–1914', in *Manliness and Morality: Middle Class Masculinity in Britain and America, 1800–1940*, ed. by J. A. Mangan and James Walvin (Manchester: Manchester University Press, 1987), pp. 52–74

——, *Youth, Empire and Society: British Youth Movements 1883–1940* (London: Croom Helm, 1977)

Summers, Anne, *Female Lives: Moral States* (Newbury: Threshold Press, 2000)

——, 'Gender, Religion and an Immigrant Minority: Jewish Women and the Suffrage Movement in Britain c. 1900–1920', *Women's History Review*, 21 (2012), pp. 399–418

Tananbaum, Susan L., 'Biology and Community: The Duality of Jewish Mothering in East London, 1880–1939', in *Mothering: Ideology, Experience and Agency*, ed. by Evelyn Nakano Glenn, Grace Chang and Linda Rennie Forcey (London: Routledge, 1994), pp. 311–32

——, 'Ironing Out the Ghetto Bend: Sports and the Making of British Jews' *Journal of Sport History*, 31 (2004), pp. 53–75

——, *Jewish Immigrants in London 1880–1939* (London: Pickering and Chatto, 2014)

——, 'Making Good Little English Children: Immigrant Welfare and Anglicization Among Jewish Immigrants in London, 1880–1939', *Immigrants and Minorities*, 12 (1993), pp. 176–99

——, 'Philanthropy and Identity: Gender and Ethnicity in London', *Journal of Social Research*, 30 (1997), pp. 937–61

——, 'To Their Credit as Jews and Englishmen: Services for youth and the Shaping of Jewish Masculinity in Britain, 1890s-1930s', in *Men, Masculinities and Religious Change in Twentieth Century Britain*, ed. by Lucy Delap and Sue Morgan (Basingstoke: Palgrave Macmillan, 2013), pp. 90–118

Tebbutt, Melanie, *Being Boys: Youth Leisure and Identity in the Inter-War Years* (Manchester: Manchester University Press, 2012)

Tinkler, Penny, 'Cause for Concern: Young Women and Leisure 1930–50', *Women's History Review*, 12 (2003), pp. 233–62

——, 'Girlhood and Growing Up', in *Women in Twentieth Century Britain*, ed. by Ina Zweininger-Bargielowska (Harlow: Pearson, 2001), pp. 35–50

Todd, Selina, 'Women, Work and Leisure in Interwar England', *The Historical Journal*, 48 (2005), pp. 789–809

Tosh, John, *Manliness and Masculinities in Nineteenth Century Britain: Essays on Gender, Family and Empire* (Harlow: Pearson, 2005)

——, *A Man's Place: Masculinity and the Middle-Class Home in Victorian England* (London: Yale University Press, 1999)

Totten, Andrew, *Straight and Ready: A History of the 10th Belfast Scout Group 1908–1988* (Belfast: Nelson and Know, 1989)

Tumblety, Joan, *Remaking the Male Body: Masculinity and the Uses of Physical Culture in Interwar and Vichy France* (Oxford: Oxford University Press, 2012)

Umansky, Ellen M., *Lily Montagu and the Advancement of Liberal Judaism* (New York: Edwin Mellen, 1983)

Valman, Nadia, 'Disraeli, Jewishness and Gender', in *Disraeli's Jewishness*, ed. by Todd M. Endelman and Tony Kushner (London: Vallentine Mitchell, 2002), pp. 62–101

——, *The Jewess in Nineteenth Century British Literary Culture* (Cambridge: Cambridge University Press, 2007)

——, '"Jewish Girls" and the Battle of Cable Street', in *Remembering Cable Street: Fascism and Anti-Fascism in British Society*, ed. by Tony Kushner and Nadia Valman (London: Vallentine Mitchell, 2000), pp. 181–94

——, 'Little Jew Boys Made Good: Immigration, the South African War and Anglo-Jewish Fiction', in *'The Jew' in Late-Victorian and Edwardian Culture: Between the East End and East Africa*, ed. by Eitan Bar-Yosef and Nadia Valman (Basingstoke: Palgrave MacMillan, 2009), pp. 45–64

Voeltz, Richard A., 'A Good Jew and a Good Englishman: The Jewish Lads' Brigade, 1894–1922', *Journal of Contemporary History*, 23 (1988), pp. 119–27

Warren, Alan, 'Sir Robert Baden Powell, The Scout Movement and Citizen Training in Great Britain, 1900–1920', *English Historical Review*, 101 (1986), pp. 376–98

Webber, Jonathan, *Jewish Identities in the New Europe* (London: Litman Library of Jewish Civilisation, 1994)

Zweininger-Bargielowska, Ina, 'Building a British Superman: Physical Culture in Interwar Britain', *Journal of Contemporary History*, 41 (2006), pp. 595–610

——, *Women in Twentieth Century Britain* (Harlow: Pearson, 2001)

Index